THE ART OF ASIAN COSTUME

AN EXHIBITION PRESENTED AT THE
UNIVERSITY OF HAWAII ART GALLERY
NOVEMBER 13 TO DECEMBER 23, 1988

Sponsored by the University of Hawaii Department of Art and the Department of Human Resources and supported by the National Endowment for the Arts, the Center for Arts & Humanities, the School of Hawaiian, Asian & Pacific Studies, the Office of Research Relations, the UH Student Activity and Program Fee Board, the Center for Southeast Asian Studies, an Educational Enrichment Grant from the UH Foundation, the A.J. Simone Kimono Culture Research Fellowship, the J. Watumull Fund, Sueko M. Kimura, Mark Masuoka Designs, Inc., and Partners of the Gallery.

(Cover)
CEREMONIAL SHOULDER
CLOTH, *SELENDANG SONGKET*
Palembang, Sumatra, Indonesia

DONORS TO THE ASIAN COSTUME COLLECTION

The Department of Human Resources, University of Hawaii at Manoa, gratefully acknowledges the following donors to the Asian Costume Collection:

Mr. Akazawa
Claudia Aoki
Jean Ariyoshi
Asia Ashraf

Elizabeth Bailey
Sunny Barnett
Mary Barstow
Mrs. Donald (Mary) Bartow
Adelaide Beste
Robert M. Blair
Desarone Boungnaseng
E. Bowman
Erma Boyen
Reed Brantley
Ruth Hock Brantley
Phil Brooks

Margaret B. Campbell
Suzanna Fok Chang
Mrs. Toy Len Chang
I-dah Chao
Theodora Chong
Herbert Choy
Diane Chuensanguansat
Kaylene Chun
Diane and Ken Chung
Barbara Cox
Virginia Crozier
Dr. and Mrs. Robert Curtis

Frances E. Davis
Burgess Dell
David C. Des Jarlais
Mary Ellen Des Jarlais
Mrs. Donald Doti
Willis and Eunice Dunne

Ada K. Erwin

Mary Farris
Linda Fong
Ethel Fukunaga
Gloria Furer
Barbara Furniss

Solou Garret
Phyllis Gocke
Jose Gould
Katherine Gruelle

Rhoda E. A. Hackler
Mrs. Halla Halm
Helen Hamada
Orpha Herrick
Joanna Higham
Betty Ho
Elizabeth Ho
Lum Chew Ho
Yung Ho
Helene Horimoto
Barbara Cox Hussey

Jean Ikeda
Harriet Iwai

Sheila James
Yeong Jung

Violet Kam
Shirley R. Kamins
Deanna Kikuchi
Maita Kindig
Lucinda King
Susan Fan Kozak
Hazel Kramer

Mary Kong Lee
Jeannie Lee
Joan Lenzer
Tony Lenzer
Anne Leung
Will Lidsker
Lianne Loo
Leanne Luke

Dr. and Mrs. W. Glenn Marders
Mrs. Archibald Mark
Jim McNeal and Associates
Phyllis McOmber
Carey D. Miller
May Moir
Marcia Morgado
Joan Moynahan
Kathleen Muirhead
Lorna Muraki

Mrs. Shizu Naganuma
Shizu Nakajima
Carol Naone

Mrs. Alfred Ono

Duane Pang
Mrs. D.D. Parker
Dora Pratt

Puri Rani
Ellin Burkland Reynolds
Florence Rishi

Gene Sawyer
Alice Scheuer
Irwin Shepherd
Mrs. Aiko Shigematsu
Amy Shimabukuro

Gregg M. Sinclair
Saku A. Skuk
Barbara B. Smith
Carrole M. Smith
Estate of Mrs. Grace Hobson Smith
John E. Smith Jr.
Garrett Solyom
Mara Sprenger
Jeerawan Sripromma
Mrs. Howard R. Starke
Pearl Steele
Jessie M. Stevens
Lola Stone
Gale Suzuki
Charlene El Swaify

Susan Tanaka
Joy Teraoka
Karen Thompson

Stephen Uhalley
Oma Umbel

Sandra Vitousek

Paula Waterman
Mrs. Gulab Watumull

Hiroko Yamaguchi
Edith H. Yamanaka
Deanna Yanigasawa
Miwako H. Yorita
Lynn Yorito
Sylvia Young
Dean Eloise Yulo

LENDERS TO THE EXHIBITION

Jim and Maria Bolman
Desarone Boungnaseng
Diane Chuensanguansat
Nancy Cooper
Dr. and Mrs. Robert Curtis
Carol Langner and Fritz Fritschel
Sheldon Geringer
Roger Lau
Asmaa Mahmud
Yoshino Majikina Nakasone
Nguyen Ngoc Nhung
G. Pang
Virginia B. Randolph
Dr. Donald H. Rubinstein
Sharon Tasaka
Fritz and Barbara Warren
Mrs. Gulab Watumull
Zoe Wolfe
UH Hamilton Library
UH Center for Japanese Studies
Anonymous collectors

Library of Congress Cataloging-in-Publication Data

The Art of Asian costume.

"Sponsored by the University of Hawaii Department of Art and the Department of Human Resources."
Includes bibliographical references.
1. Costume—Asia—Exhibitions. I. University of Hawai at Manoa. Art Gallery. II. University of Hawaii at Manoa. Dept. of Art. III. University of Hawaii at Manoa. Dept. of Human Resources.
NK4772.A7 1989   391'.0095'07496931   89-20449

Copyright 1989
The University of Hawaii Art Gallery
Honolulu, Hawaii
All rights reserved

CONTENTS

Acknowledgements

Historical Background of the University of Hawaii Asian Costume Collection
by Carol Anne Dickson

Asian Garments: Comparisons and Contrasts
by Mary Ellen C. Des Jarlais

Catalogue of the Exhibition

Bibliography

ACKNOWLEDGEMENTS

The Art of Asian Costume represents a major collaboration between two departments at the University of Hawaii: the Department of Human Resources and the Department of Art. Selected for the quality of their design and execution, the objects in the exhibit present a range of personal apparel from twenty Asian countries. Assembled over a period of twenty-four years, the Asian Costume Collection of the Department of Human Resources contains over 2500 objects of clothing and accessories, including many items not previously exhibited or published. It ranks among the largest and most significant collections of 19th and 20th century costumes at a United States university.

The Asian Costume Collection exists because of the dedication and continuing work of two individuals, Emeritus Professor Oma Umbel whose foresight is responsible for the origination of the collection and Dr. Mary Ellen C. Des Jarlais, Professor of Textiles and Clothing, who, as curator since 1974, has continued to expand, conserve and study the collection of Asian textiles. Her selection, coordination and preparation of the University's costumes for exhibition is sincerely appreciated. Additionally, I want to thank Dr. Carol Anne Dickson, Chairperson of the Department of Human Resources, for her assistance and that of her department.

The exhibit has been supplemented substantially by the addition of selected works from private collections in Hawaii. To each of the collectors our appreciation is extended for their generosity in helping to present more thoroughly the costume heritage of specific Asian cultures. It is to Karen Thompson, Associate Gallery Director, that the deepest appreciation is extended. It was she who searched for and made arrangements to obtain the additional costumes and accessories.

Likewise Karen Thompson conducted the research and wrote the catalogue entries from the documentary information developed by Professors Oma Umbel and Mary Ellen Des Jarlais for the Department of Human Resources and from information provided by lenders to the exhibition. Dr. Donald H. Rubinstein, former Executive Director of Centers for Asian and Pacific Studies, assisted in the compilation of the Indonesian section. With the exception of the Japanese armor which was researched and compiled by Dr. Willa Tanabe, Associate Professor of Art, graduate art history student Sharon Tasaka researched and wrote the entries for Japan. Karen Lum developed the entries for Korea; graduate student Kevin Chang selected the Philippine and Chinese jewelry and wrote the catalogue entries. Gallery faculty assistant Jeanne Wiig served as catalogue editor with the assistance of Carol Langner as proofreader. The continuing help of student secretaries Velma Yamashita, Divina Corpuz and Monica Bacon has been essential to the exhibition program at the University of Hawaii.

Former University of Hawaii design student Thomas Tsuhako deserves special recognition for the sensitivity to design evident in this catalogue and the exhibition announcement. Nathan Chung and Man To Wan are to be commended for the quality of photographs for this publication. I appreciate the many hours each has put into this project. The Honolulu Display Co. Inc. is to be acknowledged for the preparation of custom-made mannequins for the exhibition.

Students play a key role in the installation of all exhibitions at the University of Hawaii. The installation of an exhibition of this scope requires the help of many people. Graduate student Wayne Kawamoto assisted in the development of the exhibition installation. Special thanks are extended to him and to student gallery assistants Scott Katano, Darrell Takaoka, Roger Shelley, Dennis Bader, Adriene Harrison, Robert Shintani, Martin Baxter, Sarrah Parrish, Paul Utu, Robert Delgado and Jeff Woodyard for their concern and care in helping to prepare the exhibit. Likewise students in Art 360, Exhibition Design and Gallery Management, Robyn Doo, Stacy Hoshino, Asmaa Mahmud, Alisa Mitchner, Jean Pritchard, Abraham Raguindin, Sandy Sandelin, Alan Saltiban and Cara Yoshimura assisted in the installation of the exhibit. Their help and that of volunteers Carol Langner, Lisa Yoshihara, Catherine Dunning, Sally Lagundimao, Tanya Lagundimao, Marilyn Wagner, Mary Mitsuda, Hobby Norton, Delmarie Klobe, Michael Mitchner, Tony Lee, Lisa Lee, Ahlan Diroex, John Koga, Ivan Treskow and Edwin Koh is greatly appreciated.

Students in Textiles and Clothing 491, Museum Management, Lisa Aito, Tracy Ching, Doris Ho, Kam Kok, Laurie Okimoto, Yvonne Thai, Traci Uwono, Ann Williams, Mary Etta Abromaitis, Mariette Chong, Maria Lora, Teresa Heard, Barbara Procham, Jose Gould, Reba Isibashi, Laurie Izumi, Bryna Jones, Cass Tudor, Norma Williams, Jenny O'Flaherty, assisted in the restoration, conservation and preparation of the objects for the exhibition. Faculty, staff and students who helped in this process include: Gloria Furer, Joy Teraoka, June Gibson, Helene Horimoto, June Yoshimura, Ron Wall, Diane Chung, Marcia Morgado, Melanie Kusake, Donna Paik, Susan Teruda, LaVerne Williams, Susan Davis, Sarah Ussery, Gene Sawyer, Dean Nagasako, Laurie Woodward, Terry Ann Akasaka, Lydia Iwamoto and Barbara Harger.

Once an exhibition is prepared for public viewing an indispensable part of the presentation is our student gallery attendants, Adriene Harrison, Xuan Dai Tran, Wai Kit Young, Phithoun Lau, Vone Xaysengsouk, Jessica Gambsky, Paul Utu, Liang Rasachak, Sarah Parrish, Tynia Grace, Martin Baxter, Glenn Thielk and many volunteers, Helen Kuhlman, Elly Brodsky, Adriana Jimenez, Edward Holt, Amy Lee, Stacy Hoshino, Robyn Doo, Asmaa Mahmud, Lisa Kamae, Linda Robertson, Daisy Kurashige, Jenny Lau, Doris Ogawa, Kimiyo Fujioka, Grace Fukunaga, Edith Kondo, Nellie Chang, Joan Kurashige, Hazel Hee, Lorna Klobe, Dorothy Dimond, Carol Perrey, Violet Gaspar, Toshiko Tasaka and Grace Kohatsu who assist us in guarding the exhibit and welcoming visitors.

Providing public education through guided tours enhanced the understanding of objects and the context in which they were created. Professor Des Jarlais and Karen Thompson led many of these tours as did graduate art students Sharon Tasaka, Kevin Chang, Teddie Ching, Esther Tanaka and Zoe Wolfe.

I am pleased to acknowledge the National Endowment for the Arts for its generous support of this project and the opportunity it presents of bringing this collection to the attention of a larger audience through the publication of this catalogue. Additionally, I thank the University of Hawaii Foundation Educational Innovations Fund, the A.J. Simone Kimono Cultural Foundation and the Student Activity and Program Fee Board for their support of this exhibition. Partners, the Department of Art's community support group, presented a splendid reception with ethnic food. Musical accompaniment, under the direction of Professor Ricardo Trimillos, was provided by the University of Hawaii Department of Music.

In conclusion I want to thank the many individuals who, over the years, have given a part of their family heritage in the form of clothing and accessories to the safekeeping of the Department of Human Resources at the University of Hawaii. Future generations will have the opportunity to study and appreciate the complex cultural origins of the peoples who make Hawaii so unique and so beautiful.

Tom Klobe
Director
The University of Hawaii
Art Gallery

HISTORICAL BACKGROUND OF THE
UNIVERSITY OF HAWAII ASIAN COSTUME COLLECTION

A course in Costumes of Asia was first offered at the University of Hawaii during the summer session of 1960. The history of European costume had long been taught at the University of Hawaii as it was at many universities, but this was the first time any university had offered a course regarding the history of costumes of Asian peoples. With Hawaii's widely diversified Asian population, it was appropriate that this first course in the history of Asian costume be introduced at the University of Hawaii. The increased emphasis on Asian Studies at the University of Hawaii, the introduction of a new major in fashion design and merchandising, and the influx of thousands of mainland students for summer sessions during the 1960s made this a timely innovation. Professor Oma Umbel planned and taught this course using fabrics and snapshots from her trips to Asia, filling in with illustrations from a collection of very old National Geographic magazines.

In 1963-64, Umbel took sabbatical leave in order to continue her study of clothing and textiles in Asia. She traveled extensively in Asia: Japan, Korea, Taiwan, the Philippines, Cambodia, Thailand, Malaysia, Indonesia, Nepal, India, Vietnam, Okinawa, Hong Kong, and West Pakistan. In each country Umbel searched for scholarly studies in clothing and textiles, and interviewed specialists in the field. She visited research institutes, museums, craft centers, and mills, photographing examples of historical, traditional and modern costumes in exhibits, displays, private collections, dance recitals, and festivals.

Umbel, despite a limited budget, shipped to the University of Hawaii more than 125 cartons of fabrics, costumes, tribal jewelry, accessories and crafts as well as books and thousands of slides with which to enrich and expand the work in costumes of Asia. The acquisition of these items greatly enhanced the Costumes of Asia course and the course became a requirement for Fashion Design and Fashion Merchandising students. Through the use of the artifacts, students were introduced to the history and culture of Asia and its people. The collection was also used as a source of design inspiration for contemporary apparel.

The articles acquired by Umbel during her sabbatical leave provided the nucleus for the Asian Costumes Collection at the University of Hawaii. Over the years, students and friends of the University learned of the collection, and generous donations of artifacts came from the closets of Hawaii and the mainland. By 1968-69 the single course, Costumes of Asia, had outgrown its one semester time allotment. Two courses were developed to fill the needs of the department's students: Costumes of East Asia and Costumes of South and South East Asia.

When Professor Emeritus Oma Umbel retired in 1974, Professor Mary Ellen C. Des Jarlais became curator of the Asian Costume Collection and took responsibility for teaching the Asian costume courses. Since Des Jarlais had lived in Asia periodically, she brought with her a rich knowledge about the area — its customs and costumes.

Des Jarlais' interest in ethnic costume and textiles began when she was a Costume and Interior Design student at the University of Wisconsin-Madison. As a student, Des Jarlais worked for costume collector and curator, Professor Helen Allen. Allen's South American textile and costume collection was not well organized since no systematic cataloging system had been devised for costume collections, but her enthusiasm for collecting and teaching was contagious.

Shortly after the end of World War II, Des Jarlais accompanied her Army officer husband to an assignment in Japan. The customs and costumes, as well as the wartime destruction, of Japan were a sharp contrast for Des Jarlais and her midwestern background. Des Jarlais was enchanted with her first taste of Asian culture, from the women with lacquered hair to the young girls in silk factories who dipped their hands in hot water to catch a silk filament to ply with another silk filament. Using their Japan assignment as a base, Des Jarlais traveled all over Asia and Southeast Asia- Hong Kong, the Philippines, Thailand, and Taiwan. As she traveled she began to collect textiles, costumes, and household items of interest.

In the 1960s and 1970s the Des Jarlais were assigned to the Philippines and, later, to Hawaii. Des Jarlais continued her study and collection tours to exotic faraway places including Japan, Korea, Taiwan, the hills of northern Thailand, Cebu City and Zamboanga in the Philippines, Singapore, Vietnam, Indonesia, and China. Des Jarlais photographed scenes ranging from the prince and villagers' funeral in Bali, to the opium smoker of the Golden Triangle, to the toothless Hmong indigo-batik skirt dyer—so she could bring to life the culture and customs of Asia for her students.

As Des Jarlais traveled and studied in Asia and Southeast Asia, and collected textiles, costumes, and photographs, she observed and noted differences and similarities between and among cultures and their costumes, defining costume as garments, hairstyles, and accessories. She compared the dairy farms of Wisconsin to the cocoon-raising *minka* or farms of Honshu, Japan. She also compared the Western fitted dress with the non-sexist cylindrical kimono. She analyzed the cultural contrasts and similarities she observed and shared those analyses with her students.

In the Asian Costume Collection held by the University of Hawaii Department of Human Resources, it is the individualism and master craftsmanship of each piece that researchers, students, and collectors have found most intriguing. Some of these same students and collectors have facilitated the growth of the collection.

The costume and decorative arts holdings of the Department of Human Resources are on continuous display throughout the fall and the spring semesters. Every two weeks the displays in a lecture room and an entrance hallway are changed so that students—majors in Design, Merchandising, Theater, and Art—will have the opportunity to study them. Each student investigates a topic of his or her own choosing related to the collection.

Students, as well as collectors, have contributed many items from their mother's or grandmothers' wardrobes. Snatches of history come with the gifts:

My grandmother told me that this kimono was hidden behind the wallboards during World War II. She had worn it for special occasions until that time, but it was never worn again.

My grandfather visited the Chinese village of his birthplace, and this robe was given to him by his relatives. We wish that it become [sic] part of the University's collection so that others can learn about their heritage.

I was born in Korea and worn [sic] this dress as a child. Perhaps you would like to have it for the University collection.

Several friends of the collection donate textiles and apparel items annually. Oma Umbel and Mary Ellen Des Jarlais have donated part of their personal holdings to the collection each year.

Such gifts are deeply appreciated and it is through such generosity that the University of Hawaii has been able to acquire one of the finest and most extensive University collections of Asian costumes in the country. We know that we are the only University in the United States offering two courses specializing in Asian Costume. Another course, Museum Management, has been developed and is being taught. This course gives students the opportunity to learn the essential operations of a museum with special attention given to those items in the Department collection.

Time has increased the value of the Department's holdings and the Department is conserving the collection by storing it in a temperature and humidity controlled environment. Ultraviolet light protectors have been installed in display areas, as well as work and storage areas. The Campus Women's Club generously made a grant of $4,700 for the building of custom-made display cabinets for the lecture room. They protect the garments and enhance their visual appeal.

Several special exhibits of the collection have occurred in Hawaii. In 1976 a $2000 conservation grant was received for the presentation of the exhibit, "Costumes of East, South, and Southeast Asia." In 1978, the "Chinese, Tibetan, Vietnamese, Korean, and Japanese Costume" exhibit contributed to the celebration of the United Nations week. In 1982, the "Reflections of Rare Treasures" exhibit was held as a part of the University of Hawaii's 75th Anniversary. "The Cultural Influences on the Ornament of Chinese Costumes" exhibit and presentations were given to the Pacific Friendship Fibre Arts National Conference in 1982 and the exhibit and presentation, "Oriental Costume: Fine Arts of Craftsmanship" was presented to the national meeting of the Association of College Professors of Textiles and Clothing. Additionally, eleven slide-lecture presentations and journal publications have been prepared and given by Des Jarlais. However, this is the first large exhibit to be presented to the people of Hawaii who have so generously given to our fine Asian Collection.

Carol Anne Dickson
Chairman
Department of Human Resources

ASIAN GARMENTS: COMPARISONS AND CONTRASTS

The typical Asian garment is a flat rectangle worn folded and draped on the body. The width of the fabric is determined by the width of the loom on which it is woven. Rectangular sashes, ties, or belts secure the garment at the waist. There is greater choice regarding the length of the rectangle than its width. The fabric is generally wrapped horizontally on the body—in contrast to the lengthwise placement generally preferred by Westerners. Lengths of rectangular fabrics have become somewhat standardized in favor of the presumed largest wearers. A slender individual uses excess fabric by adding extra tucks or pleats when draping the garment.

The advantages of these garments are both utilitarian and aesthetic. In the preparation of the rectangular garment, no time is wasted for machine construction of the garment. The fabric is simply removed from the loom and securely twisted around the body. The garment adjusts to an individual's weight loss or gain by adding more pleats or tucks or by using fewer of them. There is no labor cost involved in sizing of garments for the individual wearer. Also, treasured garments can be passed from one generation to the next with the knowledge that there will be no problems of fit.

The rectangular garment is also easy to clean. It can be washed in a river and stretched flat on a river bank to dry. No pressing is required. Additionally, the garment is easy to store since it can be simply folded and placed on a shelf.

The type of fiber, the weight of the yarn, and the type of weave are adjusted relative to climatic conditions. To increase the warmth of the garment, silk and wool fibers, heavy yarns, and close or double weaves are used. To decrease the warmth of the garment, cotton, linen, or ramie fibers are used, the yarns have fewer plys, and weaves are likely to be open.

The Indian sari is a good example of a rectangular garment. For everyday wear the sari has a standard width of about forty-two inches and a length of about six yards. The selvage edge of one end of the sari is tucked into the waistband of a snugly secured half slip and then the fabric is wrapped twice around the waist and hips, with tucks and pleats for fullness and ease of movement. The last third of the rectangle is wrapped about the lower body and the free end is carried upwards over the left shoulder to hang down the back of the wearer.

Another example of the Asian flat rectangular garment is the women's or men's wrap-around skirt which is worn in Malaysia, Indonesia, Thailand, and the Philippines. The names of these garments depend on the country in which they are worn. The width of these garments, too, depends on the width of the looms on which they are woven, and the length is dependent on the desires of the weaver or the wearer. These wrap-around skirts are held in place with sashes, ties, or strings.

The Japanese *kosode*, or everyday kimono, is a variation on the rectangular wrapped Asian garment. The standard width of fabric used in Japanese *kosode* is fourteen inches. The length of fabric is cut into six pieces: two lengths of twenty-six inches for the sleeves, two lengths of fifty-seven inches for the front and back panels and one length of fifty inches which is split vertically into two strips measuring seven inches wide. One of these seven inch strips is then cut into two pieces, each twenty-five inches long to form extensions on either side of the center front panels. The remaining piece, which is seven inches wide, is cut into three pieces. Their lengths depend on the designer's wishes regarding placement of the motifs on the garment. These last three pieces form the collar which is folded three times before it is sewn to the garment. All of the fabric in the original kimono length is used, and all as rectangles. The traditional sash, the obi, is also a flat rectangle given stiffness by the addition of an inner lining or use of a very heavy fabric. Since it is Japanese custom to have the kimono folded precisely when worn, the body of the woman is padded, concealing her curves.

The kimono is handsewn and, when soiled, it is taken apart to be washed and resewn. When the fabric begins to show wear, perhaps where it rests upon the wrists, that part of the garment would be shifted to another area or reversed to reduce the stress on it.

Chinese men's trousers and the Indian man's *dhoti* are additional examples of rectangular cut, wrapped body covers. Each can be folded and stored flat, thus eliminating the need for Western hangers in closets.

As the above discussion demonstrates, Asian garments that wrap around the body are useful and convenient. Whether comparing the cost or the steps in construction, adjustment of a particular garment to a changing physical size or to another individual, or ornamenting the garment, in comparison with Western garments, the Asian garment can be clearly defined as utilitarian.

Asian color and motif selection carry a different meaning from that known in the West. Asian colors are symbolic: red means happiness, white indicates death, in China blue is the color for the commoner while bright yellow, during the Empire, was reserved for the Emperor. Oriental motifs are also symbolic. They express a desire for beauty, longevity, children, happiness, and wealth. In China, the dragon motif is the most powerful and most beneficent; it brings the rain to nourish the crops; it is the overlord of protection. In contrast, the Western World's dragon is evil and needed to be slain by St. George. In Occidental countries, color and motif choice is often made believing it will enhance the individual's hair, skin color, or personality.

Most costumes of Asia are designed and made by a single person. Exceptions were those made by groups of workmen in the Imperial workshops of China. As the masterpieces of Western literature and art were created by individuals, so is the design and mastery of the Asian costume the work of individual artists.

Mary Ellen C. Des Jarlais
Professor of Textiles and Clothing

AFGHANISTAN

MUSLIM WOMAN'S HEAD AND BODY COVER, *CHADRI*

1970s
Rayon
Length (back panel to top of crown) 143.5 cm
Length (front panel to top of crown) 89.2 cm
Length (face covering) 7.5 cm
Width (face covering) 14.4 cm
1977.05.20
Gift of Oma Umbel, 1977

"O Prophet! Tell thy wives, thy daughters and the wives of all believers to wrap their veils tightly about them! This will be the simplest way for them to be recognized and not insulted. Allah is forgiving and merciful." (*Koran*, 33:59)

While the *Koran* (24:31) decrees that women "...draw their veils over their bosoms," there is no mandate for complete concealment of the body, nor for veiling the face. Nevertheless, *purdah*, the seclusion and veiling of women, became customary, and in some instances law, in many Muslim countries including Afghanistan, where women enveloped themselves in a garment called the *chadri*, which covered the face and body. According to Wikan (1982:101-03), some anthropological research has shown that many Middle Eastern women consider the veil, and the secluded status it signifies, a sign of prestige.

In Afghanistan, *purdah* was made voluntary almost twenty years ago and the majority of modern women in Kabul appear in public unveiled, although the *chadri* may still be seen in towns and villages.

This Afghani Muslim woman's garment, in embroidered rust-colored rayon, fits closely to the head and envelops the shoulders and body in accordion pleats. The face is covered by a drawn-work screen. Some sources (Fairservis, 1971:72) identify this pleated style robe and headpiece as a *burqua*, the word generally used in Northern India and Pakistan.

MAN'S ENSEMBLE

1960s
Kabul
A.1977.04.04 a,b,c,d
Gift of Lola Stone, 1977
Illustrated p. 12

TROUSERS
Rayon
Length 103.5 cm
Waist (with elastic) 64 cm

SHIRT
Rayon
Center back 97.5 cm
Sleeve (sleeve tip to sleeve tip across shoulders) 168 cm

VEST
Silk velvet; gold metallic braid; cotton
Center back 50.4 cm
Width (shoulder) 47.5 cm

HAT
Cotton; glass beads
Height 7.5 cm
Circumference 51.1 cm

Finely embroidered cutwork ornaments the front of this long white shirt. It is worn with white trousers and a vest of heavy royal blue velvet embellished with wide metallic gold braid in an intricate design. The small, crocheted cotton hat is trimmed with rows of tiny, cut glass beads.

MAN'S ENSEMBLE
Afghanistan

PAKISTAN

WOMAN'S ENSEMBLE

1950s
Kalat, Baluchistan
A.1987.08.01 a,b
Gift of Karen Thompson, 1987

LONG SHIRT, *PUSHK KURTA*
Rayon; cotton
Center back 96 cm
Sleeve width 164 cm

PANTS, *EJAR*
Rayon
Length 96 cm
Waist (drawstring) 380 cm

Evidence that embroidery was used to ornament clothing in the Indus Valley Civilization (2500-1500 B.C.) is suggested by raised patterning on garments of some images from Mohenjodaro and the disovery at that site of bronze needles of the type used for embroidery. Mantles embroidered with gold thread are mentioned in the ancient text, *Rig Veda* (c.1000 B.C.). Figures in 5th century A.D. cave frescoes at Ajanta and Bagh are depicted with elaborately embroidered costumes.

The Baluchi, who live in modern Pakistan, Iran and Afghanistan, have carried on the tradition of embellishing their costumes with ornate embroidery. The town of Kalat is especially noted for this skill. Geometric motifs predominate. Long tunic-like shirts, *pushk kurta*, with almost solidly embroidered fronts, matching sleeve cuffs and a front pouch are very popular in this region. The shirts are worn with voluminous trousers, tapered at the ankles and tied at the waist with a drawstring.

WOMAN'S DRESS, *CHOLO*

1980s
Baluchistan
Cotton; silk, mirrors, shells
Center back 123 cm
Sleeve width 129 cm
Loaned by Asmaa Mahmud

The marvelously embroidered front panels from old shirts and dresses are often saved to be used for new garments, such as this black *cholo*. The bodice is almost solidly embroidered in satin-stitched, geometric patterns and decorated with small white shells, mirrors and a border of small pompons of multi-colored yarn. The *cholo* has long sleeves and a gathered, ankle-length skirt which ties at the back like an apron. The style is popular with Muslim women in certain areas of Pakistan today. This type of garment may be a descendant of the *pasvaj*, a long-sleeved, ankle-length garment similar to a dress, apparently imported in the Mughal period.

WOMAN'S SHOES
1963
Punjab
Suede
Length 25.5 cm
Height 9.5 cm
Width 8 cm
A.1987.08.03 a,b
Gift of Oma Umbel, 1987

WOMAN'S SHOES,
SALIM SHAHI
1980s
Multan, Punjab
Leather; metallic gold thread
Length 24.5 cm
Width 8 cm
Loaned by Asmaa Mahmud

Shoes with extended curled toes are worn by both men and women in the Punjab. The shoes are called *Salim Shahi*, after the Mughal ruler who first wore this style. The right and left shoes are identical.

MAN'S HAT
1960s
Sind or Baluchistan
Cotton; mirrors, *abla*
Height 8 cm
Circumference 50.5 cm
Loaned by Karen Thompson

MAN'S HAT
1964
Karachi
Cotton; metallic gold thread
Height 7.5 cm
Circumference 54 cm
62-3
Departmental purchase, 1964

An all-over design in couched gold thread decorates this white muslin hat.

MAN'S HAT
1965
Karachi
Cotton; machine quilted
Height 7 cm
Circumference 52 cm
62-2
Departmental purchase, 1965

MAN'S SHOES
1960s
Multan
Suede; gold thread
Length 28 cm
64-4
Departmental purchase, 1964

MAN'S SHOES
1960s
Chakwal
Leather; metallic gold thread
Length 28.5 cm
64-3
Departmental purchase, 1964

SHAWL, *CHADDAR*
(OR BEDCOVER)
1930s
Hazara, North-West Frontier Province
Cotton; *phulkari* embroidery
Length 262 cm
Width 136 cm
62-1
Gift of Carey D. Miller, 1962

Phulkari are embroidered textiles from the Punjab and the North-West Frontier Province. The word has also become synonymous for a type of embroidered shawl, *chaddar*, worn by women in this area. *Phulkari*, "flower craft," is used for everyday wear and has more sparsely patterned embroidery. This textile from Hazara is identified as a *bagh tara*. The heavily embroidered head shawl called *bagh*, meaning "garden," is mostly for ceremonial occasions and is sometimes worn as a wedding shawl. (Peebles, 1981:24)

Yacopino (1977:42) describes some traditional uses of *phulkari*: In Hazara, a bridegroom's family often makes a *phulkari* to place over the palanquin which carries the bride to her husband's home. For several days afterward the bride wears it as a symbol of the consummation of her marriage. In northern Punjab villages, a *chaddar* called *suber phulkari* is held like a canopy over the bridegroom after he takes a ritual bath at his home prior to the ceremony. He wears this textile on his shoulders in procession to the bride's home and then presents it to her.

These heirloom textiles, which are part of a trousseau, take many years to complete and are traditionally begun by a girl's mother and grandmother shortly after her birth. While *phulkari* generally refers to shawls, these embroidered fabrics are also used for tablecloths, bed and cushion covers and shirts, *kurtas*. The patterns, which are principally geometric, are done with a darning or satin stitch in untwisted yellow, orange, white, green or red silk floss worked from the reverse on a coarse, homespun cotton dyed a deep red, blue or brown.

Phulkari SHAWL, *CHADDAR*
(OR BEDCOVER)
1930s
North-West Frontier Province,
Pakistan

TABLECLOTH

c. 1950
Swat, Northwest Frontier Province
Cotton; silk
Length 78.7cm
Width 77.8 cm
A.1988.15.01
Departmental purchase, 1964
Illustrated p. 19

The design motifs of Swati embroidery reflect a Greek influence unique in Pakistani textiles. (Yaccopino 1977:12) Symmetrically arranged series of triangles, squares and rectangles surround a central diamond. The Greeks first came into the region during the conquest of Alexander the Great. Traces of Greek influence remain in the art, drama and language of Swat.

BED COVER

First half of 20th century
Punjab
Cotton; *phulkari* embroidery
Length 244 cm
Width 130 cm
A.1986.01.01
Gift of Orpha Herrick, 1986

The principal motifs, identified in Department of Human Resources files as flowers, birds and feathers, are rendered in *phulkari* embroidery on this textile which was probably used to cover a bed.

SHAWL OR BED COVER

Sind
Cotton; mirrors, *abla*
Length 188 cm
Width 153 cm
80-8
Departmental purchase, 1964

Tiny mirrors, *abla*, fastened with a variety of embroidery stitches in combination with floral or geometric motifs are often used to decorate Pakistani clothing and textiles, such as this tie-dyed cotton shawl or bedcover.

BEDCOVER

1950s
Lahore
Cotton
Length 246 cm
Width 147 cm
A.1988.16.01
Departmental purchase, 1964

The ancient art of block printing textiles, widely practiced in Pakistani villages today, is often combined with hand painting. This bedcover is hand painted within printed outlines. The tree of life motif dominates the design.

TABLECLOTH
North-West Frontier Province,
Pakistan

INDIA

THE SARI

An Indian woman in a sari is the epitome of graceful movement. The draped garment has always been a part of traditional Indian costume. Small terra cotta images from the Indus Valley civilization (2300-1750 B.C.) display a short length of fabric wrapped about the hips in the manner of a sarong. This piece was gathered or pleated in front and secured below the navel by a girdle or *kamarband* (belt or knotted cord). Some scholars (for example, Chandra, 1973:4) refer to these and similar early costumes as saris. The word sari, or a similar term, is found in ancient literature, but neither the costume nor the way it was worn, as a lower body cover only, resemble the modern sari. Draped garments, shawls and scarves existed in the Vedic era (1500-450 B.C.) and the *Vedas* (texts sacred to the Hindus) mention a strip of cloth worn above the knees called *nivi*, "gathered," which was apparently much like the short garment described above.

In the fourth century B.C., women wore the *nivi*, and ankle-length *lungi*, which was something like a skirt, an upper body cover, *adivasa*, and a scarf-like overgarment (Chandra 1973:8). In the opinion of Fabri (1960:8), the present day sari may have evolved not from the *nivi*, or a like garment, but from the scarf, or *dupatta*, which simply became longer over time. On the other hand, there also appeared, by 320 B.C., a sari-like wrapped garment, with one free end called *pallu*, which could be used to cover the upper body. By the second century A.D., the *pallu* came to be worn over the head, as the very elaborate headdresses worn in early India became less fashionable.

Another possible influence on the development of the sari may have been softly draped Grecian garments said to have been brought into India by the Greek wife of Chandragupta Maurya (r. c.323-298 B.C.), founder of the first great Indian empire. Men and women in the time of Asoka, Chandragupta's grandson (r. c. 272-231 B.C.), wore one-piece draped garments.

Sculptures from the subsequent Sunga and Kushan periods show sari prototypes, and in Ghandara (now northern Pakistan and part of Afghanistan) under the Kushans (late first century to third century A.D.), images are clothed in "saris" wrapped around the waist with the free end either pleated and tucked into the back waistband, or thrown across the upper body and over the shoulder. Many variations of the basic sari-type garment appear in succeeding centuries, culminating in the sari as designed in the eighteenth century.

The modern sari may be plain or woven with endless variations and combinations of patterns. Generally five meters to 8.2 meters in length, it is draped in a variety of ways according to personal preference and styles prevalent in certain areas. The sari is worn with a long slip and a *choli*, a tight-fitting blouse with a rounded neck, either sleeveless or having short or elbow-length sleeves. Most *choli* leave the midriff bare. While they usually fasten in the front, some are backless and tied with cord at the neck and lower back, reflecting earlier garments with the same name that were worn as breast supports.

SARI
Benares, India

Sari

Mid 20th century
Benares
Silk; metallic gold thread
Warp 549 cm
Weft 112 cm
Loaned by Mrs. Gulab Watumull

The *Rig Veda* tells of cloth of "shining gold," and silk garments woven with gold thread are especially favored by Hindus. The metal may be drawn or the gold leaf wrapped around a core, usually of silk, to create these shimmering metallic threads. Silk brocades with floral motifs, *kimkhab*, have delicate patterns of woven gold. The most famous of these silks come from Benares, with other manufacturing centers at Hyderabad, Bombay and Madras.

Sari

Early 1900s
Benares
Silk; metallic silver thread
Warp 537 cm
Weft 112 cm
Loaned by Diane Chuensanguansat

According to the lender, this is a wedding sari worn by a member of the Rana family of Nepal in the early 1900s. The Ranas came to power in Nepal in the 19th century as hereditary prime ministers. The present queen of Nepal is a member of this family.

Professor Mary Ellen Des Jarlais states that it is likely that the magenta and silver sari was woven in Benares, India, where much of the silk fabric woven with metallic threads is produced and she describes the process of obtaining the gold or silver thread. This involves beating metal bars until flat. The metal is then drawn through progressively smaller holes of a steel plate until it is reduced to a fine wire. It may be used in weaving at this stage or flattened into ribbons of metal leaf to be wound about a core fiber. Both types of metallic threads are used in this sari. Because there are few impurities in this particular metal, it tends not to tarnish.

The metallic designs are woven into the fabric using the loom embroidery technique. The pattern "was created with a 'small needle-like spool (which) is carried in and out of the exact number of threads of the warp that may be necessary in the production of the pattern.'" (Sir George Watt quoted in Nordquist, 1986:141). Des Jarlais notes that the costly silver threads do not pass from one selvage to another. The motifs are spaced farther apart in the body of the sari than in the more decorative *pallu* with designs superimposed over an elaborate border of stylized flowers, leaves and pomegranate-like shapes. Metallic designs forming a continuous border along both selvages add to the beauty and value of this sari.

Sari

Mid 20th century
Benares
Silk; gold thread
Warp 549 cm
Weft 113 cm
Loaned by Mrs. Gulab Watumull
Illustrated p. 21

Woven gold elephants and peacocks in a lattice design fill the field of this brilliant turquoise silk sari. The borders and *pallu* are woven with gold on a red ground.

Sari

1980s
Silk
Warp 549 cm
Weft 113 cm
Loaned by Mrs. Gulab Watumull

This sari in purple silk has an all over design of *buti*, with *pallu* and borders in an intricate pattern of tiny flowers. The ornamentation in finely woven, off-white silk, has an effect of shimmering gold or silver. The principal motif, seen on a multitude of Indian textiles, is known to Westerners as paisley. There are differing theories on the origin of this ubiquitous design, but it is most likely the *buta*, a floral cluster contained in a form variously called a cone, flame or mango. The motif derives (according to Irwin in Chandra, 1973:246) from the Safavid Persian patterns of the sixteenth century. The Persian motif is a combination of a stylized vase and flower design fused within the shape of a cypress tree with a bent tip.

Sari

1980s
Silk
Warp 549 cm
Weft 112 cm
Loaned by Mrs. Gulab Watumull

Subtle splashes of silk *ikat* in shades of purple, green and gold create a shimmering iridescent effect in this sari. *Ikat* threads are resist-dyed, according to a preconceived pattern, prior to weaving. A woven gold stylized floral motif provides a bright accent. There is some indication of indigenous Indian silk originating in pre-Vedic times. Jayakar (1982:59) believes silk fiber may have been cultivated in the deep forests from wild tussah cocoons, which produce a brownish silk so coarse it is referred to in early texts as "bark cloth." Silk from China arrived in India via the great silk route from the first century A.D. onward, and *Chin-suhk*, Chinese silk, from mulberry cocoons, was subsequently manufactured in India. Silk manufacturing technology was zealously guarded by the Chinese. Silk worms feed on mulberry leaves, and there is a legend that the mulberry tree was smuggled into India by a Buddhist monk. (Jayakar, 1982:60).

Sari

1980s
Silk
Warp 549 cm
Weft 112 cm
Loaned by Mrs. Gulab Watumull

The emerald green center field of this sari has wide orange borders with *ikat* woven green peacocks. Purple *ikat* peacocks decorate the orange *pallu*.

Sari

1950s
Benares
Silk; gold thread
Warp 472 cm
Weft 110.5 cm
A.1987.04.01a
Gift of Karen Thompson, 1987

Woven gold stripes are often used to define the borders and *pallu* of saris, which may also be accented with tiny sprigged designs in gold. The most popular is the *kalka*, or flame motif, and the *buta* (pl. *buti*) floral cluster. A favorite color combination is shades of red or red-orange with complimentary green. This sari has a matching *choli* in red-orange silk.

Sari

Mid-20th century
Silk chiffon; silver sequins
Warp 549 cm
Weft 112 cm
Loaned by Mrs. Gulab Watumull

This sari in pale turquoise was once a white wedding sari. The entire garment is ornamented with tiny silver sequins hand sewn in a custom floral pattern. After the sari was completed, the design was destroyed. Indian women often have saris re-dyed. The color change does not effect gold or silver, either applied or woven in the fabric.

SARI

1980s
Silk georgette; gold thread
Warp 549 cm
Weft 112 cm
Loaned by Mrs. Gulab Watumull

The color of this sari changes gradually from emerald green on one end of the weft to a bright magenta on the other. It is accented with gold flowers strewn over the field, and a gold border and *pallu*.

SARI

1950s
Benares
Silk
Warp 434 cm
Weft 114.5 cm
Loaned by Diane Chuensanguansat

Stylized floral bouquets in vases decorate the brocaded borders and *pallu* of this fine quality green silk sari with a hand-knotted fringe.

SARI

1950s
South India
Rayon; imitation gold threads
Warp 498.4 cm
Weft 114.3 cm
Loaned by Diane Chuensanguansat

SARI

1960s
Sholapur
Cotton, rayon
Warp 663.3 cm
Weft 111.7 cm
20-11
Departmental purchase, 1964

SARI

1960s
Kerala
Cotton; metallic gold thread
Warp 542 cm
Weft 118 cm
20-8
Departmental purchase, 1964

Indian cotton of very fine quality is often gossamer sheer. Ancient sculptures often look as if they are unclothed; their garments, essentially transparent, are indicated only by a few folds or a hemline. Fragments of cotton cloth were found in Indus Valley excavations. However, the pre-Vedic fabric from Harappa was dyed with madder and relatively coarse. The famous cotton muslin of later manufacture was exported to Egypt, Greece, and Rome. Fine textured cotton has been cultivated extensively in India from the seventh century B.C.

Gold thread is used for ornamentation on cotton as well as silk saris. Several cotton saris with woven metallic gold stripes and other designs, such as the peacocks seen in this example, are featured in the exhibition.

SARI

1960s
Kailam-Madurai
Cotton; metallic gold thread
Warp 498 cm
Weft 116 cm
20-7
Departmental purchase, 1964

SARI

1960s
Kerala
Cotton; metallic gold thread
Warp 546 cm
Weft 121 cm
20-9
Departmental purchase, 1964

SARI

1960s
Cotton; metallic gold thread
Warp 564 cm
Weft 120 cm
20-12
Departmental purchase, 1968

SARI

1950s
Cotton; *ikat*
Warp 542.3 cm
Weft 114.6 cm
Loaned by Diane Chuensanguansat

SARI

1960s
Benares
Cotton
Warp 475 cm
Weft 112 cm
20-6
Departmental purchase, 1964

SARI

1960s
Orissa
Cotton; *ikat*
Warp 245 cm
Weft 112 cm
20-4
Departmental purchase, 1964

SARI

1960s
Pochabpalli, Andhra State
Cotton; *ikat*
Warp 110.5 cm
Weft 535 cm
20-5
Departmental purchase, 1964

BRIDE'S ENSEMBLE

1980s
Silk; silk chiffon, gold thread
Loaned by Mrs. Gulab Watumull
Illustrated p. 29

SKIRT, *GHAGHARA*
Length 115 cm
Waist (drawstring) 88 cm

BLOUSE, *CHOLI*
Center back 13.5 cm
Sleeve length (from shoulder) 24 cm

SCARF, *ODHNI*
Length 280 cm
Width 116 cm

Vertical meanders of couched gold flowers and vines pattern the skirt and scarf of this wedding ensemble in bright red silk. Royal blue borders on skirt, scarf and sleeve hems are sparked with emerald green and red beading and gold paisley and flower designs.

The skirt in India has a prototype in the *lungi* dated to the 4th century B.C. The full, ankle-length *ghaghra* appeared in the Mughal period and is worn with a *choli* or a *kameez* (shirt) and a scarf. The gathered skirt is usually tied around the waist or below the navel with a drawstring. Some skirts require as much as twenty or thirty yards of fabric.

The *odhni*, a large scarf or shawl about half the size of a sari, is usually draped over the head. It is often worn with a full skirt and *choli*.

WOMAN'S ENSEMBLE

1980s
Rajasthan
Cotton; mirrors, *abla*
Loaned by Mrs. Gulab Watumull

SKIRT, *GHAGHRA*
Length 85 cm
Waist (drawstring) 98 cm

SHIRT, *KAMEEZ*
Center back 85 cm
Sleeve 82 cm

SCARF, *DUPATTA*
Length 242 cm
Width 76 cm

This full skirt, *ghaghra*, has a tie-dye pattern of red-orange dots on black cotton. Large saffron yellow circles, with multi-colored embroidery and a mirror in the center, are appliquéd onto the skirt. The short-sleeved *kameez*, in matching fabric, has a red overlay on the front with embroidered designs and mirror work. The border of the lightweight *dupatta*, with orange and saffron tie-dye dots, is embroidered cotton and mirror work.

WOMAN'S SHAWL, ODHNI

1960s
Cotton
Length 237.5 cm
Width 166.5 cm
62-16T
Departmental purchase, 1964

This *odhni* combines a wide, red tie-dyed border surrounding a center field in red and the color of spring and earth, saffron. The design and these brilliant colors are typical of Jaipur.

GIRL'S ENSEMBLE

1980s
Rajasthan
Cotton
Loaned by Mrs. Gulab Watumull

SKIRT
Length 62 cm
Waist (drawstring) 65 cm

BLOUSE, CHOLI
Center back 24 cm
Sleeve 56 cm

SCARF, DUPATTA
Length 152.5 cm
Width 65 cm

An ensemble to delight any little girl is this outfit in saffron polished cotton and red print that is intended to look like tie-dye. The skirt and *choli* have a delicate, gold embroidered vine and flower motif, gold braid and red borders. The sheer *dupatta* is red 'tie-dye" bordered in saffron cotton.

WOMAN'S TIE-DYE ENSEMBLE
India

WOMAN'S ENSEMBLE

Mid 20th century
Delhi
Silk; metallic gold cord, sequins
Loaned by Mrs. Gulab Watumull
Illustrated p. 32

SHIRT, KAMEEZ
Center back 95 cm
Sleeve width 105 cm

PANTS, SHALWAR
Length 89 cm
Waist (drawstring) 104 cm

In the Maurya period (third century B.C.), men and women sometimes wrapped a length of cloth around their hips and placed the gathered end between their legs from front to back tucking it in the waistband. This created a sort of trouser. The concept of pants was not foreign to India, but many sewn garments, including the pants called *churidar* and *shalwar*, became more prevalent in the time of the Muslim invasions. During the British Raj, according to Biswas (1985:34), tight-fitting shalwar were considered immodest and, except for a band about the ankles, the pants became considerably wider and less revealing.

Shalwar are worn with a tunic-like shirt called *kameez*. The *kameez* varies in style and length according to prevailing fashion, in the same way as do Western dresses. In the 1960s, for example, the *kameez* was fitted at the waist, knee-length, and so tight at the hem, it made walking difficult. The *shalwar* and *kameez* are usually worn with a scarf, *dupatta*, draped across the front with the two ends flung back over the shoulders. Some women wear the *dupatta* as a head covering.

The front, neckline, and borders along the hem, side slits and sleeves of this navy blue silk *kameez* are encrusted with an Islamic-inspired design created in gold wrapped cord and gold sequins applied with an embroidery technique called *zardozi*. Similar ornamentation is found on the hem of the *shalwar* in matching navy silk with a sprinkling of tiny woven gold dots and small couched flowers.

WIDE PANTS, GHARARA

Mid 20th century
Lucknow
Rayon
Length 95 cm
Waist (drawstring) 128 cm
Width of pants hem 288 cm
Loaned by Mrs. Gulab Watumull

The tight fitting *shalwar* introduced in the Mughal period were gradually widened for modesty's sake. Dancers, perhaps coincidentally, greatly increased the width of their trousers, especially the hem. The style caught on and influenced the full, flaring women's pants called *gharara*.

Woman's ensemble

1980s
Silk; silk georgette
Loaned by Mrs. Gulab Watumull
Illustrated p. 26

SHIRT, *KAMEEZ*
Center back 98 cm
Sleeve 118 cm

PANTS, *CHURIDAR*
Length 100 cm
Waist (drawstring) 112 cm

SCARF, *DUPATTA*
Length 212 cm
Width 29 cm

Bright red and green enamel buttons fasten the front placket of this emerald green *kameez* with an all-over tie-dye, *bandhana*, pattern. Both the red and green *dupatta* and the *churidar*, in complementary red, have a matching design. The tight pants called *churidar* are very long and are gathered on the legs when worn to compensate for the extra length.

Woman's ensemble

1980s
Silk; georgette, metallic gold and silver threads, sequins
Loaned by Mrs. Gulab Watumull

SHIRT, *KAMEEZ*
Center back 65 cm
Sleeve 161 cm

PANTS, *GHARARA*
Length 105.5 cm
Waist (drawstring) 102 cm
Width of pants hem 165 cm

SCARF, *DUPATTA*
Length 233 cm
Width 85.5 cm

Cerise silk, in white tie-dye diamond-shaped patterns with metallic embroidery and sequins, creates this stunning ensemble. The wide pants, *gharara*, and the sheer *dupatta*, are ornamented with rows of large, stylized *buti*, flanked by birds and accented with gold and silver embroidery. The *kameez* has metallic embroidered borders of tiny flowers and sequins.

Bangle

18th century
Jaipur
Gold, foil-backed beryls, rock crystal, enamel
Outside diameter 7.9 cm
Inside diameter 6.7 cm
Collection of Virginia B. Randolph

Stylized lotus blossoms and pads in bright red and emerald on a wavy pond are enameled on the inside of this bangle. The exterior is ornamented with stones set in gold. Women were adorned with jewelry from the very beginnings of Indian civilization. It is often worn for symbolic and religious purposes. The *Code of Manu* mentions certain occasions on which it is obligatory to wear ornaments. On religious festival days, even the poorer women are transformed with their bead necklaces and bangles. Indian women also wear jewelry as a sign of wealth, social standing and simply for the love of it. Jewelry is often part of a dowry, and young women will wear as many ornaments as they, or their families, can afford. The exhibition contains, in addition to this bangle, several pieces of Indian women's costume jewelry.

Pendant

1960s
Silver alloy, glass
Length 43.5 cm
A.79.08.12
Gift of Oma Umbel, 1979

This pendant, which would be worn by a village woman, has red and green hand-cut glass set between metal strips on a fan-shaped base edged with pendants of twisted wire loops. The crescent shape of the largest piece of glass suggests a Muslim influence. This is a copy of an expensive necklace made of enamel and jewels, according to Department of Human Resources files.

Necklace

Beads, metallic foil, glass
Length 36 cm
Loaned by Zoe Wolfe

This necklace is a copy of Mughal jewelry, which would be made of gold set with precious stones.

Necklace

1960s
Brass, cotton
Length 40 cm
A.82.04.01
Gift of Oma Umbel, 1979

Two rows of thirty handmade brass bells are attached to twisted strands of orange, purple and natural colored yarns to make this necklace.

Bride's ensemble
India

Amulet necklace

1960s
Silver, cotton thread
Length 34 cm
A.79.08.15
Gift of Oma Umbel, 1979

This ornament is typical of those worn in rural areas. It is made of silver, pounded flat and then shaped into cylinders which were filled with wax or dirt to create the appearance of unaffordable solid silver.

Necklace

Rajasthan
Silver
Length 39 cm
Loaned by Zoe Wolfe

Bangles

1960s
Mirrored glass, plastic, metal
Circumference 16 cm
1979.08.06 a,b
Gift of Oma Umbel, 1979

Tiny blue and white plastic beads and diamond-shaped gold mirror fragments are set into base metal to make these sparkling bangles.

Nose ring

1960s
Kalimpong
Gold, glass
Length 3.5 cm
A.79.08.02
Gift of Oma Umbel, 1979

This nose ring of gold filigree with an insert of orange glass, is worn suspended from the septum of the nose. Other nose ornaments may be a small stud, usually a precious gem, worn in the side of the nose, or a large metal stud supported by a chain over the ear.

Pendant, *lalatika*

1980s
Gold (?), imitation gems, coins, pearls
Length 37 cm
A.1982.01.01
Gift of Helene Horimoto, 1982

The *lalatika* is a pendant worn on the center of a woman's forehead. The ornament is suspended from a chain which is placed along the part line and then fastened to the woman's coiled hair. This pendant is partly handmade using imitation gems, miniature coins, and pearls, and has been adapted for American use as a necklace.

Toe ring

1960s
Silver alloy
Length 5 cm
Width 6.7 cm (including extension)
1979.08.03
Gift of Oma Umbel, 1979

Toe rings with an extended bar were used to tap out the rhythm to folk music sung in Indian villages.

Earring

1960s
Silver
Length 6.7 cm
A.79.08.02
Gift of Oma Umbel, 1979

Hoops of twisted silver wire, small flowers, chains and tiny pendants on this earring make a pretty tinkling sound when the wearer moves her head.

Earrings

Beads, metallic foil, glass
Length 5 cm
Loaned by Zoe Wolfe

These earrings are a copy of Mughal jewelry.

HEAD CHAIN

Kashmir or Uttar Pradesh
Silver
Length 64 cm (with chain)
Length of earrings 7 cm
A.79.08.18
Gift of Oma Umbel, 1979

Since Indian women's pierced ear lobes are often heavily decorated with earrings, ear ornaments are sometimes suspended from a chain looped over the head to alleviate their weight. The long, drop earrings, with miniature flowers and ball pendants, jingle with the wearer's slightest movement. This jewelry is popular in Kashmir and Uttar Pradesh.

FOURTEEN STAMPS FOR A WOMAN'S FOREHEAD, BAINDI

1960s
Lead
Length (longest stamp) 2 cm
79.08.16
Gift of Oma Umbel, 1979

As noted in Department of Human Resources files, Indian women use lead stamps, *baindi*, which they dipped into a thick solution of colored yogurt, to mark their foreheads with various designs including the star, crescent and star, *tumpal*, stylized flowers, mango and *naga*, a mythological serpent.

MAN'S COAT

Early 20th century
Silk; metallic gold thread
Center back 99 cm
Sleeve 150 cm
A.1979.09.02a
Gift of Lola Stone

The luxurious coat from the British colonial period, is reportedly a type worn by the upper classes and Indian nobility. The purple silk coat is lined in magenta and bordered with gold floral scrolls and *buti*.

BELT

1960s
Silver
Length 120 cm
A.79.08.14
Gift of Oma Umbel, 1979

Stylized flowers and figure eights make a silver chain-link belt with filigree "tassels," ornamented with tiny silver bells at the ends which jingle with the wearer's movement.

TURBAN

1950s (?)
Silk chiffon
Height 12 cm
Circumference 54.5 cm
1979.09.26b
Gift of Lola Stone

Turbans of every size, shape and variety are traditional in India from ancient times. This twentieth century, pre-formed version based on the later Mughal style, is in sheer purple silk chiffon, woven with gold threads and ornamented with an aigrette of peacock feathers and imitation gems, possibly replacements for genuine originals.

SCARF, DUPATTA

1960s
Jaipur
Georgette
Length 155 cm
Width 72.5 cm
62-17
Departmental purchase, 1964

Bandhani (Hindi for "tie," or "bind") textiles come mostly from Gujurat and Rajasthan (where it is called *chundari*). Also known in India by the Indonesian term *plangi*, it is an ancient tie-dye process with conventionalized designs based principally on motifs from nature. The fine, linear patterns made of tiny dots (called *tritik* in Indonesia) are accomplished by the following method: first, the fabric is folded in four, dampened, and then pressed over a wooden block with pins in it, placed in the configuration of the design. The raised portions over the pins are picked up between the thumb and finger and tied. A single piece of binding thread is carried from one point to another. The cloth is dyed in the lightest color first, then the process is repeated. In a variation of the technique (Buhler, 1982:102), the design is outlined on the top layer of folded fabric with burnt sienna mixed with water and placed on a cord. The individual motifs are stamped on by means of a wooden block, the parts to be tied are lifted from below, pinched together and wrapped with thread.

SHAWL, *ODHNI*

1980s
Cotton
Length 242 cm
Width 109 cm
Loaned by Mrs. Gulab Watumull

This shawl, in splashes of vivid purple, saffron and magenta, is a contemporary version of an ancient tie-dye process.

SHAWL, *DUPATTA* (UNFINISHED)

1960s
Jaipur
Cotton
Width (open end) 115.5 cm
Length 565 cm
62-20
Departmental purchase, 1964

This length of fabric for a *dupatta* is used in University textile classes as a tie-dye demonstration piece. In the technique called wrap-resist-dyed, fabric is rolled and tightly bound at evenly spaced intervals. The tied areas will resist the dye and a striped, checked or plaid pattern will result. The process must be repeated for each successive color. These fabrics are frequently used for turbans.

WOMAN'S ENSEMBLE
WITH *ZARDOSI* EMBROIDERY
Delhi, India

TEXTILE SQUARE, *PATOLU*

1960s
Gujurat
Silk; double *ikat*, *patola*
Length 67 cm
Width 68 cm
62-9
Departmental purchase, 1964

Patola, the magnificent silk double *ikat* from Gujurat was traditionally used for wedding saris. The mother and female relations of a bride may wear *patola*, as well as the bride herself. In a certain part of some ceremonies the groom also wore a *patolu*, as a shoulder cloth. (Buhler, 1982:110)

Associated with birth as well as weddings, *patola* were used by the expectant mother to sit upon during a pregnancy ritual. These silk *ikat* textiles served both Jains and Hindus in religious rituals, as temple hangings and possibly as clothing for cult images and canopies placed over their heads. It was believed that *patola* had magical properties and it is said that small fragments of the cloth may have been charred and used as medicine. (Solyom, 1976:221) While much of their use was ceremonial, head scarves, *odhnis*, and a particular kind of *choli* were also traditionally made of *patola*.

The word *patola* appears in ancient literature but it is unclear if these textiles were silk, or if they were woven in the double *ikat* process. The *patola* with which we are familiar reliably date back to the 18th century. There are three main styles of *patola*: two are essentially floral patterns and the third, Patan style (from the town where the textile is made), contains motifs of elephants, human figures and birds as well as flowering shrubs.

There is less traditional use of *patola* in India today. While they are still worn as saris on festive occasions, modern *patola* is also used for items like kerchiefs and curtains. The relatively small square textile in the exhibition may have a similar purpose. The design consists of white elephants and green parrots arranged within a lozenge grid on a maroon silk ground.

SHAWL (?), *CHADDAR*

Cotton; silk
Warp 205.7 cm
Weft 132.3 cm
Loaned by Tom and Delmarie Klobe

Rows of hand embroidered toadstool-like shapes in pink and and black cover the field of this natural colored textile. The motif is identified as fan-shaped flowers in a very similar late 19th-early 20th century shawl or veil from Gujarat in the collection of the Honolulu Academy of Arts. (*Festival of Fibers*, 1977:38) Wide borders on both ends feature large floral bouquet medallions.

KASHMIR

SHAWL, *CHADDAR-RUMAL*

19th century
Wool, twill weave; wrapped gold threads
Warp 157 cm
Weft 152 cm
Loaned by Mrs. Gulab Watumull
Illustrated p. 35

According to literary sources, including Ksemendra (c. A.D. 990-1065), a writer of the medieval period in Kashmir, the shawl industry was thriving in the area at least as early as the eleventh century. (Chandra, 1979:236) In the 13th century shawls and other woolen goods from Kashmir reached Western India. The emperor Akbar (1556-1605) was a great admirer of Kashmiri shawls and their manufacture and use flourished during the Mughal period. Shawls with a square format (often called *rumal*), are sometimes said to reflect patterns similar to those of 17th century Mughal canopies. Some square shawls are still used for this purpose, as well as worn. (Fermenias, 1984:18)

In subsequent centuries, the famous shawls of Kashmir were exported in great numbers to Europe. Many shawls reflect Islamic influence in their design, including the paisley pattern and its derivatives. Embroidered shawls from Kashmir appeared in the 19th century. Until that time designs apparently had been woven, or woven and embroidered. *Zardozi* embroidery, with gold metallic threads, is one of the more elaborate techniques used to ornament these popular textiles. The fine, red wool challis shawl in the exhibition is appliquéd with paisley and other Islamic inspired motifs in green, purple and blue, and the design is further embellished with intricate gold embroidery.

EMBROIDERED SHAWL,
CHADDAR-RUMAL
19th century
Kashmir

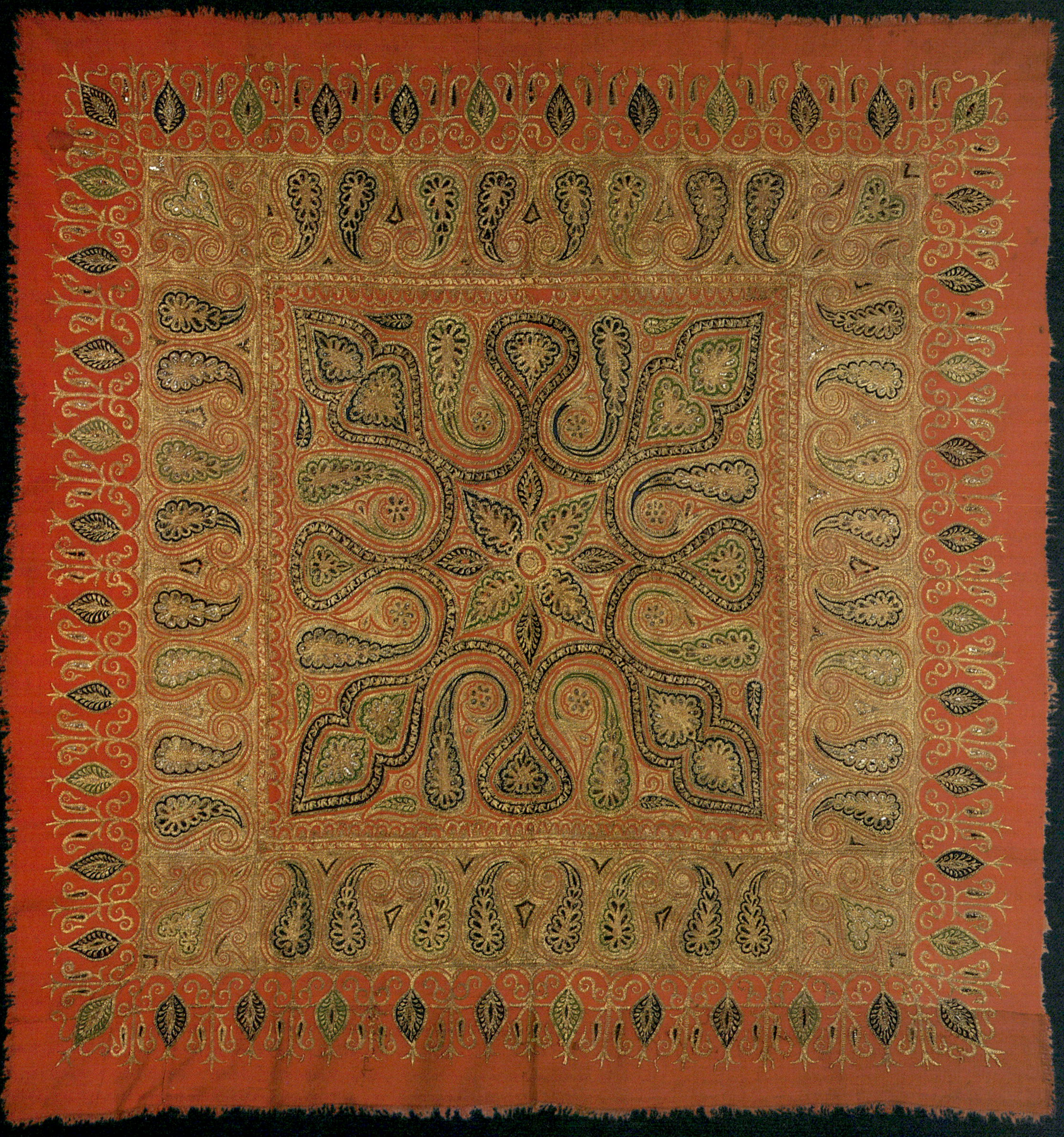

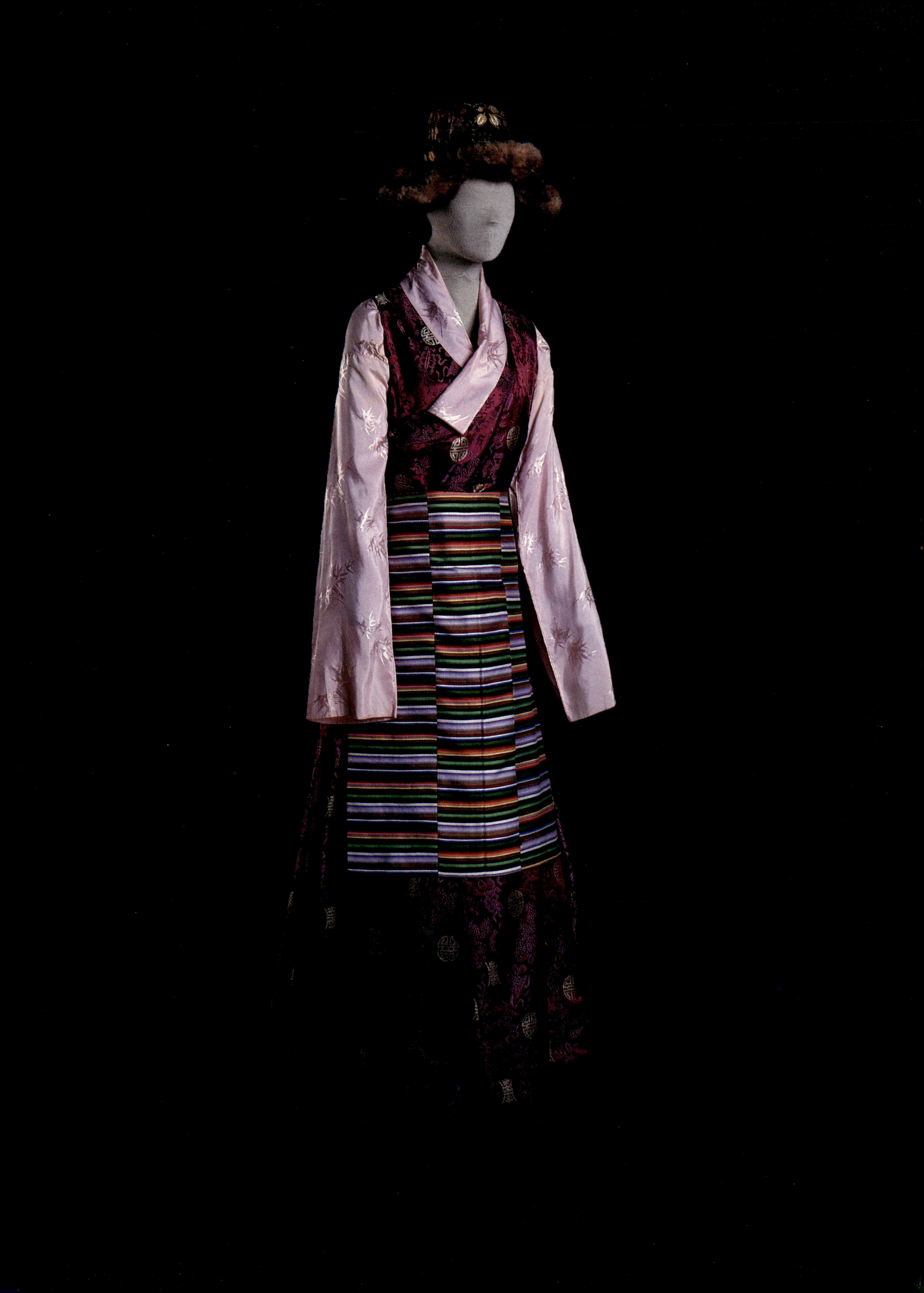

SIKKIM

WOMAN'S
INFORMAL ENSEMBLE

1960s
Gangtok
A.1979.10.06 a-f
Gift of Lola Stone, 1979
Illustrated p. 36

OUTER-GARMENT, *MO-KHO*
Silk, cotton, metallic gold
Center back 144 cm
Width (across shoulders) 31.6 cm

BLOUSE, *HANJU*
Silk brocade
Center back 55.8 cm
Sleeve 88.7 cm

HAT, *TSERING KENGYAP SHAMBU*
Silk brocade; marten fur
Height 14.4 cm
Circumference (outer edge) 95 cm

APRON, *PANGDEN*
Silk, rayon velvet, cotton
Length 65.4 cm
Width 48 cm

SCARF
Silk
Length 114.6 cm
Width 33.3 cm

SCARF
Silk
Length 114.6 cm
Width 34 cm

According to the donor, this ensemble belonged to former Queen Namgyal of Sikkim, the American-born Hope Cooke. Sikkim, once a small Himalayan kingdom bordered by Tibet, Nepal and Bhutan, is now an Indian state.

As queen of Sikkim, Hope Cooke dressed in traditional costume. This informal outfit consists of a sleeveless, full-length outer garment in plum silk brocade with woven gold Chinese longevity symbols, worn over a pink silk blouse. Scarves may be placed about the neck, or wrapped around the waist as a sash. They are often ceremonially exchanged between Sikkimese friends on important occasions. (Wilcox, 1965:36) A striped apron is traditionally worn with this costume. This example is handwoven multi-colored silk, lined in maroon cotton with a floral motif and tied with cotton and velvet. The silk brocade hat has four fur-lined flaps, which may be lowered as protection against the mountain winds.

NEPAL

MAN'S HAT, TOPI

1960s
Katmandu
Velvet
Height 11 cm
Circumference 51 cm
62-1
Departmental purchase, 1964

MAN'S HAT, TOPI

1960s
Katmandu
Velvet
Height 11 cm
Circumference 54 cm
62-2
Departmental purchase, 1964

MAN'S HAT, TOPI

1960s
Katmandu
Cotton
Height 15 cm
Circumference 52 cm
62-5
Departmental purchase, 1964

MAN'S HAT, TOPI

1960s
Katmandu
Cotton
Height 14 cm
Circumference 53 cm
62-4
Departmental purchase, 1964

MAN'S HAT, TOPI

1960s
Cotton
Height 17 cm
Circumference 52 cm
64-7
Departmental purchase, 1964

NECKLACE

Gurung and Tamang peoples
Glass, string, thread
Length 80 cm
Loaned by Zoe Wolfe

A bead necklace such as this signifies that the woman who wears it is married.

NECKLACE

Pohkari region
Gurung people
Silver, yarn, string, bone or teeth
Length 59 cm
Loaned by Zoe Wolfe

Gurung women in the Pohkari region wear this type of necklace. The major pieces are often recycled and restrung.

NECKLACE

Gurung people
Stone, rope
Length 36 cm
Loaned by Zoe Wolfe

Stone beads are an inexpensive substitute for the preferred material, coral, in this necklace.

BANGLES

Glass
Diameter 26.3 cm
Loaned by Zoe Wolfe

All Nepalese women and girls wear large quantities of bangles.

EARRINGS

Garung and Tamang peoples
Brass
Length 41.5 cm
Width 4.3 cm

TIBET

EARRING

20th century
Turquoises, corals, gilt copper
Length 9.5 cm
Depth 1.7 cm
Private collection

This drop earring from Tibet, consists of a large, tubular coral bead, flanked by rows of beading and a band of leaves.

EAR ORNAMENT

20th century
Turquoises, corals, rubies, emeralds, lapis lazuli, gilt silver
Length 11.4 cm
Width 7.4 cm
Depth 4.3 cm
Private collection

Large ear ornaments such as this are fastened to hoop earrings and, in order to alleviate weight on the earlobes, further attached to a headdress. This mandala-shaped ear ornament is created with rows of turquoise lotus petals and a jeweled phoenix set within a floral design.

HAIR ORNAMENT

Silver, brass, turquoises, corals, cord
Length 59 cm
Width 3 cm
Loaned by Zoe Wolfe

BRACELET

Silver
Diameter 6 cm
Loaned by Zoe Wolfe

This bracelet of forged, hollow silver alloy is worn by both Tibetan and Sherpa women.

BRACELET

Cast bronze
Diameter 6.5 cm
Loaned by Zoe Wolfe

MAN'S RING

Silver, coral
Height 3 cm
Width 2.2 cm
Depth 3 cm
Loaned by Zoe Wolfe

Because of its distinctive shape, this is called a "saddle ring."

TIBETAN OR SHERPA WOMAN'S BELT BUCKLE

Mixed silver; silver plate
Height 13 cm
Width 8.8 cm
Loaned by Zoe Wolfe

BELT BUCKLE

Silver alloy
Height 9 cm
Width 6 cm
Loaned by Zoe Wolfe

TIBETAN OR SHERPA WOMAN'S BELT

Yak wool
Length 97 cm
Width 16.5 cm
Loaned by Zoe Wolfe

MAN'S BELT

Leather
Length 110 cm
Height 11.5 cm
Loaned by Zoe Wolfe

Central Asia

Woman's Boots

Late 19th century
Pamir Plateau, West Central Asia
Sheepskin (?); cotton
Length 23 cm
Width 8 cm
Height 30 cm
A.1982.14.01 a,b
Departmental purchase, 1982

According to research by Mary Ellen Des Jarlais, these carefully crafted, handmade boots are worn for very special occasions. She describes the construction as follows: "The leather has been tanned and dyed in shades of red, beige, green and black. Traditional motifs, following a symmetrical arrangement, were cut and sewn together with the seams on the inside of the boot. The soles have been attached using hand stitching and glue, while the upper edges of the boot were bound with a red cotton fabric which extends one-half centimeter down the inside of the boot."

The Pamir Mountain region where the boots were made is bordered by China, Afghanistan and the area which is now the Soviet Union and was for centuries traversed by East-West trade routes. Des Jarlais states that the design of the boots reflect international influences: the shape is Russian; the wide scrolls, medallions and leaf motifs are inspired by both China and the Middle East. Today, similarly styled boots are worn by Uzbek women living in the Bokhara region of Russia and the Xinjiang Uygus Autonomous Region of China.

BURMA

FABRIC FOR
WRAPPED SKIRT, *LONGYI*

1960s
Silk; weft *ikat*
Warp 174 cm
Weft 100 cm
A.1981.01.06
Departmental purchase, 1981

The Burmese *longyi*, worn by both men and women, is a long skirt cloth which is wrapped about the hips. Men usually tie the *longyi* at the front, while women secure it at the waist with a black belt which is hidden by an overblouse.

WRAPPED SKIRT,
LONGYI (UNSEWN)

1960s
Silk; warp *ikat*
Warp 180 cm
Weft 99 cm
A.1981.01.03
Departmental purchase, 1981

WRAPPED SKIRT,
LONGYI (UNSEWN)

1960s
Silk; warp *ikat*
Warp 177 cm
Weft 99.5 cm
40-3
Departmental purchase, 1971

FABRIC FOR
WRAPPED SKIRT, *LONGYI*

1960s
Silk
Warp 386 cm
Weft 111.5 cm
1981.01.10
Departmental purchase, 1981

GIRL'S CEREMONIAL
HEADDRESS, *SEEPON*

Mandalay
Cotton; metallic gold thread; sequins
Height 27 cm
Circumference 55 cm
62-1
Departmental purchase, 1971

This elaborate, helmet-shaped headdress ornamented with peacocks was worn in an ear piercing, or *nat win*, ceremony which marked a girl's passage from puberty to womanhood. In the ritual, which would be followed by refreshments for friends and relatives, a group of young women dressed in their finest attire would have their ears pierced by golden needles. (Fairservis, 1979:112; Fraser-Lu, 1988:75)

MAN'S JACKET, *THAIPOME*

1960s
Cotton
Center back 58 cm
Sleeve 163 cm
15-2
Departmental purchase, 1971

MAN'S FORMAL HAT,
GAUNG BAUNG

1960s
Silk; basketry
Height 27 cm
Circumference 52.5 cm
62-2
Departmental purchase, 1964

Pink silk draped on a basketry frame creates this turban-like man's hat in a traditional style. Burmese men wear these for important occasions such as weddings. The hats are also worn for certain events by members of Parliament.

Laos

BRIDE'S ENSEMBLE

1970
Loaned by Desarone Boungnaseng

JACKET
Silk brocade, metallic gold thread
Center back 48 cm
Sleeve 133.5 cm

SARONG, SIN
Silk; *ikat*; metallic thread
Length 71.6 cm
Waist 56 cm

SASH, PHA BEANG
Silk; metallic brocade, gold colored balls, mother of pearl
Length 179.5 cm
Fringe 10 cm
Width 16 cm

This ensemble was worn by the lender for her wedding ceremony. The sarong, *sin*, in purple silk, has narrow, vertical stripes of red and gold metallic yarns, and a wide hem border with *ikat*-patterned geometric and stylized animal motifs. Pink silk metallic brocade is used for the tightly fitted, long-sleeved jacket enhanced with heavy metallic gold embroidery along the neckline. It fastens at the left with handmade buttons and fabric loops. The sash, which is worn over the shoulder, is of silk metallic brocade with an elaborately fashioned fringe of tiny gold-colored balls and little birds of mother-of-pearl.

BRIDE'S WEDDING RECEPTION ENSEMBLE

1970
Loaned by Desarone Boungnaseng

BODICE
Raw silk
Length (from top of shoulder) 42.4 cm
Width 38.5 cm

SARONG, SIN
Silk; *ikat*
Length 79.1 cm
Width 110.8 cm

It is customary for a bride to wear different costumes at the wedding ceremony and the reception. This ensemble is typical of the fine silks that are traditionally woven in the lowland regions near Vientiane and Luang Prabang. The sarongs (tubular wrap skirts), *sin*, are patterned with vertical stripes, or small geometric or floral designs of woven gold threads. *Sin* always have a separately woven hem border, called *tdinjok*, decorated with discontinuous supplementary weft patterning. This example has a design of interlocking gold zigzags and floriate motifs. The royal blue and gold *sin* is worn with a beige raw silk blouse.

Vietnam

Woman's ensemble

Tunic, *áo dài*; pants, *quần*
Silk crepe
Center back 116.5 cm
Sleeve 147.5 cm
Loaned by Nguyen Ngoc Nhung

The Chinese influenced *áo dài*, like the form-fitting Hong Kong *cheongsam*, which it resembles, evolved from the *jipao (chi-p'ao)* worn by Manchu women in the later years of the Qing dynasty. The tunic-like dress is fitted at the waist, has long, tight sleeves and a stand-up, "mandarin" collar. It fastens at the right with fabric loops and frogs or buttons. The sides are slit to the waist to reveal wide-hemmed, ankle-length pants, *quần*, worn underneath. A large sun hat, *nón lá*, is worn with the costume.

The Vietnamese were under the rule of China from the first century B.C. to A.D. 939. Sericulture (the production of raw silk including the raising of silk worms) and the weaving of fine silks flourished in Vietnam for centuries until European fabrics began to be imported into French Indo-China.

This lilac silk crepe *áo dài* was hand-painted with a floral design by the atelier Thanlé, now in Paris. The garment is worn with white *quần*.

Woman's ensemble

Tunic, *áo dài*; Pants, *quần*
Synthetic
Center back 138 cm
Sleeve 140 cm
15-1
Gift of Matia Kindig, 1969

Woman's hat, *Nón lá*

1950s
Saigon
Palm leaf, bamboo; cotton, velvet, gold paper
Diameter 43.5 cm
Height 16 cm
Loaned by Karen Thompson

The wide brimmed, conical sun hats, *nón lá*, are made of split palm leaves on a stripped bamboo frame. They are often embroidered on the underside with brightly colored floral or geometric designs, sometimes enhanced with gold paper cutouts. The hats are held in place by wide chin-straps of silk, velvet or other fabrics in colors which complement the costume. *Nón lá* come with fitted plastic covers to protect them, and the wearer, from rain.

Torque (neck ring)

20th century
Silver
Length 14 cm
Width 13 cm
Private Collection

The traditional Chinese motif consisting of a dragon and phoenix with peony and prunus blossoms is worked in repoussé on this silver torque. The serrated ring on the upper section unscrews and the back section swivels open, allowing the torque to be slipped around the neck.

Man's ensemble

Departmental purchase, 1963

TUNIC, *ÁO DÀI*
Synthetic fabric
Center back 99.5 cm
Sleeve 158 cm
15-6a

PANTS, *QUẦN*
Length 108 cm
Waist 64 cm
15-6b

HAT, *KHĂN DÓNG*
Circumference 54 cm
Crown 9 cm
64-4

The man's tunic, also called *áo-dài*, is knee length, has narrow sleeves, and is more loosely fitted than the woman's garment. Floral medallions and the Chinese symbol for longevity are woven into the fabric of this black *áo-dài*, which is worn with white trousers. An opened-crowned hat, *khăn dóng*, consisting of a cardboard base covered with black rayon crepe draped in a turban-like fashion, completes the costume.

Following page

IKAT WALL HANGING
Cambodia

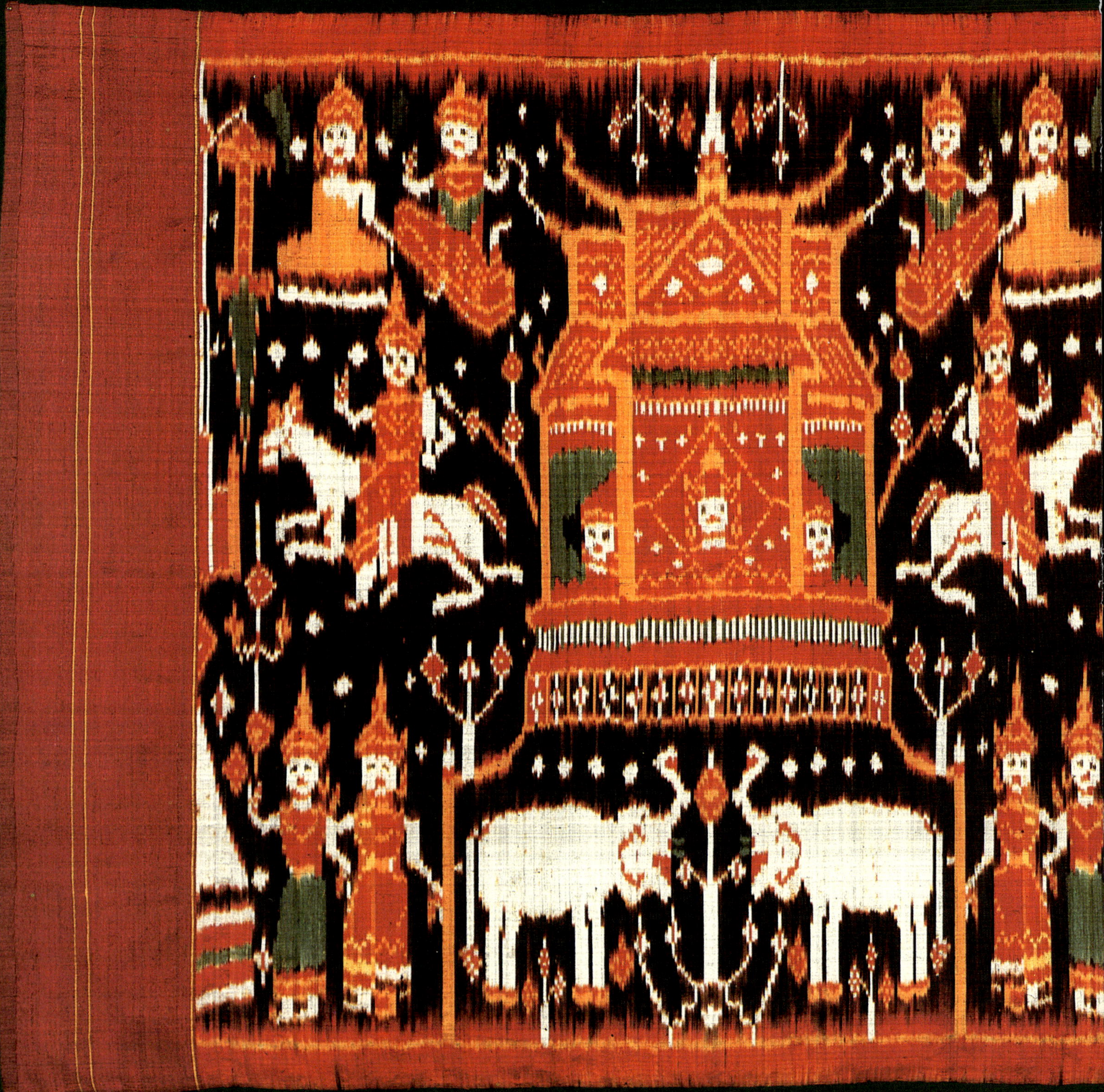

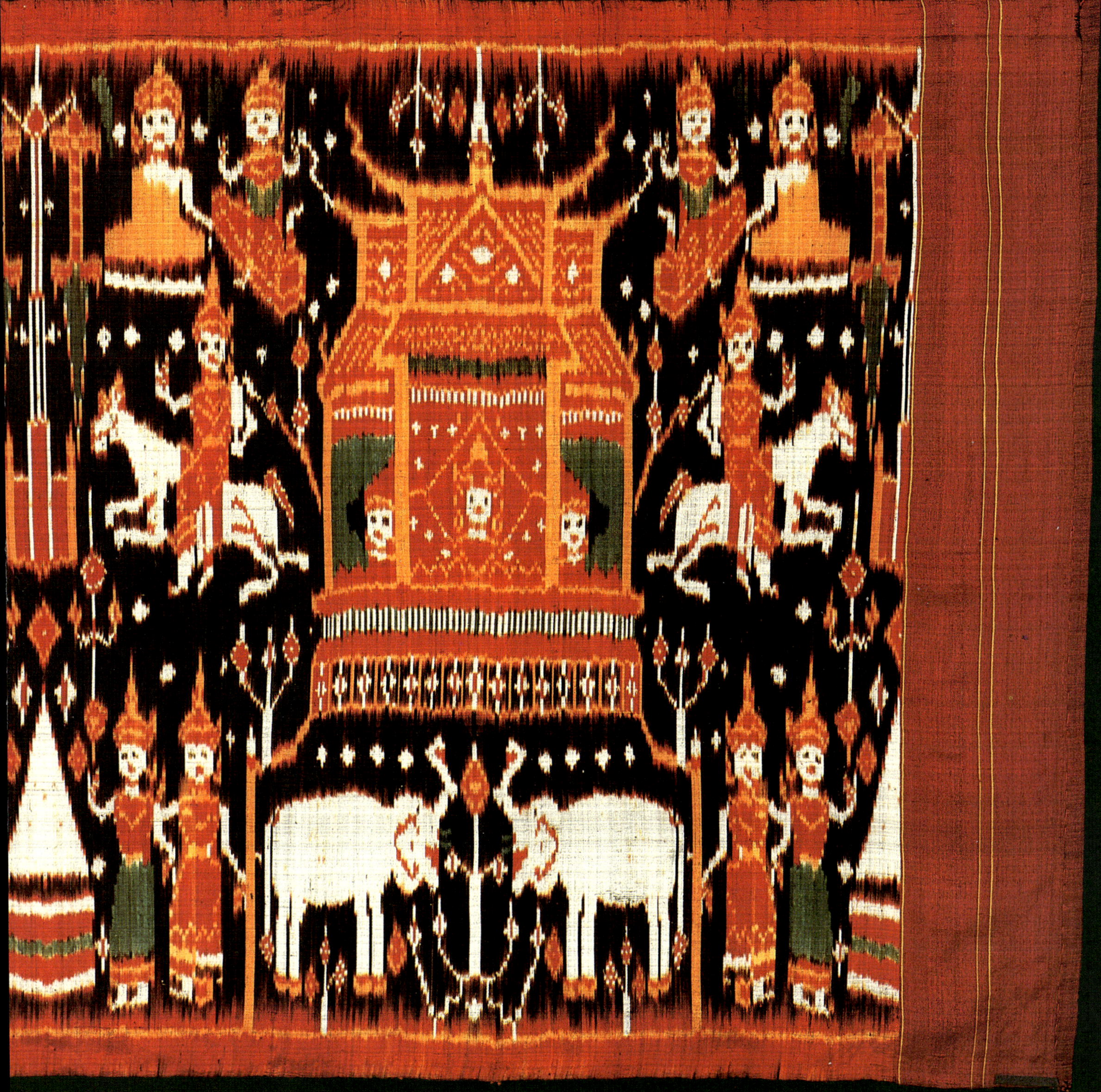

CAMBODIA

WALL HANGING

c. 1963
Silk; weft *ikat, hol*
Warp 171 cm
Weft 70 cm
80-1
Departmental purchase, 1963
Illustrated p. 44-45

The silk industry in Cambodia dates to the twelfth or thirteenth century, when silk worms began to be imported from China and Siam (Thailand). Cambodian textile craftspersons were especially known for silk weft *ikat* (*hol*) fabrics with rich, shimmering colors obtained by immersing them for long periods, or successively, in the dye-bath. (*Kambuja*, No.7, Oct. 15, 1965:47)

Pictorial wall hangings, or banners, which were used primarily to decorate the Cambodian house on ceremonial occasions such as marriages or funerals (Fraser-Lu, 1988:132), are examples of excellence in weft *ikat*. The naturalistic imagery is often associated with Theravada Buddhism. Some have inscriptions from Buddhist scriptures.

Unfortunately, this type of weft *ikat* textile seems not to have been made in Cambodia since the 1970s. Fraser-Lu (1988:pl 20) depicts a far less skillfully executed funerary banner, with imagery similar to the wall hanging in the exhibition, which was woven by Laotian refugees at a camp on the Thai border.

FABRIC FOR WRAPPED SKIRT, *SAMPOT*

1967
Seim Reap
Silk; *hol*
Warp 118.0 cm
Weft 82.0 cm
40-5
Gift of Oma Umbel, 1967

The *sampot* is a length of fabric that may be wrapped about the hips with the end gathered and tucked in at the waist or pulled between the legs to form trousers. The *sampot* may also be sewn into a tube skirt like the Indonesian sarong.

This vivid textile is produced by the weft *ikat* process known as *hol* in Cambodia. According to Mary Ellen Des Jarlais, the weaver, in an attempt to keep the outlines of each motif as distinct as possible, is obliged to sacrifice absolutely straight selvages. This is one indication that the fabric is handwoven. The placement of a border on one end of the textile is unusual and suggests that this is a fragment cut from a larger piece of cloth.

WRAPPED SKIRT, *SAMPOT*

1960s
Silk; ikat
Warp 164 cm
Weft 83.5 cm
40-2
Gift of Barbara Smith, 1969

WRAPPED SKIRT, *SAMPOT*

Silk; *ikat*
Warp 170 cm
Weft 85 cm
40-6
Departmental purchase, 1967

WRAPPED SKIRT, *SAMPOT*

1960s
Silk; *ikat*
Warp 174 cm
Weft 85 cm
40-1
Departmental purchase, 1963

PILLOW COVER

Silk
Square, 56.5 cm
80-2
Departmental purchase, 1967

An excellent example of the *plangi-tritik* tie-dye process is this cerise pillow cover patterned in bright yellow, blue and green. The puckering and ruffled edge are a result of binding the fabric very tightly with dye resistant material. The Cambodian *plangi-tritik* textiles are much like those from Sumatra and Java. The motifs are contrived with short lines, triangles and other geometric shapes. (Larsen, 1976:28, 38)

THAILAND

Among the most interesting and colorful Asian costumes are those worn by the tribal peoples of the hill country of northern Thailand who have migrated into the area during the current century from China, Burma and Laos. Their diverse ethnic backgrounds and cultures are reflected in their clothing styles, which vary greatly from one group to another. Ornamentation is important to all groups; the most lavishly decorated costumes (except in the Karen tribe) are worn by unmarried women.

WOMAN'S ENSEMBLE

1960s
Lahu (Mussur) people
Cotton; silver, coins
15-18
Departmental purchase, 1967
Illustrated p. 48

JACKET
Center back 39 cm
Sleeve 112 cm

SKIRT (TUBULAR)
Length 108 cm
Width 128 cm

Plain or petal-shaped round buckles engraved with geometric and floral patterns are used by the Lahu to fasten tunics or jackets. The jacket in the exhibition, in black and red cotton, has three large buckles and a silver button trim. At center back, and at either side of the front placket, is a vertical row of Indian rupees and annas from the 19th and early 20th century; the earliest dates to 1862. A horizontally striped, sarong-like skirt is shown with the short jacket. Leggings (not in the exhibition) would be worn under the skirt. Costumes with elaborate ornamentation, which would include several pieces of silver jewelry, are usually reserved for festive occasions.

SHOULDER BAG

1960s
Lahu people
Cotton; wool
Length 33.5 cm
Width 28.5 cm
Strap 82 cm
Fringe 15 cm
72-1
Departmental purchase, 1967

Embroidered shoulder bags are part of the Lahu costume worn by both men and women. This bag, in black cotton with red stripes, is ornamented with geometric designs in patchwork appliqué, decorative fringe, and multicolored wool pompons.

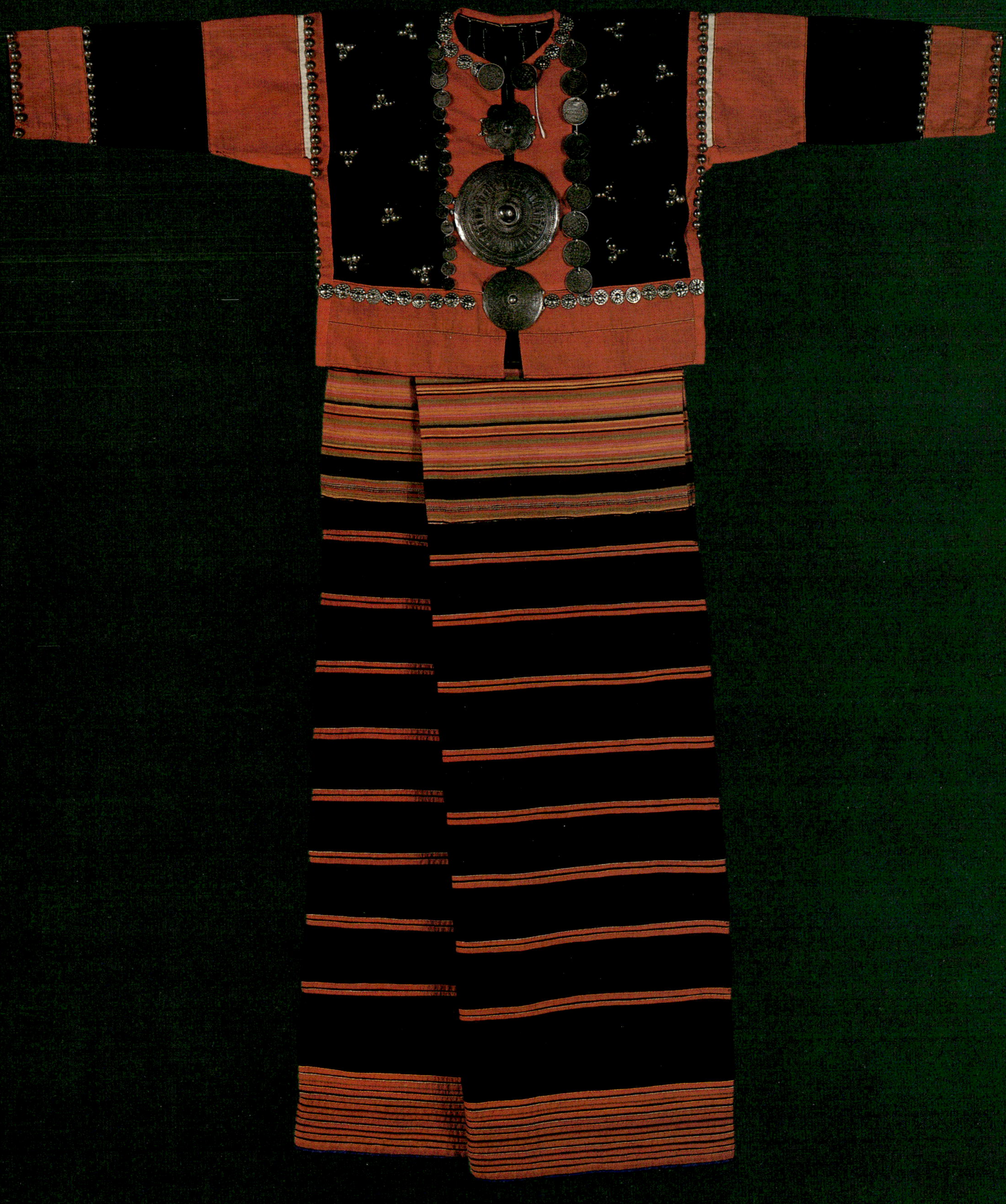

Woman's Jacket

1980s
Akha people
Cotton
Center back 76.5 cm
Sleeve 142.5 cm
A.1982.13.01
Departmental purchase, 1982

Akha women wear hip length jackets in blue-black, indigo-dyed cotton. Except for a bright, colored binding, the front of the jacket is generally plain; decoration is confined to the sleeves and the back, which is appliquéd with complex, multi-colored geometric designs. The jacket would be worn over a halter-like garment. A short skirt, leggings, a sash with ends ornamented with pompons, coins, beads and other objects, and an ornate headdress would complete the costume. The Lewises point out that most Akha ornamentation is attached to their clothing. The basic style varies somewhat among three sub-groups of Akha people.

Girls dress in essentially the same style as their mothers, their costumes becoming more elaborately ornamented as as they grow older. The change from one type to the next occurs as part of four rites of passage ceremonies. The girl is first allowed to wear a halter. In the next stage she adds Job's tears seeds (small, white bugle-bead shaped seeds from a tropical grass), red and white beads, and silver to her cap. She then adds a sash to her costume and, finally, changes to an adult-style headdress. Her unmarried status is indicated by tiny gourds worn at the waist and on the headdress. (Lewis, 1984:203-217)

Woman's Headdress

1960s
Akha people
Cotton; palm, silver, glass, feathers
Height 29 cm
Circumference
62-3
Departmental purchase, 1967
Illustrated p. 51

The elaborate Akha headdress is worn even when working at home or in the fields. Constructed with a high framework of palm fiber covered with coarse indigo cloth, this typical headdress is embellished with rows of hollow silver buttons, shirt buttons, beads, feathers, pompons and old coins.

Woman's Belt

Akha people
Cotton; beads, buttons, cowrie shells, Indian coins
Length 70 cm
Width 5 cm
Loaned by Zoe Wolfe

The Ahka woman's belt, decorated with cowrie shells, beads, buttons and coins, is worn over her jacket. Marital status is indicated by the width of the belt; unmarried women's belts are wider and usually have more shells. (Lewis, 1984:211)

Two Necklaces

Akha people
Silver beads; glass
Length 55 cm
Loaned by Zoe Wolfe

Pendant

Ahka people
Silver, beads, fiber
Length 60 cm
Loaned by Zoe Wolfe

Woman's Skirt

Early 1960s
Hmong (Meo) people
Cotton
Length 60.5 cm
Waist (wrap-skirt) 66 cm
Hem width 712.6 cm
15-10
Departmental Purchase, 1967
Illustrated p. 53

Patterning on the "skirt of one hundred pleats" worn by Hmong women is made by the batik wax-resist process, drawing the designs in melted beeswax and dipping the fabric in cold indigo dye. After the dye has set, the wax is removed by boiling, and recycled. The Blue Hmong sub-group are apparently the only Thai hill people working in batik.

A strip of plain fabric is sewn to the top of the skirt and a wide border of multi-colored, cross-stitch embroidery is attached to the bottom. The skirt is pleated by anchoring the pleats down with a herringbone stitch, and the running threads which hold the pleats together remain in place until the skirt is worn. Teen-age girls have the widest hem borders on their skirts. This is in keeping with the general custom among the hill tribes of marriageable girls wearing the most elaborate ornamentation on their costumes. (Lewis, 1984:11,108)

Lahu Woman's Ensemble
Thailand

MARRIED WOMAN'S ENSEMBLE

1960s
Chieng Mai
Pwo Karen people
Cotton; seeds
15-12,13
Departmental purchase, 1967

BLOUSE
Center back 63 cm
Sleeve 60 cm

SKIRT (UNSEWN)
Length 92 cm
Width 132 cm

Bright yellow and red checks, zigzags and rectangles are satin-stitched over the entire surface of this blouse in the bold patterning favored by Pwo Karen women. Job's-tears seeds enhance the design.

Married women in the Pwo Karen tribal group wear a horizontally striped skirt and a tunic-like blouse, which is constructed from two widths of cloth folded in half at the shoulders and seamed at underarms, center front and center back, leaving an opening for the neck.

The Karen are known for fine weaving. This is evident in their hand-woven skirts, made of two strips of cloth which are stitched together horizontally and then at the sides to form a tube. Of varying lengths, the skirts usually overlap at the front and are belted at the waist. According to the Lewises (1984:77), skirts with *ikat* stripes are woven by mountain women, each having a special way of binding the threads before dying to produce an *ikat* pattern exclusively hers. The skirt in the exhibition has stripes in a herringbone *ikat*.

MARRIED WOMAN'S BLOUSE

1960s
Skaw Karen people
Cotton; seeds
Length 52 cm
Sleeve 70 cm
15-8
Departmental purchase, 1964

Skaw Karen women wear skirts similar to those of the Pwo Karen group. Their blouses have a more subtle decoration, often confined to the lower portion, neck and sleeve borders of a plain, indigo-dyed homespun cotton garment. This blouse is ornamented with multi-colored embroidery and Job's tears seeds.

MAN'S SHIRT

1960s
Skaw Karen people
Cotton
Center back 56 cm
Sleeve 52 cm
15-15
Departmental purchase, 1967

The construction of the upper body cover worn by men and married women of the Karen tribal groups is the same, except that men's are usually longer. This Skaw Karen man's shirt, in red with vertical stripes, is fringed at the lower edge. Men wear peasant style pants or knee-length tube skirts with two wide, horizontal stripes.

AKHA WOMAN'S HEADDRESS
Thailand

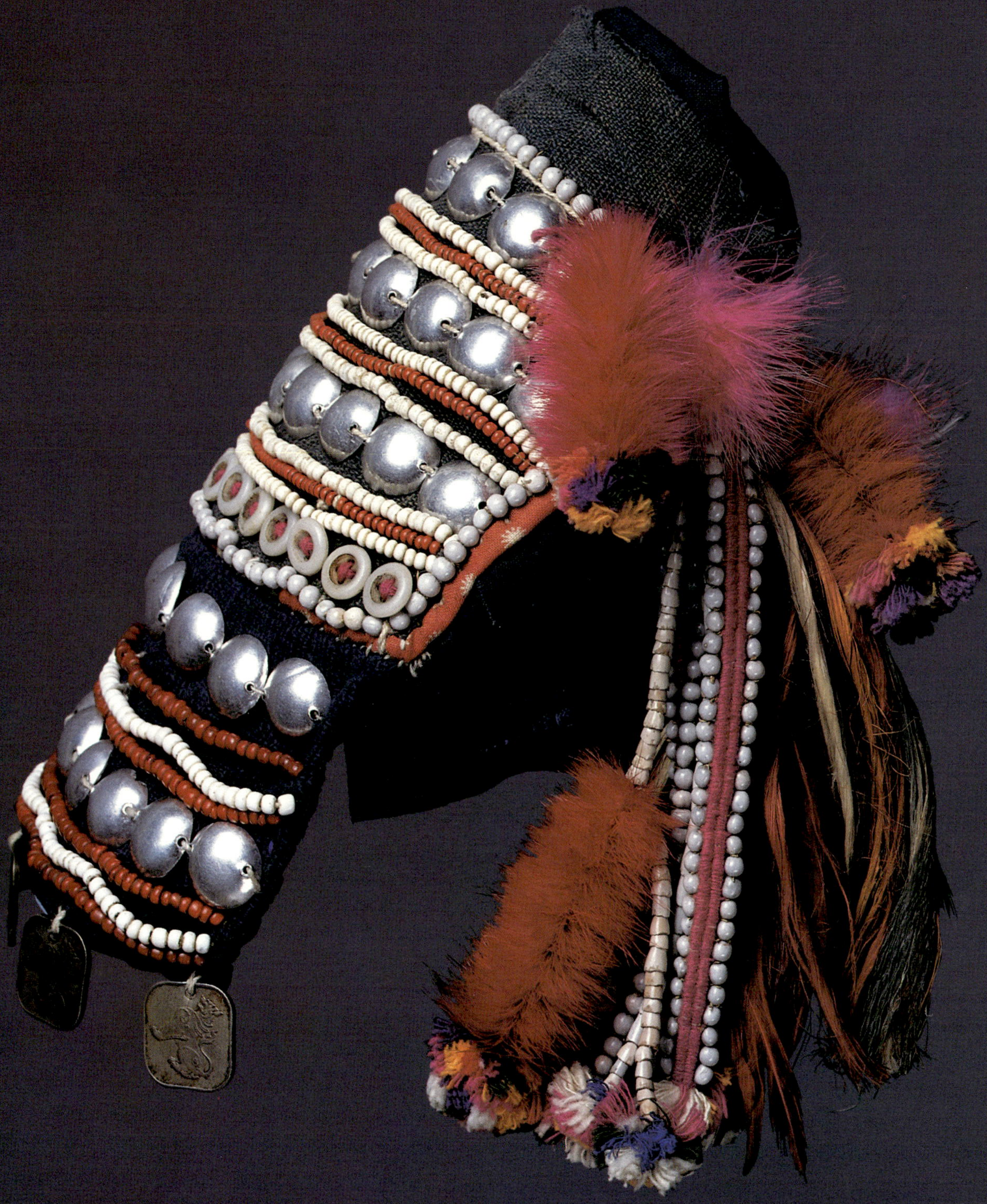

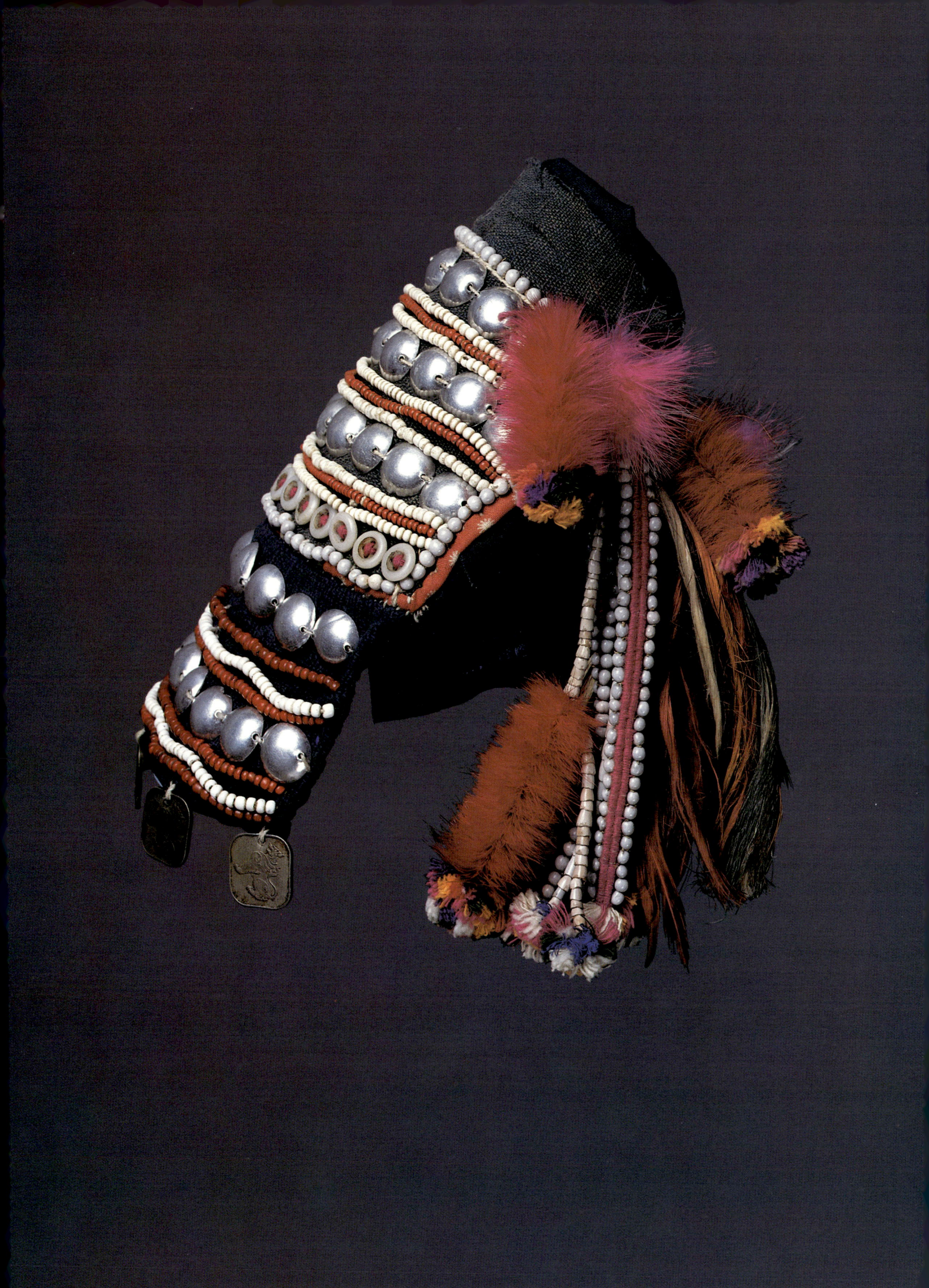

Unmarried Woman's Dress

1960s
Chieng Mai
Pwo Karen people
Cotton
Center back 114 cm
Sleeve 60.5 cm
15-11
Departmental purchase, 1967

White cotton dresses are worn by Pwo Karen females until marriage. Girls learn to make these garments when they are very young. Constructed in the same manner as the married woman's blouse, they are simple to sew but the trim becomes more sophisticated as the girls grow older. (Lewis, 1984:74)

The high waistline of this dress is indicated with heavy red, yellow and black threads and a long fringe at the center front and sides. The lower part of the garment has a design of satin-stitched black and red diamonds.

Tribal Jewelry

1960s
Silver
Departmental purchase, 1967

Silver jewelry, ingots and artifacts are a primary medium of exchange among Thai tribal peoples and an indication of one's wealth and status. The following pieces of silver jewelry from the Department of Human Resources collection are included in the exhibition:

Neck Ring

Circumference (outside) 16.5 cm
Width (widest part) 2.7 cm
60-5

Plain neck rings of flat silver with ends curled in a spiral are worn mostly by Akha women. (Lewis, 1984:48)

Neck Ring

Circumference 42 cm
60-6a

The flattened ends of many round neck rings resemble the heads of sharp-beaked birds. These terminals often serve as hooks from which pendants, chains and other ornaments are suspended. These are from the Lahu group.

Neck Ring

Circumference (outside) 47.5 cm
60-6b

Neck Ring

Circumference 33.6 cm
60-6c

Torque Bracelet

Circumference (outside) 17.9 cm
60-3a

Open ring torques made of twisted silver wire are worn by several Hill Country tribal peoples.

Torque Bracelet

Circumference 18.1 cm
60-3b

Torque Bracelet

Circumference 18.3 cm 60-3c

Bracelet

Circumference (outside) 20.8 cm
60-4a

Silver spiral bracelets such as these heavy, open-ring torques, are mostly of Chinese origin. Akha women in particular wear this style bracelet. (Lewis, 1984:43)

Bracelet

Circumference 21.6 cm
60-4b

Bracelet

Circumference 14.5 cm
Height 3.6 cm
A.1988.24.01a

Some bracelets worn by Lahu, Akha and Lisu women are made of flattened silver, plain or with engraved designs, which are bent to conform to the wrist.

BRACELET

Circumference 16.3 cm
Height 3.5 cm
A.1988.24.01b

BRACELET

Circumference 16.1 cm
Height 3.6 cm
A.1988.24.01c

BRACELET

Circumference 14.2 cm
Height 3.6 cm
A.1988.24.01d

EARRINGS

Length 3.2 cm
Circumference (outside) 8.7 cm
60-7a

HMONG WOMAN'S SKIRT
Thailand

EAR PLUGS

Length 3.4 cm
60-7b

There are many styles of ear ornaments including large and small cylinders, buttons, cup-shapes, and plugs, such as this pair with designs on the caps.

HAT, MWA NON

1960s
Palm, bamboo
Height (crown) 15 cm
Diameter (brim) 40 cm
Height (inner hat) 14 cm
Circumference (inner hat) 43 cm
62-1
Departmental purchase, 1963

The *mwa non* is worn by Thai women on the farm and in the markets. Shaped like a lampshade, this wide brimmed hat is made of palm leaf strips and is worn over a separate inner hat with an open crown, to which it is attached by thin bamboo pins.

HAT, MWA NON

1960s
Bamboo
Height (crown) 15 cm
Diameter (brim) 44.5 cm
Height (inner hat) 13 cm
Circumference (inner hat) 48.5 cm
62-2
Departmental purchase, 1964

Both the hat and inner hat are made of open weave bamboo.

WOMAN'S FORMAL DAYTIME ENSEMBLE, *CHITRLADA*

Silk; brocade, gold metallic thread
15-22
Departmental purchase

JACKET
Center back 60 cm
Sleeve 140 cm

SKIRT
Length 95 cm
Waist 72 cm

There are five principal styles of national costume decreed by Her Majesty the Queen for wear by the women of modern Thailand. These garments, which derive from the traditional dress of earlier historical periods, are categorized according to degree of formality, from casual to full-dress wear. The *chitrlada* is worn for formal daytime occasions. The jacket in this exhibition, in peacock blue, iridescent Thai silk, has a stand-up "mandarin" collar and fastens in front with five gold-colored buttons. Formal daytime jackets usually have long, tight sleeves, but may have three-quarter length sleeves. The sarong-like skirt, *paisin*, has a center pleat and is sewn to a waistband. The skirts for this costume may be plain, of all-over brocade or designed with a wide, lower brocaded border, such as this example in metallic gold.

MALAYSIA

WOMAN'S FORMAL ENSEMBLE

1964
Kuala Lumpur
Departmental purchase, 1964

BLOUSE, *KEBAYA BANDUNG*
Cotton
Center back 58.6 cm
Sleeve 145.6 cm
15-2

SKIRT, *KAIN LEPAS*
Cotton
Length 94 cm
Waist 59 cm
15-1

SHOULDER CLOTH, *SELENDANG*
Cotton and rayon lace
Length 177.8 cm
Width 57 cm
62-1

The *kebaya, kain lepas* and *selendang* make up the traditional costume for festive occasions. This hip-length *kebaya* in green and white floral patterned lace has a shawl collar and a shirred insert at the center front closing. The long sleeves end in shallow points which extend over the hands. The *kebaya* is worn with an imitation batik skirt, patterned with leaves, vine scrolls, cocks, representations of family shrines, and wings of the mythical bird, Garuda. The skirt is sewn with front pleats to give the appearance of the draped, wrap-skirt, *kain lepas*. Complementing this costume is a shoulder cloth, *selendang,* of copper colored imported French lace, which is worn around the head and shoulders or over the left shoulder.

WOMAN'S SKIRT, *KAIN LEPAS*

1960s
Penang
Cotton
Warp 228 cm
Weft 108 cm
20-6
Departmental purchase, 1964

The *kain lepas* (lit. "escaped," or "free" cloth), also known as *kain panjang,* is a long, unsewn skirt cloth. It is wrapped around the hips and worn with the right end pleated over the left at the center front. A geometric and floral design in medium pink and dark blue is featured on this kain *lepas* produced in the *tulis*, or hand drawn, batik method.

FABRIC FOR WOMAN'S SARONG
(UNFINISHED BATIK)

1964
Kota Baharu, Kelantan
Cotton
Warp 194.2 cm
Weft 104.7 cm
20-3
Departmental purchase, 1964

This unfinished sarong shows the initial steps in the Malaysian stamped batik process, using a metal stamp, *cap,* with a design of stylized birds and flowers. The *cap* was dipped in melted wax and stamped on the fabric, recreating the pattern in wax resist. Blue indigo dye was then hand painted on portions of the pheasants, flowers, scalloped arches and floral borders. The ground is still the natural colored fabric.

WOMAN'S SARONG
(FINISHED BATIK)

1964
Kota Baharu, Kelantan
Cotton
Warp 193.7 cm
Weft 106 cm
20-4
Departmental purchase, 1964

In this finished version of the batik sarong (20-4, above), mustard yellow dye has been handpainted on the fabric in addition to the indigo. Yellow applied over blue resulted in the green background color. When all dyeing was completed, the wax was removed by boiling.

WOMAN'S SKIRT CLOTH,
KAIN PANJANG
(UNFINISHED BATIK)

1964
Kota Baharu, Kelantan
Cotton
Warp 234.4 cm
Weft 106.5 cm
20-1
Departmental purchase, 1964

The batik process is demonstrated on this unfinished fabric. The design has been stamped on. Birds and flowers are painted and wax resist applied. The background has not yet been dyed.

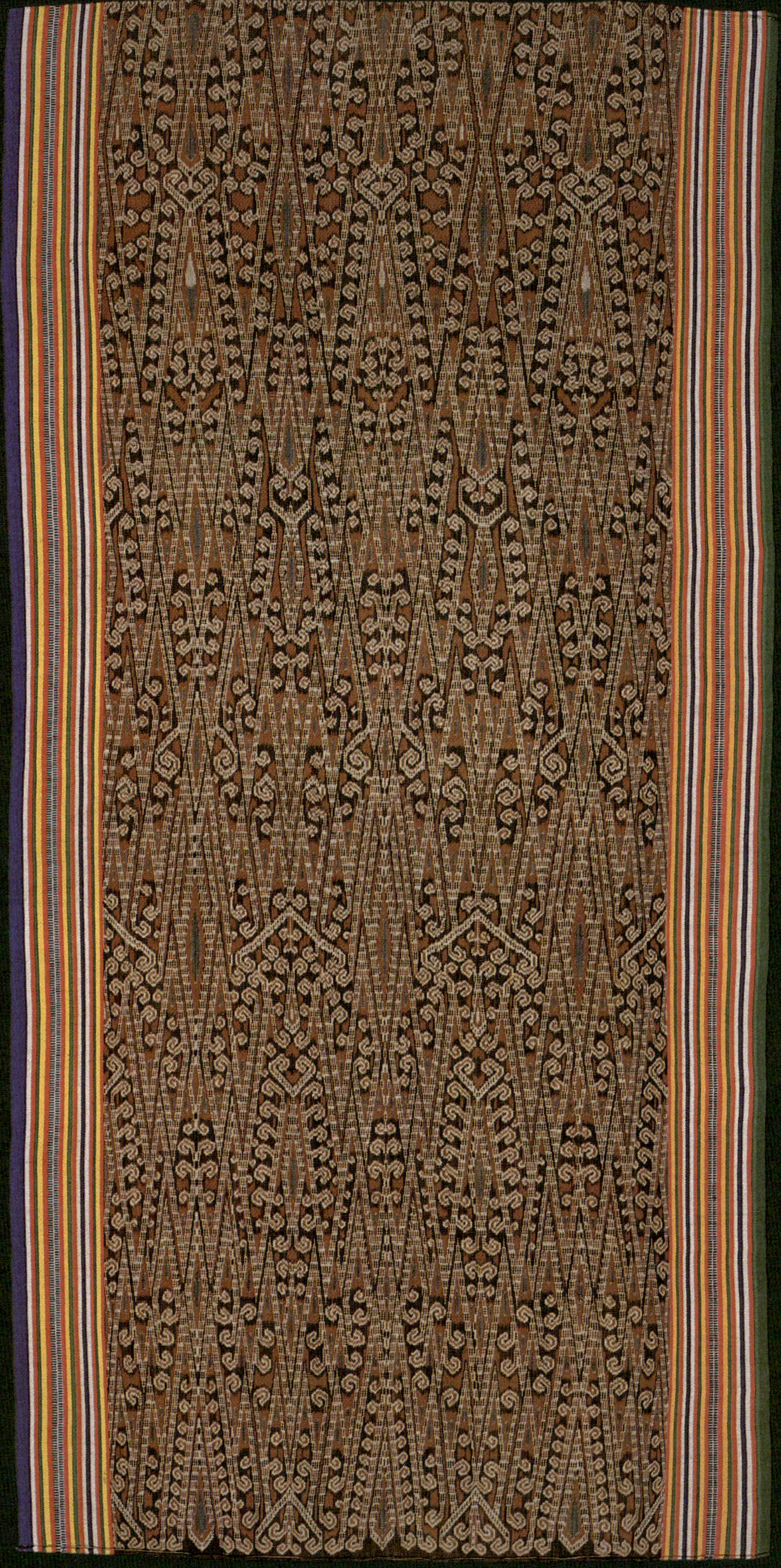

WOMAN'S SKIRT CLOTH,
KAIN PANJANG

1964
Kota Baharu, Kelantan
Cotton
Warp 234.4 cm
Weft 106.5 cm
20-2
Departmental purchase, 1964

This batik *kain panjang* is a variation of a type of skirt cloth called *pagi sore*, or "morning-evening", which is divided diagonally and has two distinctively different patterns and colors. The batik is similar to the unfinished textile (20-1), above.

WOMAN'S SHOULDER CLOTH,
SELENDANG

1964
Kelantan
Silk; metallic gold tinsel threads
Length 146.8 cm
Length (fringe) 11 cm
Width 53 cm
62-3
Departmental purchase, 1964

This subtly patterned *selendang* would be folded vertically in half and worn over the woman's left shoulder. The plain weave ground consists of orange warp yarns and black tie-dye weft yarns. Metallic gold supplementary threads enhance the geometric motifs, the borders, and fringe.

WOMAN'S SKIRT, *BIDANG* (UNSEWN)

1970
Iban people, Sarawak
Cotton
Warp 116 cm
Weft 58.7 cm
15-5
Departmental purchase, 1971
Illustrated p. 56

Young Iban women wear short wrapped skirts of handwoven cotton called *bidang*. Gittinger (1979:213) refers to these skirts as "normal clothing," but generally they are reserved for festive and ceremonial occasions, when making offerings to ancestral spirits and deities, for example. (Solyom, 1984:53). The *bidang* had its origins in myth; it had once been the possession of the daughter of an important god. The textile is also instrumental in rituals for the dead. A *bidang* is presented to the shaman who conducts souls to the beyond to protect her and insure her return from the underworld. (Gittinger, 1979:218).

The central band on a *bidang* has warp *ikat* tendril, hook and scroll patterns, often highly complex and sometimes having zoomorphic or anthropomorphic connotations. Selvages, which form borders at the top and bottom of the skirt when it is worn, can be plain or, as in this example from the exhibition, narrow, brightly colored stripes. These provide a great contrast to the subtle browns, blacks and beiges of central, *ikat* designs. These borders of commercially dyed threads appeared as early as the 1880s. (Kahlenberg, 1977:16)

WOMAN'S SKIRT, *BIDANG*

1960s
Iban people, Sarawak
Cotton
Warp 53.4 cm
Circumference 114.0 cm
15-6
Departmental purchase, 1971

WOMAN'S SKIRT, *BIDANG*

1960s
Iban people, Sarawak
Cotton
Warp 104.7 cm
Weft 50.7 cm
15-4
Departmental purchase, 1971

MAN'S SARONG,
KAIN SAMPIN

1961
Kelantan
Silk; gold thread
Warp 190.9 cm
Weft 104.7 cm
20-9
Departmental purchase, 1961

The *sampin* is a short sarong that is worn over a traditional loose fitting shirt and trousers for festive occasions. A heavy silk textile in deep burgundy, this *sampin* is ornamented with a metallic gold, supplementary weft, *songket*. The principal motif is identified (Fraser-Lu, 1988:143) as *pucuk rebung lawi ayam* (bamboo shoot resembling cock's tail feathers). *Sampin* are generally folded in half lengthwise, and wrapped around the hips with the decorative panel in back.

IBAN WOMAN'S SKIRT,
BIBANG
Malaysia

INDONESIA

CEREMONIAL CLOTH, *TAMPAN*

Early 20th century
Lampung Region, Southern Sumatra
Cotton
Warp 72.5 cm
Weft 62.3 cm
Collection of Barbara and Fritz Warren

The *tampan*, a small, almost square cloth, has not been woven in Indonesia for at least three-quarters of a century. This unique textile played a prominent role in ritual gift exchanges and rites of passage: birth, circumcision, puberty, marriage and death. It served as a symbol of transition from one status to another, or bonding between individuals or groups.

In some ceremonies the honored person sat on a *tampan,* and in other rituals groups of celebrants gathered around *tampan.* In south Sumatra, funeral biers were wrapped with *tampan.* In the Krui area, the head of the deceased person rested on a *tampan* while the body was washed and dressed. At house ceremonies a *tampan* was tied to a ridgepole and remained for the duration of the house's existence.

Large numbers of *tampan* were included in a bride's dowry. Ceremonial use of *tampan* in marriage rites began with negotiations between parents when, as part of the bride price, small bundles of food or sweet cakes wrapped in *tampan* were sent by the bridegroom's family to the bride's family. At the marriage ceremony, a *tampan* placed atop a spear symbolizing the cosmic tree was positioned behind the couple. Called *dewas*, it represented the spirits that witnessed the ceremony. In some areas, *tampan* were used to wrap token gifts of food from the family of the bride to the family of the groom.

In most *tampan,* including the pieces in this exhibition, the ship is the dominant motif. According to Galerie Mabuhay (1980:34), the multi-level ship is a visual indication of the Lampung concept of society as a "ship-like structure" with the members of a village as the crew. "Thus, during the 'rites of passage' the ship stands for the transition (movement) and for the structure (social). Via the ship the novice is, as it were, brought from a temporary uncertain place outside the society to a sure position inside." Some interpretations give *tampan* a cosmological significance, comparing the decks, or tiers, to a diagram representing the sacred realm. (Solyom, 1984:33)

CEREMONIAL CLOTH, *TAMPAN*

Lampung region, Sumatra
Cotton
Warp 65 cm
Weft 60.5 cm
Collection of Virginia B. Randolph
Illustrated p. 60

CEREMONIAL CLOTH, *TAMPAN*

Lampung region, Sumatra
Cotton
Warp 94 cm
Weft 74 cm
Collection of Virginia B. Randolph

CEREMONIAL CLOTH, *TAMPAN*

Early 20th century
Lampung region, Sumatra
Cotton
Warp 66.2 cm
Weft 59.8 cm
Collection of Barbara and Fritz Warren

CEREMONIAL CLOTH, *TAMPAN*

Late 19th century
Lampung, Sumatra
Cotton
Warp 86 cm
Weft 72 cm
Collection of Donald H. Rubinstein

Two ships, in reverse orientation, are bearing human figures and mythological elephant-like creatures of enormous size, indicated by their juxtaposition against the human images. Canopies, umbrellas and other objects used in ceremonial processions are also represented.

THREE CEREMONIAL CLOTHS, *TAMPAN (UNCUT)*

Early 20th century
Lampung region, Sumatra
Cotton
Warp 136 cm
Weft 43.3 cm
Collection of Barbara and Fritz Warren

This interesting example shows how tampan can be woven in strips and cut off as needed for use in ceremonies. The designs are created with supplementary weft.

CEREMONIAL CLOTH, *TATIBIN*

Early 20th century
Lampung region, Sumatra
Cotton
Warp 99 cm
Weft 40.7 cm
Collection of Barbara and Fritz Warren

Tampan are one of three types of ceremonial textiles known to Westerners as "ship cloths." While *tampan* were made and used by all levels of society, the other two were reserved for the upper echelons of the aristocracy. The largest of these, which is about three meters long, is called *palepai* ("ship") or *sesai balak* ("big wall"). In rites of passage ceremonies, *palepai* were generally hung as backdrops behind the honored person or persons.

The third type of ship cloth, *tatibin*, may be thought of as shorter versions of *palepai*, measuring up to one and a half meters long. They were used only in the Banding area; few *tatibin* were made, so they are extremely rare. (Lin, 1987:3) In certain ceremonies *tampan*-covered cushions and a stack of thin mattresses covered with a *tatibin* were arranged to make a sort of couch which was placed in front of the *palepai* wall hanging. (Gittinger, 1972:91)

SHOULDER CLOTH, *ULOS GODANG*

1875-1900
Propat region, North Sumatra
Toba Batak people
Cotton
Length (with fringe) 173 cm
Width 72.2 cm
A.1983.01.03
Gift of Mr. and Mrs. Will L. Lidsker, 1983

The *ulos godang* is presented by grandparents to a new grandchild. *Ulos* are important articles in all ritual gift exchange ceremonies of the Batak. According to Warming and Gaworski (1981:95), "...some of the essence of the giver is passed along with the cloth to the receiver. When goods change hands, a bond is formed, ties are strengthened or some result (such as protection, or prosperity) is sought."

This *ulos godang* is hand spun and handwoven, with narrow warp stripes and warp *ikat* in a diamond pattern on a deep maroon ground throughout the central area, contrasted with supplementary weft stripes and borders. The warp ends are plied and twisted to form a fringe.

Ikat is a term used for both a textile and, more precisely, the technique by which it is created. The word derives from the Malay-Indonesian *mengikat*, to "tie" or "bind." For each color used in the pattern, portions of yarn are bound with dye-resistant material, such as palm leaf or vegetable fiber, to prevent color penetration. After dyeing, the resist material is removed. The textile may be woven with dyed warp *ikat* yarns, weft *ikat* yarns, or both. This complex double *ikat* process requires great precision and expertise in matching warp and weft threads to form the design.

Supplementary weft yarns, usually thicker or of a different material than those used in the ground fabric, are added to the woven textile in a discontinuous manner in order to create decorative patterns.

HAIR CUTTING CLOTH OR HEAD COVERING CLOTH, *SINGEP*

Sumatra
Minangkabau people
Silk; metallic gold threads
Warp 72.2 cm
Weft 68.7 cm
A.1983.01.02
Gift of Mr. and Mrs. Will Lidsker, 1983

The *singep*, which is used to cover a child on the occasion of his first haircut, can also be worn as a head covering. In the Minangkabau gift-exchange tradition, the *singep* is presented to the child by his paternal grandparents. In this example, supplementary weft of metallic gold accents the red and blue-green striped fabric, bordered with connecting squares and small checks. The central area has a repeat pattern of eight-pointed stars.

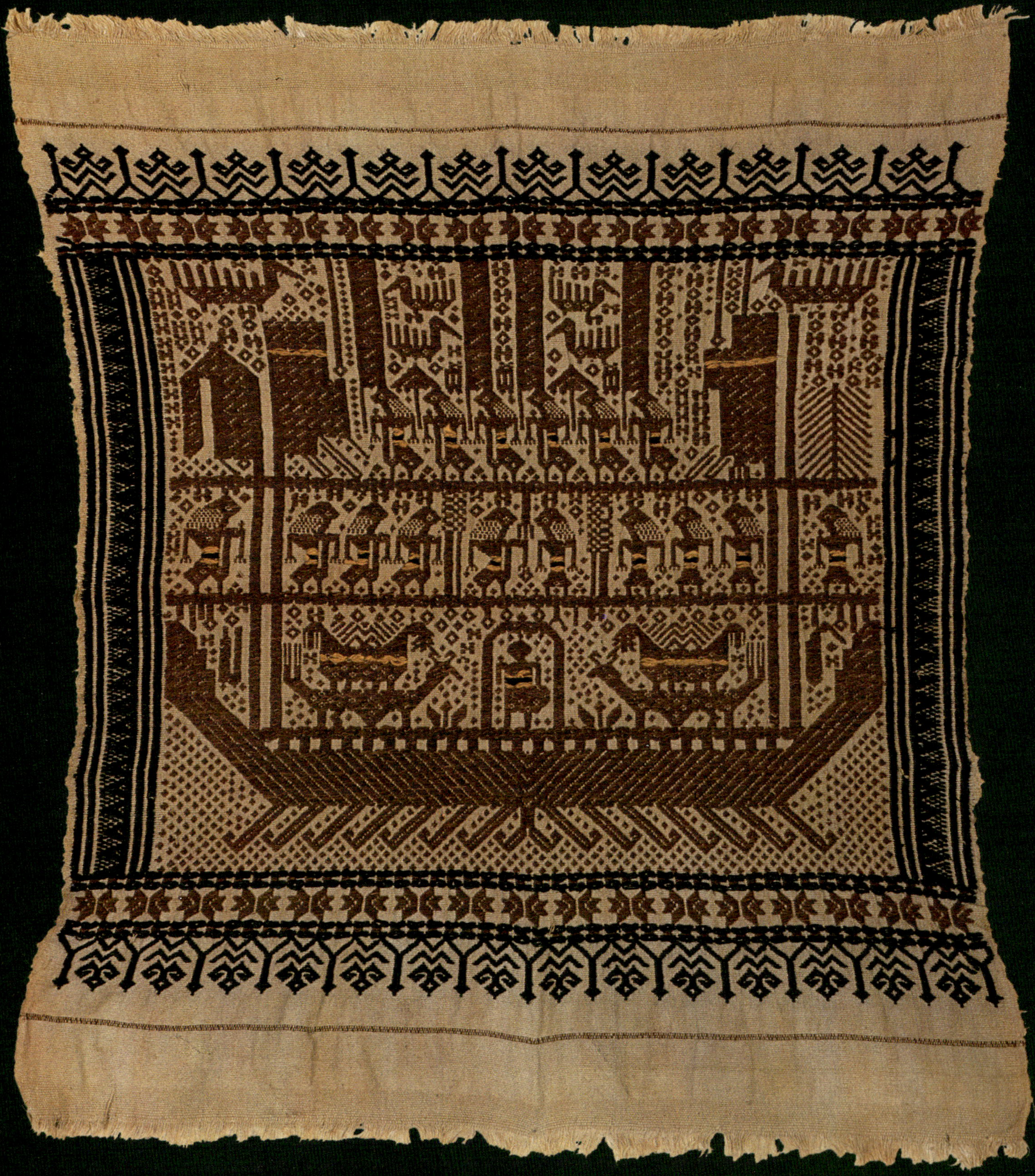

MAN'S SHOULDER WRAP OR HIP WRAP, HINGGI

East Sumba
Cotton
Warp (including fringe) 271 cm
Weft (two panels) 101.6 cm
I-20
Departmental purchase, 1967

Hinggi are warp *ikat* garments woven in pairs. One is customarily worn wrapped about the hips and the other as a mantle, or shawl, draped over the shoulders. In the highly stratified Sumbanese society, decorated textiles and clothing were a mark of wealth, prestige and rank. The *hinggi kombu*, or red dyed *hinggi*, for example, was once reserved for kings. *Hinggi* are associated with ritual occasions and gift exchanges. Because its existence is believed to be eternal, the *hinggi* is often presented as a funerary gift. (Kahlenberg, 1979:23)

Hinggi generally have three to five horizontal sections on either side of a central section. This warp *ikat hinggi* is dominated by dynamic designs relating to Sumbanese life. From the fringed end upward are: rampant lions, a symbol of royal power adapted from the Dutch coat of arms first introduced into Indonesia on ships' flags and the flags of the Dutch East India Company in the sixteenth century. (Adams, 1969:137) Continuing in ascending order, according to Des Jarlais, are birds in flight, buildings (or houses and trees?), confronting simians, walking birds, and a wide central band of eight-pointed stars. The bands on *hinggi* are sometimes compared to the traditional Sumbanese village; the king resides in the center. Stars, a common motif in the central band, are "...the highest objects in the sky (therefore), they represent the highest authority in the kingdom." (Warming and Gaworski, 1981:82)

MAN'S SHOULDER WRAP OR HIP WRAP, HINGGI, KOMBU KAWURU

1952
Sumba
Cotton
Warp 274 cm
Weft 122 cm
Collection of Donald H. Rubinstein
Illustrated p. 63

This *hinggi* was made by a royal family, as indicated by the densely patterned figures and also their curvilinear style. The warp *ikat* textile is constructed in two panels; the borders are finished with a cross-woven, locking band and has *ikat* and corded fringes. The fabric is woven with complex figure-ground reversals. The central pattern, which may be derived from Indian double *ikat (patola)*, displays lunar motifs, a Chinese-influenced *naga* (a mythological serpentine creature), snakes, fish, a variety of animals, heraldic double eagles, and Dutch influenced heraldic lions.

CEREMONIAL HIP WRAPPER, DODOT BANGUN TULAK ALASALASAN PINARADA EMAS

Early 20th century
Surakarta, Central Java
Length 356 cm
Width 204 cm
Collection of Donald H. Rubinstein

The *dodot* is an extremely large wrapper worn by the nobility and court officials on ceremonial occasions. This textile reportedly survived the fire that destroyed the Surakarta court. It served as a groom's wedding garment, and still bears the marks of gold dust, perfumed oils and perspiration stains. *Alasalasan* (forest-like) motifs of plants form a lattice which is interspersed with animal forms including the centipede, scorpion, dragonfly, crab, snake, bat, fish, dog, bird, cock, elephant, deer and Garuda, a mythological bird which is the traditional mount of the Hindu god Vishnu. The edge is decorated with a vine motif.

This textile is a single panel of indigo-dyed cotton. Gold leaf was applied with fish paste to the entire cloth on one side and to the corners on the reverse, which would be visible when the garment was worn. There are a number of different ways to drape the *dodot*; it is often folded in a bustle-like arrangement in the back.

CEREMONIAL CLOTH, TAMPAN
Late 19th-early 20th century
Sumatra, Indonesia

CEREMONIAL SHOULDER CLOTH, *SELENDANG SONGKET*

1875-1900
Palembang, Sumatra
Silk; metallic gold threads
Warp 202 cm
Weft 76.6 cm
A.1981.01.01
Departmental purchase, 1981
Illustrated on catalogue cover

The sumptuous brocaded silk textiles, *kain songket*, particularly associated with Palembang and a few other areas of Sumatra, are woven with discontinuous supplementary weft (threads worked back and forth in small pattern areas) to create elegant designs in gold and silver. These extraordinary fabrics are used for sarongs, head wrappers and shoulder cloths, *selendang songket*. According to Gittinger (1975:102), they are rarely worn except at weddings and on religious holidays.

A favorite *songket* design motif, especially for borders, is the *tumpal*, which is shaped like an isosceles triangle. This design, when used on a *kain songket* from Palembang, may also be referred to as *pucuk rebung*, or bamboo shoot.

Floral, *tumpal* and star motifs in heavy gold metallic supplementary weft border the center field of this fine, handwoven *selendang songket*. Very thin sheets of gold, silver or copper alloy are cut into narrow strips and wound around yarn to create the metallic thread.

CEREMONIAL SHOULDER CLOTH, *SELENDANG SONGKET*

Bukittinggi, West Sumatra
Silk; metallic gold and silver threads
Length 171 cm
Width 43 cm
A.1983.01.01
Gift of Mr. and Mrs. Will Lidsker, 1983

The lozenge and *tumpal* motifs in supplementary weft create an almost solid patterning in shimmering gold and silver in this *selendang songket*.

MAN'S SHOULDER CLOTH OR WAIST CLOTH, *SELIMUT*

Late 19th or early 20th century
Moro Village, eastern Timor
Cotton
Warp 230 cm
Weft 72 cm
Collection of Donald H. Rubinstein
Illustrated p. 64-65

This textile is extremely rare. One of only two extant examples from an area call Los Palos, it had been made for the royal house. It was purchased in Timor by the former owners from a crocodile hunter in 1967; the other textile was taken to Lisbon by an official in the Portuguese government. Two royal houses which had been occupied by the original owners of these *selimut* had burned to the ground and may have impoverished the families.

Woven with a supplementary warp, this *selimut* has unusual tableaux of figures representing complex scenes and showing rudiments of perspective. Design motifs of mounted riders and buffaloes (which were used as currency in Timor) are not often found in Indonesian textiles. Also represented are floral forms and squirrels, probably of European influence, and cocks.

CEREMONIAL CLOTH, *GERINGSING*

Late 19th-early 20th century
Tenganan Pageringsingan, eastern Bali
Cotton
Warp 200 cm
Weft 60 cm
Collection of Donald H. Rubinstein

Geringsing are Balinese double *ikat* textiles indigenous to the village of Tenganan Pageringsingan. The literal definition of *geringsing* is "without sickness," connoting protection against illness and evil. When the warp (fringes) is cut, the cloth is worn for ceremonial and ritual purposes, otherwise it is used as an offering. (Solyom in Kahlenberg, 1977:75) This schematic floral pattern is derived from the *patola* (double *ikat*) of India.

MAN'S SHOULDER WRAP OR HIP WRAP, *HINGGI*
Sumba, Indonesia

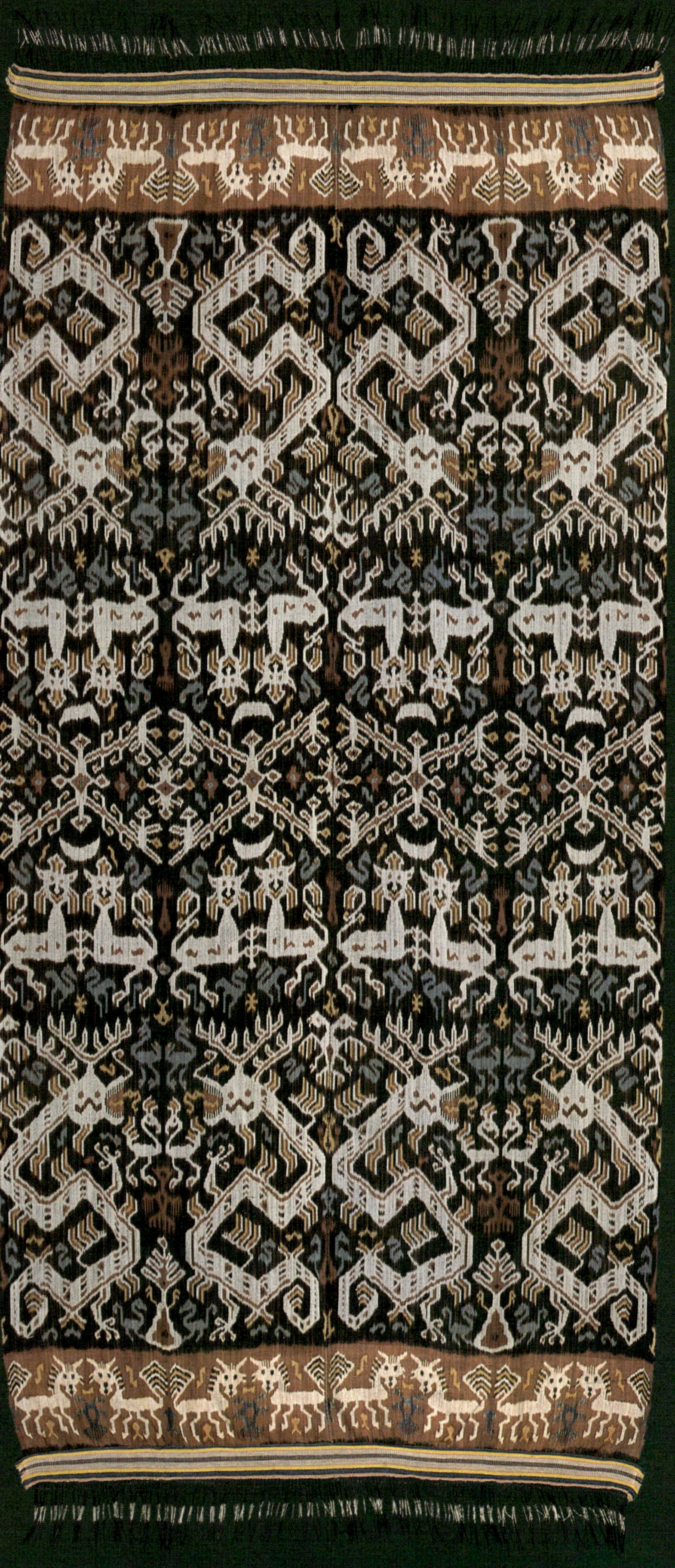

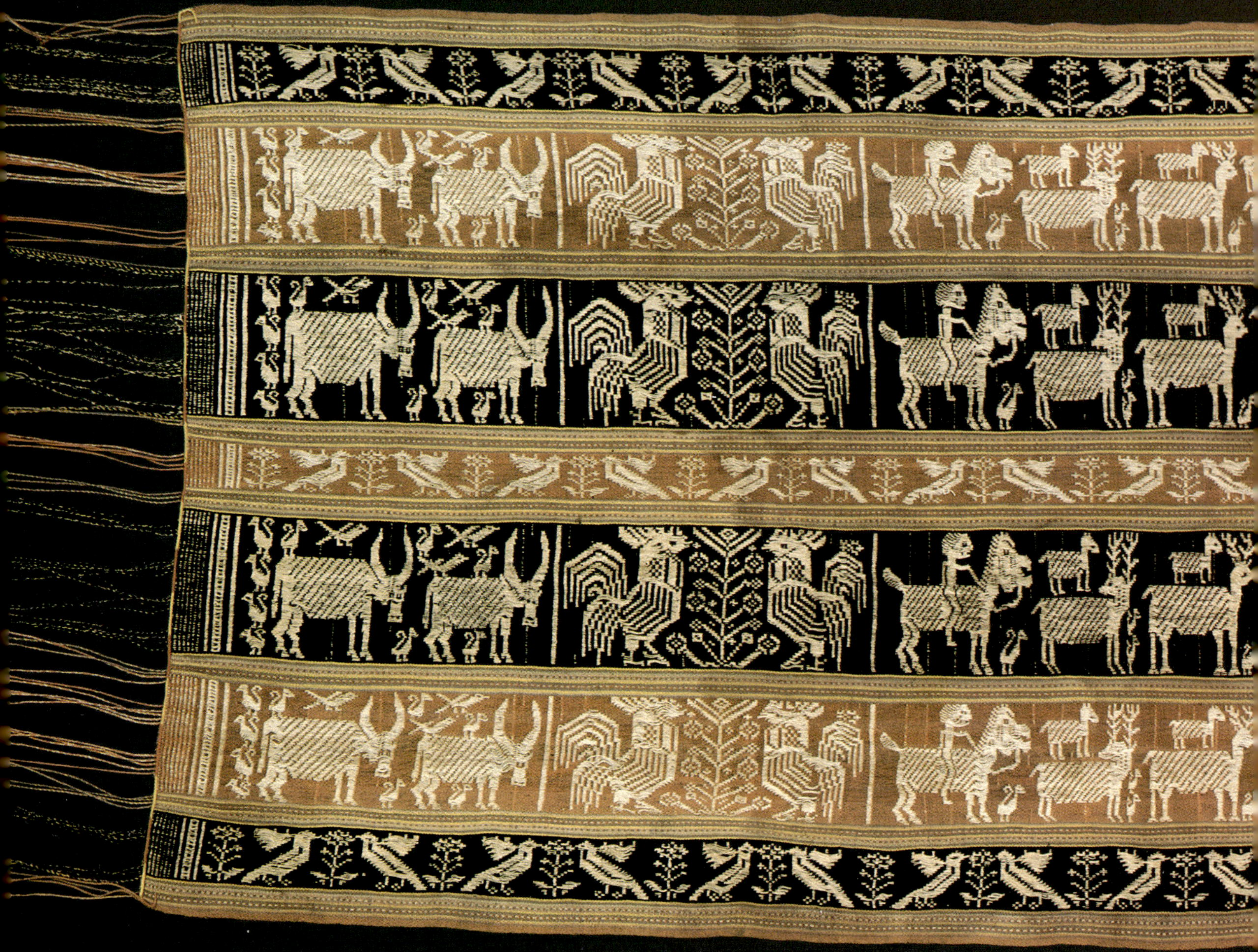

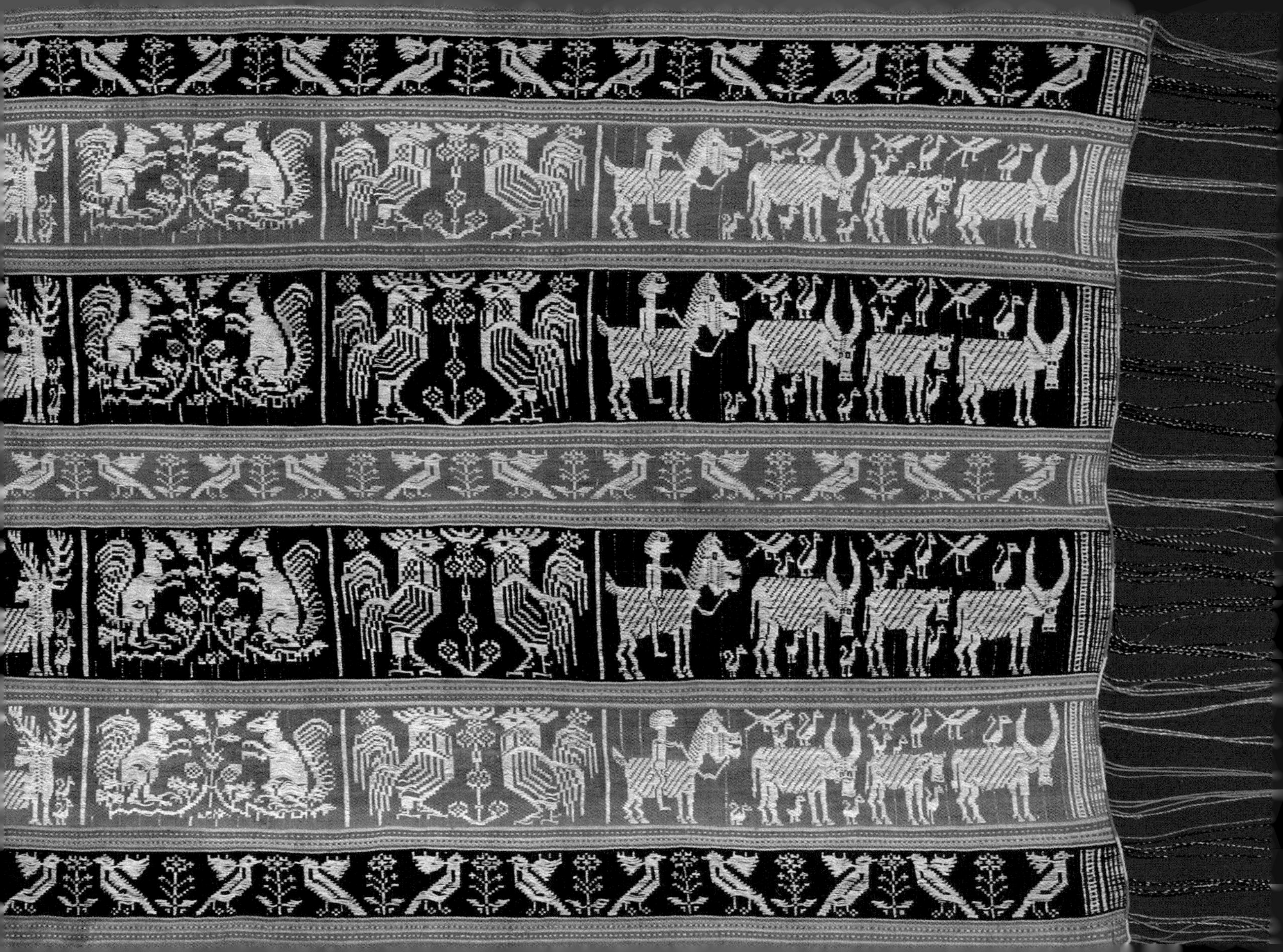

CEREMONIAL CLOTH,
GERINGSING WAYANG KEBO

Early 20th century
Tenganan Pageringsingan, Bali
Bali Aga people
Cotton; double ikat
Warp 207 cm
Weft 54.7 cm
Collection of Barbara and Fritz Warren

There is little variation in traditional *geringsing* in the *wayang kebo*, or shadow puppet pattern. The principal motif is a large, four-pointed star in the center field under the quadrants of which are repeat groupings of three figures. The central figure, generally assumed to be male, is larger than the others. He has either elaborately arranged long hair or wears a turban similar to a court headdress, suggesting he is a king or high priest. The three figures are often identified as a priest, his wife, and a kneeling devotee with one arm raised in a gesture of reverence. A similar cloth, illustrated in Gittinger (1979:147), carries this interpretation based on research by Urs Ramsayer linking these figures to prototypes on 13th or 14th century East Javanese Hindu temple reliefs at Candi Jago. (1975:plates 33,34) The ends of the cloth have "half stars," with the same figure groupings, and three rows of small star motifs which are also common in Javanese bas reliefs and batik designs.

Ramsayer (1977:208, fig 316), depicts girls wearing *geringsing wayang kebo* performing a sacrificial dance in honor of a deified king. One weaver reported to the lender of the textile in the exhibition that it takes an average of six years to create this type of *geringsing*.

Previous page

MAN'S SHOULDER CLOTH OR
WAIST CLOTH, SELIMUT
Late 19th-early 20th century
Eastern Timor, Indonesia

CEREMONIAL CLOTH, PUA

19th century
Sarawak, Borneo
Iban people
Cotton
Warp 238 cm
Weft 151 cm
Collection of Donald H. Rubinstein
Illustrated p. 67

Pua have many ritual functions. They are used as hangings to define ceremonial areas or enclosures, including those which contain the deceased and his mourners. Often referred to as a "ceremonial blanket," the *pua* serves in this capacity for someone "...sleeping in a 'dream house' on the roof of the longhouse, seeking a spirit helper from beyond." (Gittinger, 1979:217-18) Like many other ritual textiles, *pua* are instrumental in the transference of power or wealth, or important in curing disease. *Pua* may be worn as a head and shoulder covering for ceremonial occasions. Noted headhunters, the Iban also used *pua* to ceremonially receive heads taken in war. (Holmgren in Kahlenberg, 1977:41)

The geometric pattern on many *pua*, including this example, suggests abstract anthropomorphic forms. According to Donald H. Rubinstein, the *pua* contains unusual headhunting images: three monumental figures, perhaps related to spirits, receiving decapitated heads. Each large figure has a hollowed abdomen containing small paired figures and detached skulls, possibly suggesting the symbolic association of headhunting with fertility. The spirit figures appear to be enveloped by *naga* images, possibly representing the *nabau*, a mythological serpent or water dragon, which is believed to accompany the headhunter and aid him in his heroic task. The *pua* is meant to encompass the spirits.

CEREMONIAL CLOTH,
PUA SONGKET

19th century
Kapuas River, Borneo
Iban people
Cotton
Warp 275 cm
Weft 102 cm
Collection of Donald H. Rubinstein

Two warp *ikat* side panels are sewn with a running zigzag stitch to a central panel patterned with a discontinuous supplementary weft, *songket*, in this hand spun cotton *pua*. The ends are fringed. The central panel is filled with densely branching trees and foliate forms. Several small human figures and male and female genitalia appear among the branches. *Ikat* side panels contain a column of stylized figures. The use of indigo for the ground weave is highly unusual in *pua songket*, which are generally red or occasionally yellow.

CEREMONIAL CLOTH, PUA
19th century
Sarawak, Borneo, Indonesia

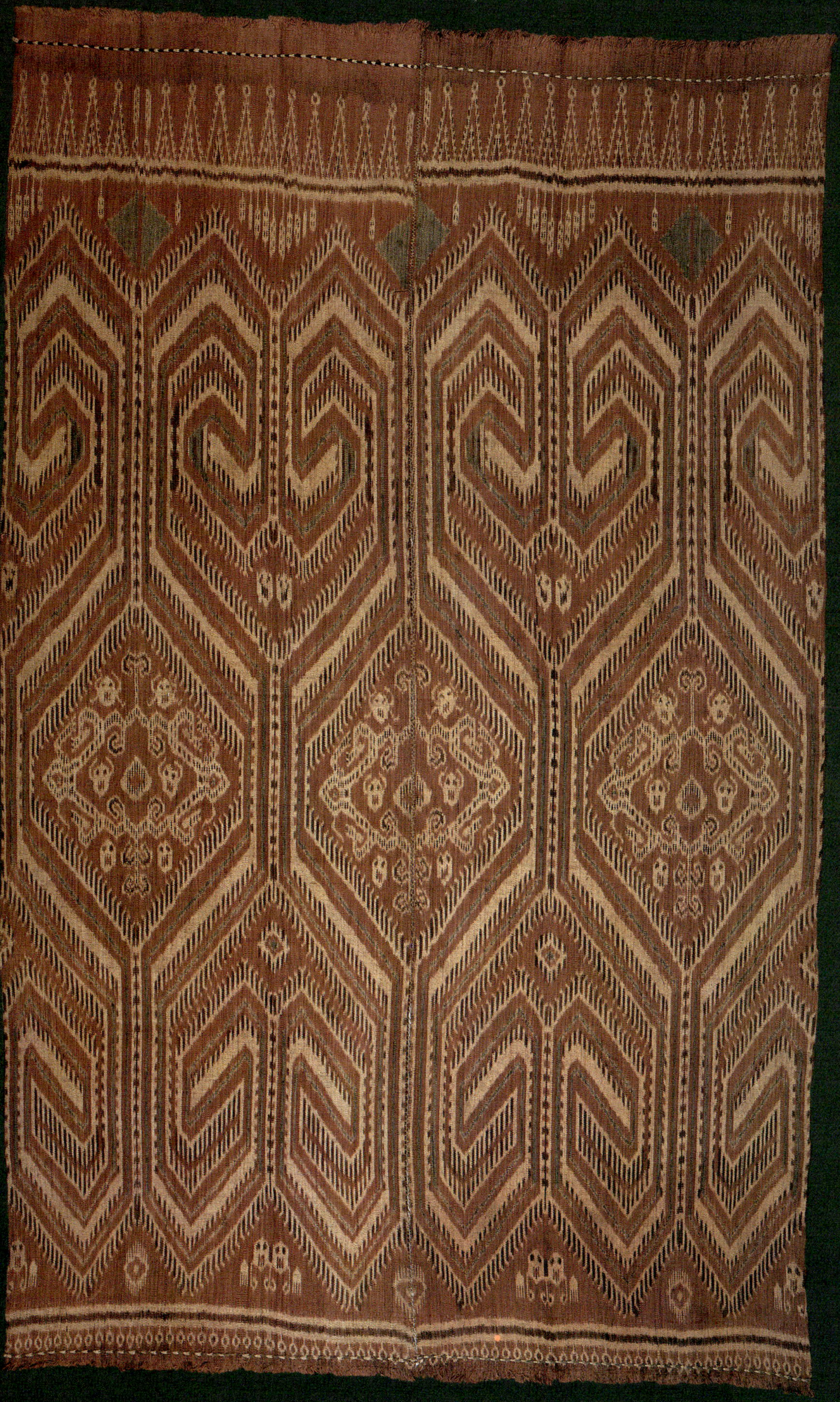

Head Cloth or Belt, *Ragidup or Hohos*

Early 20th century
Northern Sumatra
Batak people
Cotton; human hair
Warp 197 cm
Weft 36 cm
Collection of Donald H. Rubinstein

According to Sandra Niessen (letter to Donald H. Rubinstein, 1985), this textile "...is most likely a *hohos*, and *hohos* are rare. Oddly enough, I find these more in private collections than in museums. A *hohos* is a belt. It was worn around the waist of high-status persons. Indeed the supplementary weft is similar to that found in the end panels of the *ragidup* (a prestige textile with weft brocade patterning) and this is what gives the cloth its status...human hair mixed in with the weft ...is a practice found all over Indonesia, but I can't say that I've ever noticed it in Batak weavings. In myths and prayers, there are frequent allusions to the analogous properties of yarn and hair."

Woman's Jacket, *Baju*

Lampung region, Sumatra
Kauer or Smendo people
Center back 21 cm
Sleeve 45 cm
Collection of Donald H. Rubinstein

These short jackets were worn on festive occasions only by young unmarried women. The costumes, which were made by the women themselves, included a sarong, *tapis*, which was wrapped around the body and tied under the arms. The jackets were constructed from a single piece of fabric with appropriately positioned front and back decorative panels and sleeve stripes woven in. The panels were embroidered and decorated with tiny mirror-like pieces of mica, *cermuk*, before the garment was cut and sewn. Shells were fastened on afterwards. The elaborate ornamentation makes Kauer jackets extremely heavy, and "...unsuitable for the tropical climate of Sumatra's coast. As a result, young women traditionally carried their jackets wrapped in *tampan* to the vicinity of the celebration and donned them at the last moment." (Gittinger, 1979:87)

This jacket is handwoven from hand spun cotton with supplementary weft in gold thread and possibly silk. Tiny sequins of *cermuk* are scattered along the striping, and appliquéd nassa (spiraloid) shell, that has been ground flat, ornaments the back panel and is arranged in triangular patterns around the neck. The back lattice design is composed of interlocking human figures or heads.

Woman's Blouse, *Lemba*

c. 1900
Celebes
Toraja people
Bark-cloth, *fuya*
Center back 57.5 cm
Sleeve 84 cm
A.1981.01.02
Departmental purchase, 1981
Illustrated p. 69

Toraja women traditionally wore a *lemba* and sarong made of beaten bark-cloth, *fuya* (usually from the paper mulberry tree), for important ceremonial occasions. A bark-cloth headdress, sometimes covering a foundation of bamboo, strings of polished seeds, stones and feathers, and metal jewelry, completed the costume.

The blouse is cut from a single piece of *fuya*, folded at the shoulders and seamed at the sides. The *lemba* in this exhibition has a 4.5 cm sleeve extension and the side seams are reinforced at the waist with thick pieces of magenta *fuya*. The "U" shaped neck opening is bound with dark brown, handwoven fabric and accented with a hand painted rectangle in brilliant magenta, bordered with stripes and crosses in magenta and blue. A similar border is found on the sleeves, and the garment hem has borders of stripes with a dentate pattern.

Toraja Woman's
Bark-Cloth Blouse, *Lemba*
c. 1900
Indonesia

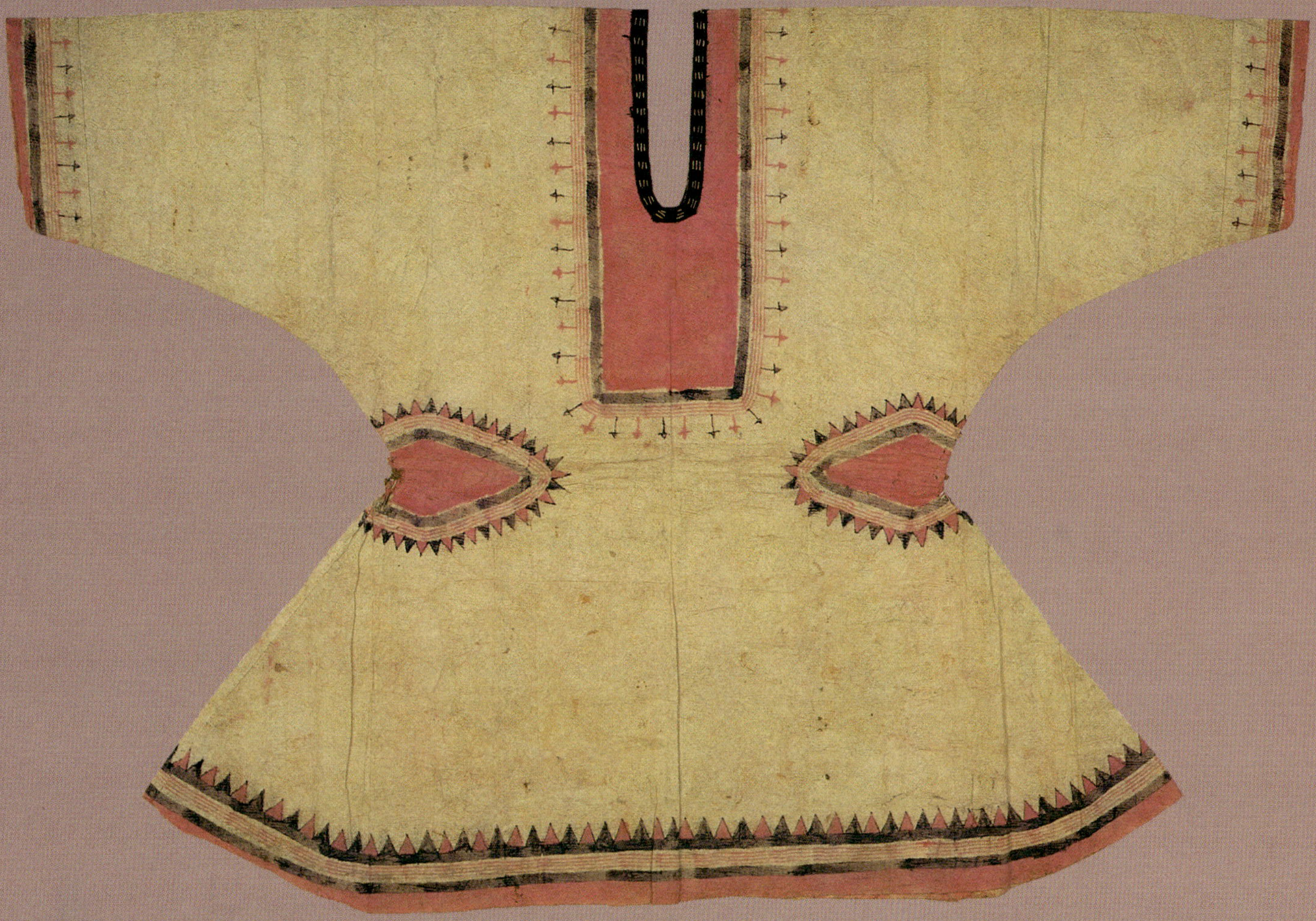

WOMAN'S CEREMONIAL
SARONG, *TAPIS*

Early 20th century
Lampung, Sumatra
Cotton; gold thread, sequins, mica, *cermuk*
Length 116 cm
Circumference 127.5 cm
Loaned by Dr. and Mrs. Robert Curtis

The elaborately ornamented heavy cotton sarongs, *tapis*, from the Lampung region are indicative of the wealth of the wearer and are prominently displayed at ceremonies marking rites of passage.

This *tapis* is shown in the exhibition with the jacket, *baju*, listed above. Hundreds of tiny square pieces of mirror-like mica, *cermuk*, are fastened with embroidery stitching to the wide horizontal bands of this *tapis*. The hem border has a pattern worked in metallic gold surrounded by *cermuk*. Narrow horizontal bands are accented with small, embroidered floral designs and gold sequins. The quantity of *cermuk* used on these garments was an important indication of wealth and status, according to Kahlenberg (1977:27). Some *tapis* took over a year to make, and could weigh as much as ten pounds.

WOMAN'S CEREMONIAL
SARONG, *TAPIS*

Late 19th-early 20th century
Lampung, Sumatra
Kauer people
Cotton; gold wrapped thread, metallic thread, sequins
Warp 140 cm
Weft 105.5 cm
A.1978.07.01
Departmental purchase, 1978

A tube-like sarong made of two pieces of fabric lengths stitched together, this *tapis* has been cut apart. The bold stripes with geometric designs and sequins are accented with fish, birds, and roosters which represent courage and fertility.

WOMAN'S CEREMONIAL
SARONG, *TAPIS*

1970s
Lampung, Sumatra
Cotton; metallic gold thread
Warp 119.5 cm
Weft 111.5 cm
Loaned by Jim and Maria Bolman

The horizontal stripes of this *tapis* are embellished with geometric designs in gold accented with red, green and turquoise and scattered with gold sequins.

TEXTILE WITH GOLD LEAF,
KAIN PRADA

1964
Bali
Warp 142.5 cm
Weft 123 cm
40-8
Departmental purchase, 1964

Textiles with designs in gold leaf, *kain prada*, are used as temple hangings, burned in funeral rites, worn at special festivals, tooth filling ceremonies and weddings. Most frequently these opulent fabrics serve as theatrical or dancer's costumes. (Gittinger, 1979:140-41)

Vine scrolls, leaves and large flowers are the most common motifs found on *kain prada*. The designs are reminiscent of Indonesian woodcarving. The gold is applied by gluing thin sheets of gold leaf onto the fabric.

PRESENTATION CLOTH

1946
Kedungwuni, Java
Cotton
Warp 53.5 cm
Weft 51.5 cm
A.1987.12.08
Gift of Oma Umbel, 1987

The finest *tulis* batik craftsmanship is found in this small textile by the famous batik artist Oey Soe Tjoen (d. 1975), patriarch of the Oey family, and founder of the noted batik factory in Kedungwuni. Some of the floral design motifs are inspired by a book of flowers given to the Oeys from a Dutch dye company, with the colors and patterns adapted to the tastes of local clientele. (Elliot, 1984:130)

Batik patterning is created by a wax resist process. Finely crafted *tulis* (from the word for "writing") batik designs are hand drawn on the fabric in liquid wax, using a pen like instrument. This tool, called a *canting (tjanting)*, has a bamboo handle, a copper reservoir for hot wax, and a narrow spout which comes in a variety of sizes and shapes according to the type of line desired. Wax is applied to larger areas with cotton attached to the spout of the pipe. The cloth is then dyed and the wax, which has resisted the color, boiled or scraped off. This process must be repeated for each color, covering the dyed areas with wax. Some Indonesian *tulis* batiks with complex patterns and many colors require more than a year to complete.

MAN'S HEAD CLOTH, *PLONGKONG*

1980s
Jogjakarta, Java
Cotton
Square 103 cm
Loaned by Carol Langner and Fritz Fritschel

A combination of tie-dye, *plangi*, and wax resist, batik, create interesting contrasts of colors and techniques in this head cloth. The diamond-shaped central portion was tied and dipped into bright saffron dye. It is surrounded by a band of brown and white batik and dark blue *plangi*. The tiny white dots in the blue fabric are accomplished by the *tritik* method—tightly wrapping a pinch of cloth with a fiber thread and, without breaking the thread, repeating the process until the entire portion of cloth to be dyed is wrapped. This results in an even, overall design of dots after the fabric is dyed and the thread removed. (Warming and Gaworski, 1981:123) The head cloth has a border of brown and white *cap* (stamped) batik.

Following pages

TULIS BATIK TEXTILES
Indonesia
(Left to right): Sarong by Oey Nio, Java; Sarong by Galinggan, Surakarta; *Kain Panjang* stamped IVA NOOR Sala, Jogjakarta; Sarong, early 20th century, Java; Sarong, Java; *Kain Panjang* by Hadiwasita, Jogjakarta

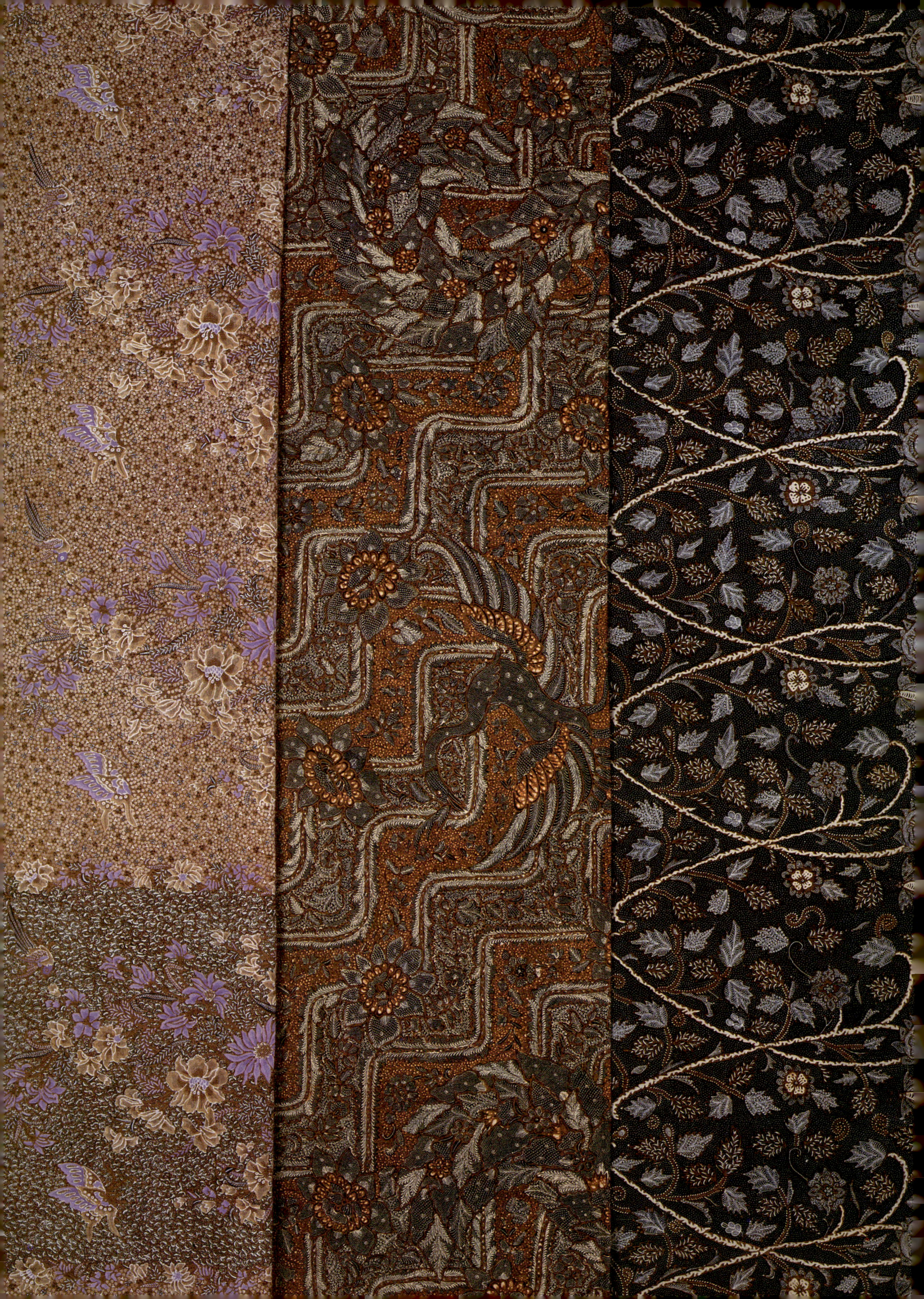

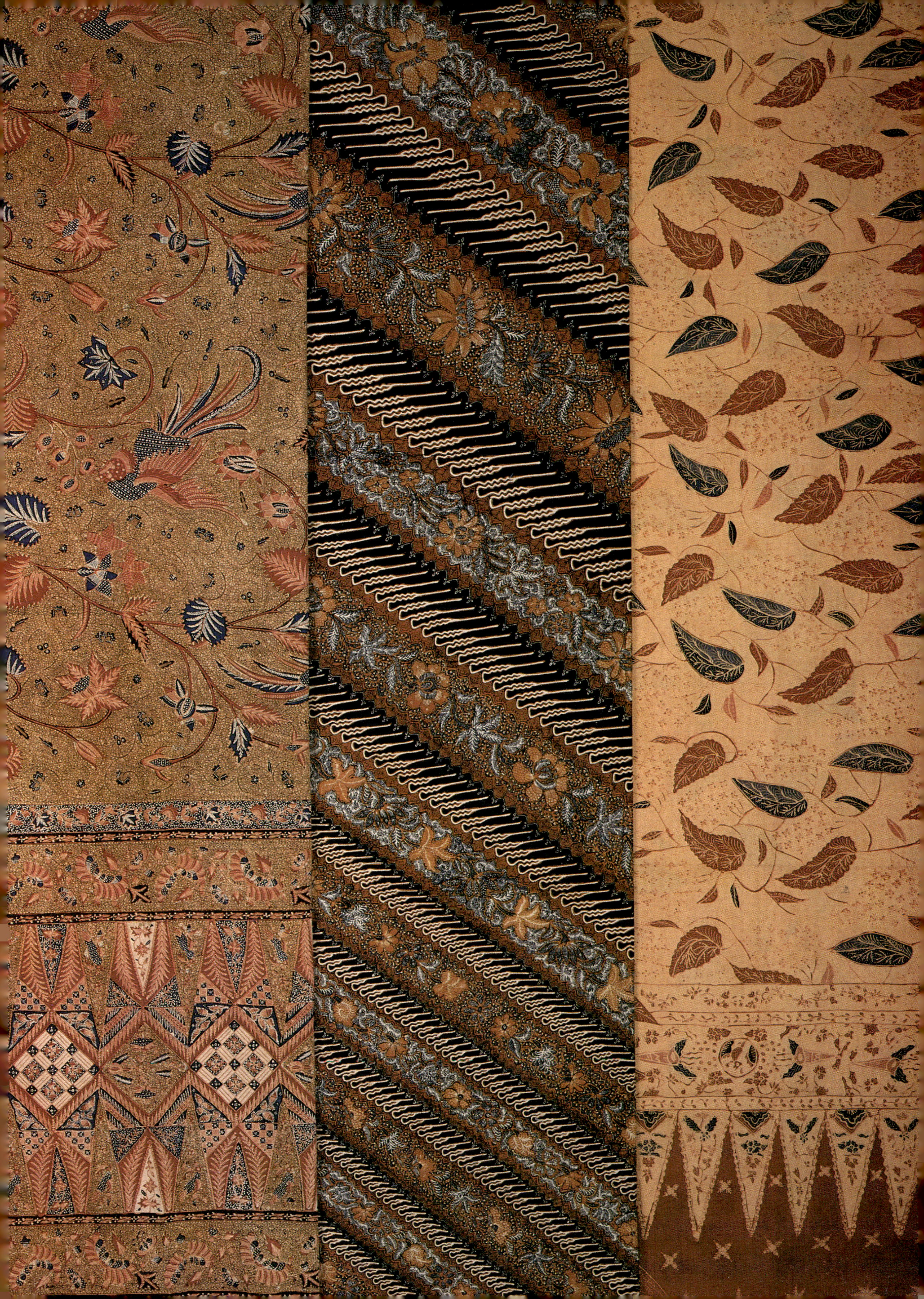

SARONG (UNSEWN)

Early 20th century
Java
Cotton
Warp 196.5 cm
Weft 106 cm
A.1988.05.01
Gift of Dr. and Mrs. Robert Curtis, 1988
Illustrated p. 73

In most Indonesian (and Malaysian) sarongs, there are two dissimilar areas. The *kepala* (lit. "head"), a decorative rectangular panel, is draped vertically at the front from waist to ankles. The *kepala* may also be worn at the sides or inside the front folds of the sarong or, for a man, at center back. The remainder of the sarong, with more subdued ornamentation, is called the *badan* or "body."

The *kepala* of this old *tulis* batik has a *tumpal* motif with birds and flowers in an intricate design usually referred to as patchwork. (Elliot, 1984:152) A Chinese-influenced design of birds, probably phoenixes, vines and leaves are rendered in red and dark blue on the tan *badan* of the sarong.

MAN'S SARONG (UNSEWN)

20th century (purchased in 1979)
Surakarta (Solo), Central Java
Cotton
Warp 242 cm
Weft 104.2 cm
Private collection
Illustrated p. 72

This *tulis* batik by the batik artist Galinggan features peacocks among zigzagging garlands as its predominate motif.

SARONG

1980s
Java
Cotton
Warp 241 cm
Weft 106 cm
Loaned by Jim and Maria Bolman
Illustrated p. 73

A diagonal *parang*, or broken sword, design alternates with floral patterns on this *tulis* batik in indigo and shades of brown.

WOMAN'S SARONG (UNSEWN)

Early 20th century (?)
Java
Cotton
Warp 200.5 cm
Weft 104.5 cm
Loaned by Dr. and Mrs. Robert Curtis
Illustrated p. 72

Flowers and lilac colored butterflies and birds were hand-drawn on this old *tulis* batik sarong by Oey (middle name illegible) Nio. Artists' signatures in batik are written in wax and are usually found in the *kepala* of a sarong or, in a *kain panjang*, in the corner. Some batiks are also stamped with the name and address of the workshop.

SKIRT CLOTH, *KAIN PANJANG* (LIT. "LONG CLOTH")

20th century (purchased 1970s)
Jogjakarta
Cotton
Warp 345.4 cm
Weft 105.4 cm
Private collection
Illustrated p. 72

In Java, the *kain panjang* is an ankle-length garment wrapped about the hips, pleated, and fastened at the waist. It differs from a sarong (generally defined as a tube) in that it is not seamed.

Decorated with butterflies among flowering vines on a stippled ground, this *tulis* batik is dyed in the traditional colors of indigo and brown. On the selvage of the fabric is a stamp indicating the name of the workshop, IVA NOOR Sala.

SKIRT CLOTH, *KAIN PANJANG*

20th century (purchased 1979)
Jogjakarta
Cotton
Warp 253.4 cm
Weft 104.5 cm
Private collection
Illustrated p. 73

Batik artist Hadiwasita created this *kain panjang* with an oriental style design of branching artemesia leaves in burgundy, pink and two shades of blue on a stippled cream-colored ground. The *tumpal* borders, on both ends, are ornamented with stylized birds on a floral ground.

Skirt Cloth, *Kain Panjang*

Late 19th-early 20th century
Pekalongan, Java
Cotton
Warp 272 cm
Weft 108 cm
A.1988.05.02
Gift of Dr. and Mrs. Robert Curtis, 1988

Signed E v Zuylen, this *kain panjang* has a floral bouquet design in blue on white. Eliza van Zuylen (1863-1947) was an *Indische*, a person of European origin whose families were long-time residents of the East Indies. They spoke the local language and had adapted to the Indonesian lifestyle. A number of *Indische* women who lived in the town of Pekalongan, Java became entrepreneurs in the batik industry. Eliza van Zuylen established a factory in 1890 and involved her entire family in the business of producing *tulis* batik. The women produced the designs, probably using books on Dutch horticulture as sources for their primary motifs of European flowers. One of Eliza van Zuylen's classic designs is large bouquets with butterflies in a formal arrangement, as seen on the piece in the exhibition. The flowers have sharply delineated edges set against clean backgrounds, "...a feat that even the best batikers in central Java were unable to match." (Elliot, 1984:102-117)

Skirt Cloth, *Kain Panjang*

1980s
Cirebon, Java
Cotton
Warp 242.5 cm
Weft 104 cm
Loaned by Nancy Cooper

This *kain* is boldly patterned with a Chinese-inspired motif resembling the *rui (jui)*—stylized, decorative clouds, and the ancient Chinese scepter, or symbol of authority, of the same name. The shape is derived from the lotus (Buddhist) or sacred fungus (Taoist), the head of which resembles the cloud form. Larson (1976:123) identifies a batik almost identical in design and color as *megamendung*, "mountains and clouds." A similar design is called *megomendung*, "threatening clouds," by Warming and Gaworski (1981:50). Gittinger (1979:137), states that the design is called *wadasan*, which means rock-like and, therefore, may be associated with the Chinese style rock formations found in some Javanese gardens.

Man's Ensemble

Jogjakarta, Java

Jacket, *Surjan*
Cotton
Center back 80 cm
Sleeve 179.5 cm
15-3
Departmental purchase, 1964

Wrapped Skirt, *Kain Panjang*
Cotton
Warp 160.5 cm
Weft 105 cm
20-9
Gift of Barbara Smith, 1959

Headdress, *Blangkon*
Cotton
Height 11 cm
Circumference 56 cm
62-18
Gift of Mrs. Archibald Marks, 1966

A square of batik cloth is draped to form a turban-like headdress, *blangkon*, accented by small, pleated blue "wings" on either side. According to Des Jarlais, the knob in the back relates to a former custom of arranging the hair in a knot. The men of Jogjakarta wear this style turban with a long-sleeved jacket, *surjan*, and a *kain panjang*. This *kain*, in a diagonal *parang*, or sword pattern, is made of batik produced by the *cap* technique.

In addition to hand-tooling, batik may be created by stamping the design onto the fabric with a *cap* (also, *tjap*). The *cap*, introduced in the mid-19th century, is a printing block made of strips of sheet copper shaped into the desired pattern. This is dipped into the liquid wax which is then applied to cloth stretched out on a padded table. Different *caps* are used for each design and color, and both sides of the fabric are waxed. Many fine batiks are made with the *cap* and there is an obvious time-saving advantage over the *tulis* batik method; the latter fabrics, however, are more highly prized.

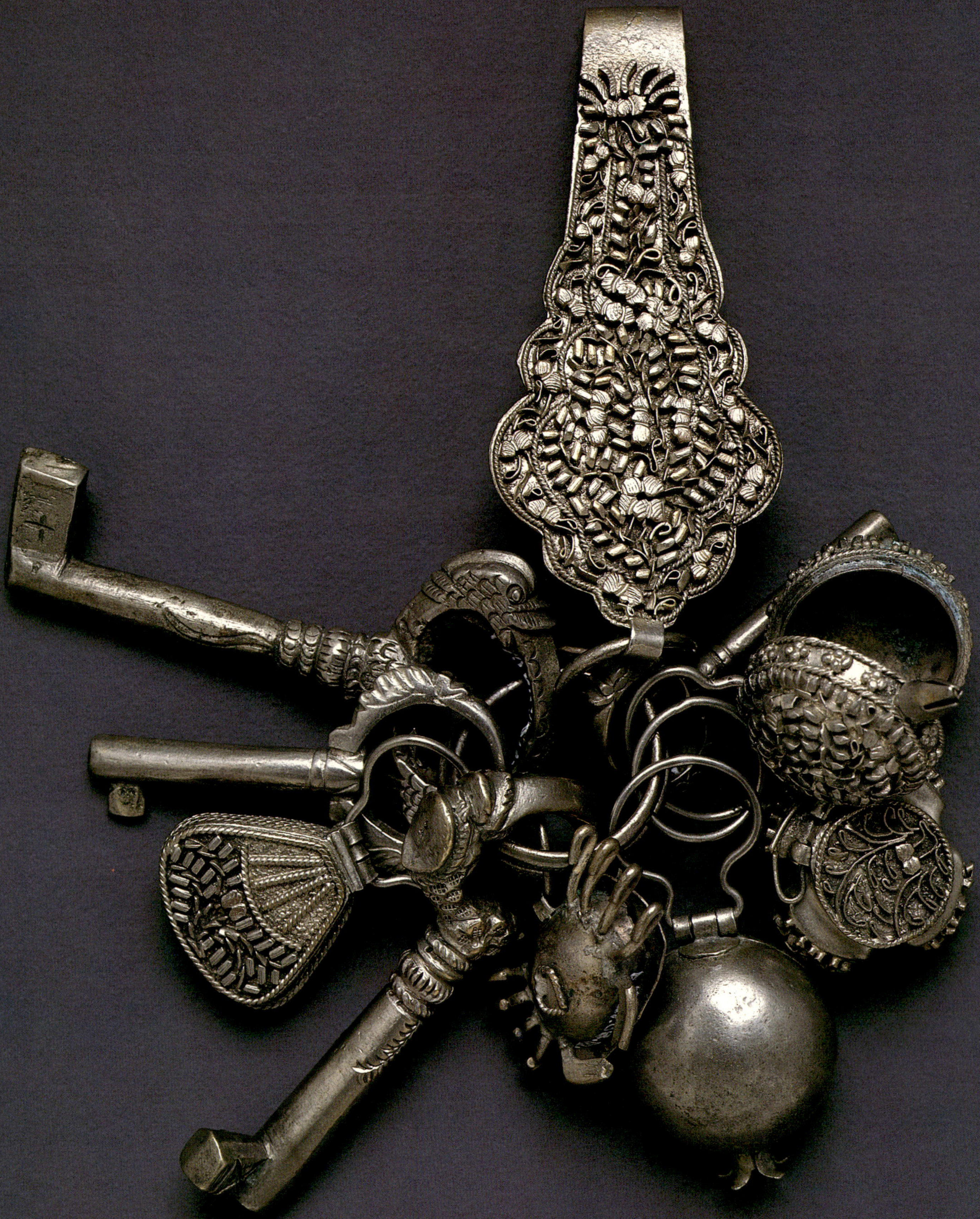

CHATELAINE WITH KEYS
AND BETEL CONTAINERS

c. 1900
Silver alloy
A.1987.08.02 a-k
Gift of Oma Umbel, 1987
Illustrated p. 76

BELT HOOK
Length 8.5 cm

RING
Diameter 2.5 cm

KEYS
    a. Length 6.3 cm
    b. Length 6.0 cm
    c. Length 4.7 cm
    d. Length 4.1 cm

CONTAINERS

    FAN
    Length 2.2 cm
    Width 2.1 cm

    CROSS
    Length 2.1 cm
    Width 2.3 cm

    CRAB
    Length 2.2 cm
    Width 3.7 cm

    BALL
    Length 3.2 cm
    Diameter 2.2 cm

    POMEGRANATE
    Length 3.2 cm
    Diameter 2.1 cm

A decorative and useful accessory to the sarong or *kain panjang* is the chatelaine, which enables the Indonesian woman to carry keys and other objects hooked to her belt. The scalloped hook in this fine example from the exhibition has an intricate foliate design accented with metal scrollwork and a border of twisted filigree. Keys and containers for ingredients used in betel chewing—betel nuts, lime, betel leaf and areca seed, and possibly tobacco—are attached to the hook by a coiled metal snake. Heads of fish and birds form the loops of the keys, and the notched ends are distinctively different.

Des Jarlais identifies the largest key as most likely a house key and the others as keys which opened drawers or chests within the home. The tiny hinged containers are shaped like a fan, a smooth-surfaced pomegranate, a stylized crab, Maltese cross and a heavily textured ball. Delicate, twisted wire, chasing, and tiny granulated beads of silver define the ribs of the fan and outline the leaves on the sphere.

The chewing of betel, a mild stimulant, is a widespread social practice throughout South East Asia.

CHATELAINE WITH KEYS AND
BETEL CONTAINERS
Indonesia

PHILIPPINES

"MARIA CLARA" BLOUSE, *CAMISA*, AND SHAWL, *PAÑUELO*

Manila
Silk
15-16 a,b
Departmental purchase, 1967

BLOUSE
Length (from shoulder) 47 cm
Bust 45 cm
Sleeve 55 cm

SHAWL
Length 80 cm
Width 77 cm

Nineteenth century Filipina elite wore the European-influenced, voluminous floor length skirt, *saya*, a blouse with wide sleeves called *baro* (also *camisa*), and a shawl, *pañuelo*. (Later, a *baro at saya*, "blouse and skirt," made of the same fabric and color evolved into the present day national dress, the *terno*, literally "matched." The *pañuelo* was eliminated in the 1940s.)

A version of this costume, which first appeared in the 1890s and is sometimes worn today, features a paneled skirt teamed with an ecru blouse, similar to this example in off-white silk in the exhibition. The blouse, with bell-shaped sleeves edged with embroidery, is worn with a matching *pañuelo*. This ensemble was later named "Maria Clara," after the heroine of Jose Rizal's popular novel *Noli Me Tangere*, published in 1909. (*Archipelago*, July 1974:38-40)

BALL GOWN AND SHAWL

Satin; beads
Center Back 153 cm
Sleeve 120 cm
A.1979.10.10 a,b
Gift of Lola Stone, 1979

Worn for very formal occasions, this "Maria Clara" inspired gown has wide, bell-shaped sleeves, a sweeping skirt with a train and a matching shawl, *pañuelo*. In white and bright pink satin, it is decorated with elaborately embroidered floral appliqué enhanced with beading.

DRESS

1890s
Manila (?)
Pineapple fiber, *piña*
Center Back 182.4 cm
Waist (skirt) 65 cm
76.260 a,b
Gift of Adelaide Beste, 1976
Illustrated p. 80

Delicate black lace is appliquéd on the bodice and skirt of this two-piece dress in sheer *piña* cloth embroidered with black and white dots. *Piña* is made from the fibrous inner layer of pineapple leaves, which is washed, bleached, dried and stripped to provide fiber threads for weaving on a hand loom. While this costume is made from indigenous fabric, European influence is evident in the styling, with its tightly fitted bodice, full, cuffed sleeves and flaring skirt with train. At the end of the 19th century "...some Filipinas, in their desire to be fashionable, imitated practically anything that was in vogue in Europe." (Cruz, 1982:4)

Dress and Jacket

1963
Iloilo, Panay
15-3,4
Departmental purchase, 1963

DRESS
Cotton
Center Back 100 cm
Width (chest) 86 cm

JACKET
Abaca
Center Back 38.5 cm
Shoulder width 40 cm

After World War II, some designers began to attach the *terno's* popular "butterfly sleeves" to bolero jackets which could be worn with Western style dresses. These sleeves, which evolved from the earlier bell-shaped style, are constructed by means of numerous tucks and resemble butterflies with folded wings poised on the shoulder. They are made of (or lined with) a stiff material or are starched to hold their shape.

A coarsely woven fiber, probably abaca, is used for this 1960s version of a butterfly-sleeved short jacket. The fiber is derived from the leaf stalks of abaca, an indigenous plant related to the banana. The jacket is combined with a strapless cotton dress, styled as a modified sarong, in a matching red, green, yellow and white plaid. Large, bold plaid was a favorite pattern for sarongs.

Man's Shirt, *Barong Tagalog*

1962
Manila
Silk
Center back 79.3 cm
Sleeve 175 cm
A.1986.02.01
Gift of Mr. and Mrs. Will Lidsker, 1986

According to "The Filipino Gentleman's Guide to Dressing" (*Archipelago*, 1978:39), "...the Filipino man is a great dandy." The "Guide" goes on to say, "Only a truly masculine man could wear such a dainty shirt...and wear it as a matter of course, with cutwork and faggoting and shadow embroidery too." The sheer, long-sleeved embroidered shirt called *barong tagalog* is worn outside the trousers, even for formal occasions. This custom is said to have originated in Spanish colonial times when authorities required Filipinos to wear their shirts in this manner to distinguish them from their more fastidious rulers. (Ibid.) The embroidered silk custom-made *barong tagalog* exhibited is shown with black formal trousers.

Woman's Shoes, *Chinelas*

1933
Abaca; crocheted
Length 25.5 cm
Width 8 cm
64-1
Gift of Mrs. D.D. Parker, 1962

Woman's Shoes, *Chinelas*

1960s
Abaca; mother-of-pearl, imitation pearls, sequins
Length 21 cm
Width 7.5 cm
64-5
Gift of Loreta Sarenas, 1963

Woman's Shoes, *Chinelas*

1960s
Manila
Abaca and hemp; woven and braided
Length 22 cm
Width 9 cm
64-6
Departmental purchase, 1964

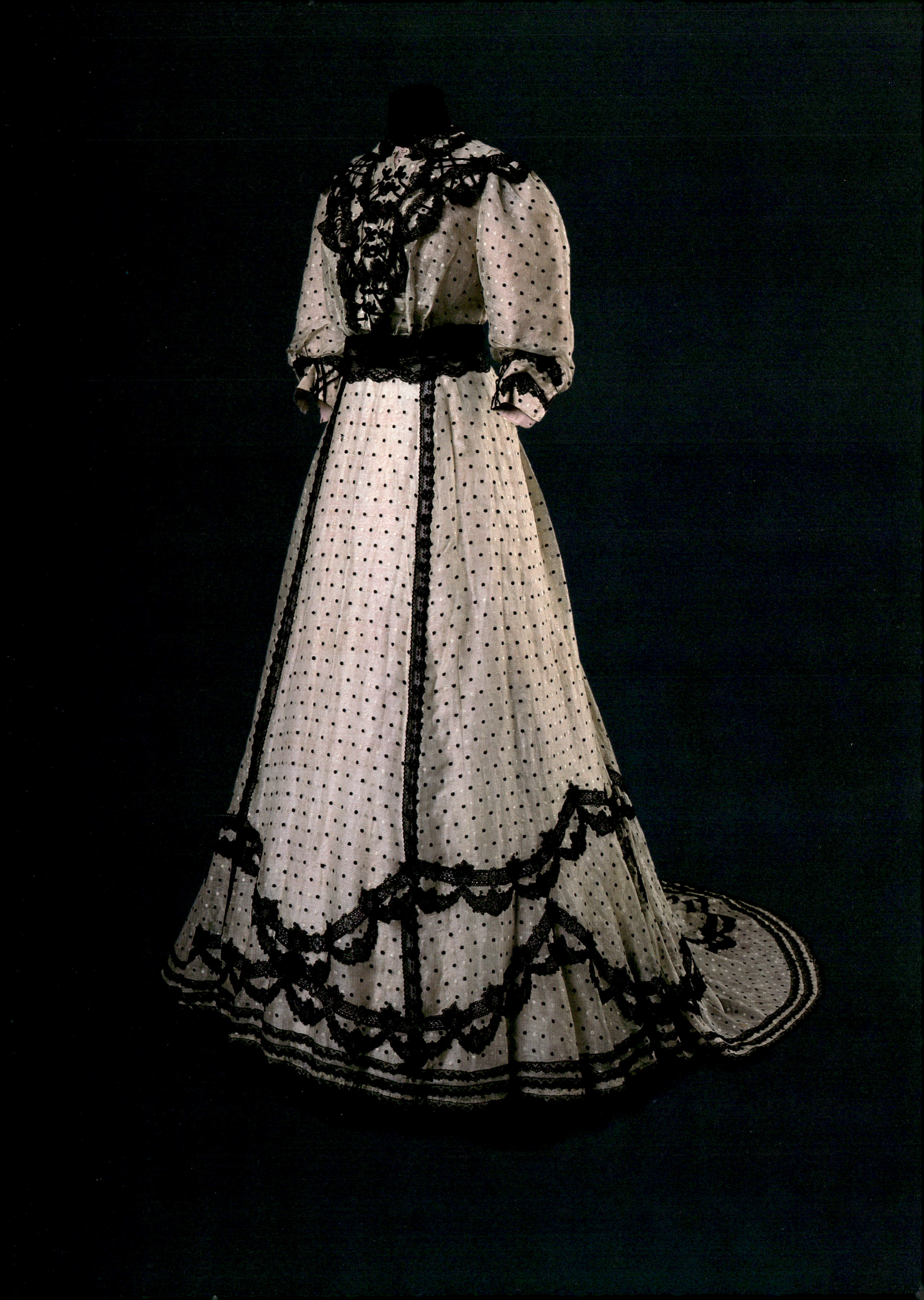

WOMAN'S ENSEMBLE

Benguet
Ibaloi people
Gift of Barbara Smith, 1961

JACKET, *SA'DY*
Cotton
Center back 50 cm (with fringe)
Sleeve 86.5 cm
15-13

WRAPPED SKIRT, *TAPIE*
Cotton
Warp 133 cm
Weft 73 cm
20-1

Indigenous aesthetic traditions are preserved among several groups which populate the mountainous north-central area of the island of Luzon. They are most noted for basketry, wood carvings and textiles. In the exhibition are clothing and accessories of the Ibaloi, Ifugao and Bontoc peoples.

The *tapis* is a wrap-around skirt, usually knee-length, worn by women of northern Luzon. Two narrow lengths of cloth are stitched together along one of the selvages. The skirt is wrapped about the hips, overlapped at the front and secured with belt or, for ceremonial occasions, a sash.

In Benguet Province, a *tapis* (called a *devit*) is worn with a matching jacket, *sa'dy*. The *tapis*, patterned in horizontal stripes, is teamed with a short, unfitted *sa'dy* trimmed on the sleeves and hem with self-fringe.

WOMAN'S SLEEVELESS JACKET, *LUBUNG*

Banaue
Ifugao people
Spun bark cloth
Center back 63 cm
Width (at shoulder) 46.5 cm
15-14
Departmental purchase, 1963

This sleeveless jacket of interworked bark fiber yarns, has vertical stripes in brown and the natural color. Before cotton became readily available in the early 20th century, some northern Luzon peoples made textiles of bark cloth. The Bontoc made a fabric of twisted bark. Today, only a very few Negrito and Ifugao groups use bark cloth. The village of Tam An produces for sale a bark cloth jacket made of yarns from the bark of a local shrub called *dami*. (Fraser-Lu, 1988:155-56)

WOMAN'S WRAPPED SKIRT, *TAPIS*

Banaue
Ifugao people
Cotton; ikat
Warp 120 cm
Weft 80 cm
20-4
Departmental purchase, 1963

This old *tapis* in faded indigo with red warp stripes features *ikat* motifs identified as dancing figures. (Fraser-Lu, 1988:160; after Lambrecht and Reyes)

WOMAN'S SASH, *MAYAD*

Banaue
Ifugao people
Cotton; wool
Length 218 cm (including tassels)
Width 20.5 cm
66-9
Departmental purchase, 1963

Mayad are worn on special occasions. These sashes, worn by Ifugao women, may have been inspired, in the past, by the almost identical Tinguian men's sash. (Ellis, 1981:183) This sash, in indigo blue cotton, has wide red patterned bands, interspersed with narrow yellow, at the ends and is edged with red and yellow wool pompons.

MAN'S HEADBAND

Banaue
Ifugao people
Cotton, wool
Length 56 cm (with fringe)
Width 9 cm
62-13
Departmental purchase, 1963

Part of a man's attire for ceremonial occasions, this headband is patterned in multi-colored stripes and topped with bright yellow and orange fringe.

PIÑA CLOTH DRESS
1890s
Philippines

MAN'S LOINCLOTH, WANO

Banaue
Ifugao people
Cotton; *ikat*
Length 398 cm (including fringe)
Width 23 cm
66-11
Departmental purchase, 1963

Traditionally, the mountain men of northern Luzon wear loincloths, either plain or striped, as in this example which is decorated at the ends with a border and fringe. Anthropomorphic figures are found on the *ikat*-patterned stripes.

MAN'S BAG, BUTUNG

Ifugao
Cotton; brass
Length (with fringe and handle) 85 cm
Width 36.5 cm
72-6
Departmental purchase, 1963

The *butung*, a pouch-like cloth bag with long, decorative fringes, is attached to an Ifugao man's belt or loincloth by a large brass-ring handle. These bags were used to carry the various ingredients used in betel chewing, pipes, spoons and other utensils.

MAN'S SASH

Cotton
Length 250 cm (with fringe)
Width 10 cm
66-7
Gift of Barbara Smith, 1966

BLANKET

1937
Northern Luzon
Possibly Ifugao
Cotton
Warp 233 cm
Weft 127 cm
62-1
Gift of Cary D. Miller, 1962

Blankets such as this (called *kidapi* in Department of Human Resources files), according to notes taken in the field by Dr. Cary D. Miller who purchased it in Bontoc, were used as protection from "chilly, rainy weather by men and women when working in the rice terraces of Northern Luzon." She also noted that, "The Ibaloy women wrap it over the left shoulder and around the body under the right arm."

The Ibaloi did not have a weaving tradition, but cotton textiles were exported by the Kanakay into Bontoc, Ifugao and Ibaloi areas from at least the second half of the 19th century and were used in ceremonial contexts as symbols of prestige and wealth. These textiles were eventually copied by local weavers in Bontoc and Ifugao, and blankets of the type in the exhibition, called *gamong*, are woven by the Ifugao. (Ellis, 1981:220-21). An almost identical example from the Musuem of Cultural History at UCLA is illustrated in Ellis, 1981, fig. 217. *Gamong* blankets are traditionally used as shrouds; however, Fraser-Lu (1988:161; fig.196), who describes the uses of the *gamong* as a funerary wrap, depicts an Ifugao man wearing a similar blanket and says they are also worn occasionally by the living.

NECK AMULET, BITUG

Banaue
Ifugao
Brass
Length 71.7 cm
60-4
Departmental purchase, 1963

THREE NECKLACES

Mountain Province
Dogs and boars teeth, Job's tears seeds
Length (longest piece) 77.7 cm
60-2
Gift of Barbara B. Smith, n.d.

MAN'S ARMLET

Mountain Province
Boar's tusks; chicken feathers
Circumference 37.7 cm
60-1
Gift of Barbara B. Smith

BRACELET

Shell
Probably Mountain Province
Height 4.5 cm
Diameter 7.4 cm
A.1988.19.01
Departmental purchase, 1960s

WRAPPED SKIRT, TAPIS

Bontoc, Mountain Province
Cotton
Length 140 cm
Width 79 cm
20-3
Departmental Purchase, 1963

Bontoc women prefer *tapis* in bright colors like this example in orange, white, yellow and green stripes.

WOMAN'S OR GIRL'S SASH, *MAYAD* OR *WAKAS*

Banaue, Mountain Province
Bontoc people
Cotton
Length 205.7 cm (with fringe)
Width 7.6 cm
66-5
Departmental purchase, 1963

BACHELOR'S HAT, *SUKLANG*

1937
Mountain Province, Luzon
Bontoc people
Rattan, mother-of-pearl, boar's teeth and dog's teeth
Height 5.1 cm
Diameter 17.4 cm
Circumference 44.7 cm
A.1988.02.01
Gift of Willis Dunne, 1988

Shaped like a shallow basket, this fine, handwoven basketry hat, *suklang*, is held securely to the back of a young man's head by a looped cord. Des Jarlais states that traditionally, mother-of-pearl buttons, wild boar's teeth, and dog's teeth were added to the *suklang* for each head taken in battle as a show of prowess. The hat was also used to carry tobacco.

MARRIED MAN'S HAT, *SUKLANG*

Bontoc people
Rattan
Circumference 44 cm
Height 7.5 cm
62-3
Departmental purchase, 1963

Married men wear a bowl-shaped basketry hat on the backs of their heads. Unlike the colorfully decorated hats worn by bachelors, these *suklang* are natural colored basketry with no ornamentation.

MAN'S CEREMONIAL HAT

1960s
Sagada Village
Bontoc people
Natural fiber; feathers
Circumference 62.5 cm
Height (including feathers) 22 cm
62-5
Departmental purchase, 1963

WOMAN'S ENSEMBLE

Mindanao
Maranao people

BLOUSE, *SUBLAY*
Cotton and tinsel lace
Center back 54 cm
Sleeve 110 cm
15-25
Departmental purchase, 1971

SARONG, *MALONG LANDAP*

Marawi, Mindanao
Maranao people
Silk
Length 167 cm
Circumference 162 cm
15-19
Departmental purchase

The Maranao, a Muslim people who live in the highlands of the southern island of Mindanao, have a strong weaving tradition. Their traditional garment is the *malong*, constructed of two lengths of cloth which are sewn together at the selvages to make a square and then seamed at the side, creating a tubular skirt. The *malong* is worn by women in a variety of ways, including draping it over one shoulder in an elegant, toga-like fashion. (Fraser-Lu, 1988:pl.32; McReynolds, 1982:99)

The *malong landap* can be one color, but often has panels of two alternating colors. It is ornamented with separately woven bands, called *langkit*. A wide band is stitched vertically across the panels on the skirt's side seam, and two narrow bands are stitched parallel to the panels. The *langkit* have decorative, tapestry-woven patterns.

SARONG, *MALONG LANDAP*

1970s
Rayon
Warp 173 cm
Weft 162 cm
A.1979.10.12
Gift of Garrett Solyom, 1979

SARONG, *MALONG LANDAP*

Marawi City
Maranao people
Rayon
Length 165 cm
Circumference 165 cm
15-20
Departmental purchase, 1971

SARONG, *MALONG ANDON*

Marawai City
Maranao Rayon
Length 148.5 cm
Circumference 178 cm
15-24
Departmental Purchase, 1971

The *malong andon* is ornamented with *ikat* patterning rather than tapestry-woven *langkit* bands. This *malong* has one section of alternating black and white *ikat* stripes. The remainder has wider stripes in magenta, blue-violet, blue-green, yellow, and dark green *ikat*. *Malong andon* in this style are considered more modern than those with traditional all-over designs, according to Department of Human Resources notes.

WOMAN'S CLOG

1930
Mindanao
Wood; abaca, mother-of-pearl, velvet, metallic thread
Length 20.6 cm
Width 6.8 cm
Height (over instep) 8.6 cm
64-3
Gift of Mrs. D.D. Parker, 1962

The dark wood platform of this clog is carved with geometric patterns into which are set diamond shaped pieces of mother-of-pearl. The strap is abaca covered with metallic embroidered velvet.

MAN'S SARONG, *MALONG PANDI*

Maranao people
Cotton
Length 172 cm
Circumference 155 cm
15-26
Departmental Purchase, 1961

Malong pandi have a pattern of horizontal stripes that usually incorporate narrow strips of tie-dye. This *malong*, in magenta with multi-colored stripes, has a matching textile square, possibly for a turban, *tubao*. According to records of the Department of Human Resources, this is a man's *malong*. Maranao men wear the *malong* over trousers for formal occasions. (Fraser-Lu, 1988:167)

MAN'S ENSEMBLE

1960s
Sulu (?)
Tausug people
Departmental purchase, 1960s

SHIRT
Rayon; gold nailheads
Center back 44 cm
Sleeve 71 cm
15-31

TROUSERS
Rayon and cotton
Length 112 cm
Width (waist) 59 cm
15-30

HAT
Early 1960s
Cotton
Height 13 cm
Circumference 54 cm
62-19

Floral shaped nailheads of gold believed to have come from Spanish or American gold coins, trim this bright orange formal shirt, notes Des Jarlais. It is worn with loose fitting pants which are cut in a fashion similar to a type of Chinese trouser, suggesting the style may have originated in China. The white hat is worn by Muslim men to signify they had made a pilgrimage to the Holy City of Mecca.

Pre-Hispanic Philippine Gold

Ornaments made of gold have been excavated from a number of gravesites in the Southern Philippines. Manufactured in the Islands prior to the 16th century Spanish conquest, the articles include jewelry, buttons and other ornaments which may have been attached to clothing. Locations in the listings refer to excavation sites.

Pendant

15th century
Cuyo Island
Gold
Length 2.4 cm
Width 2.5 cm
Private collection
Illustrated p. 87 Second row, left

This flat pendant has a star design in repoussé with two rows of beading.

Tubular Bead

12th century
Butuan
Granulated Gold
Length 1.8 cm
Width 0.5 cm
Private collection

Ring

15th century
Cuyo Island
Gold, garnet
Width 1.3 cm
Private collection

Beads

12th-15th century
Iloilo, Panay Island
Gold
Length 1.2 cm
Width 1.2 cm
Private collection

Two square-shaped gold "beads" are patterned with four rows of four tiny pierced sections which create a honeycomb effect. It is not known precisely how these beads were strung, but it would have been possible to combine them with as many as four strands of assorted beads.

Necklace

12th-15th century
Iloilo, Panay Island
Gold; glass
Length 48.2 cm
Private collection

This reconstructed necklace is comprised of gold "honeycomb" beads and glass beads of various shapes.

Hair Ornament

15th century
Cuyo Island
Gold
Diameter 3.0 cm
Private collection
Illustrated p. 87 Second row, right

The sun is a common motif in pre-Hispanic Philippine gold. This hair ornament may also have been used as a costume facing.

Hair Ornament

15th century
Cuyo Island
Gold
Diameter 10.7 cm
Collection of Sheldon Geringer
Illustrated p. 87 bottom row

Made from sheet gold, the center of this six-petaled ornament is patterned with concentric rows of stylized scrolling pounded into the metal from the reverse.

Ear Ornament

15th century
Oton, Panay Island
Gold
Length 5.7 cm
Width 3.4 cm
Collection of Sheldon Geringer
Illustrated, p. 87 Third row

Rows of braided wire and dangles ornament this simple hoop earring.

EAR ORNAMENT

15th century
Cuyo Island
Gold
Diameter 4.9 cm
Collection of Virginia B. Randolph
Illustrated p. 87 Top row, right

EAR ORNAMENTS

12th century
Butuan
Gold
Width 2.4-2.6 cm.
Private collection

These quatrefoil-shaped ornaments with a foliated palmette design most likely adorned the ears, but could possibly have been used as buttons.

EAR ORNAMENTS

15th century
Cuyo Island
Gold
Diameter 1.2 cm
Private collection

EAR ORNAMENTS

12th century
Butuan
Gold
Diameter 2.0 cm
Private collection

These simple gold ear ornaments are also referred to as "barter rings," since they may have been used as currency.

EARRING

12th century
Butuan
Gold
Length 4.7 cm
Width 1.2 cm
Private collection

Five lozenge and bell-shaped pendants dangled from a simple hoop create this twelfth century earring.

EAR ORNAMENTS

15th century
Cuyo Island
Gold
Diameter 2.0 cm
Private collection

Probably worn like ear plugs, this pair of bobbin-shaped ornaments adhere to the inside of the ear lobe.

EAR ORNAMENT

15th century
Cuyo Island
Gold
Diameter 4.1 cm
Private collection
Illustrated p. 87 Top row, left

One of a pair, this ear ornament, which adhered to the inside of the lobe, is a fine example of gold granulation.

PRE-HISPANIC
PHILIPPINE GOLD
15th century
(Left to right)
Top row: Ear Ornaments
Second row: Pendant; Hair
Ornament
Third row: Ear Ornament
Bottom row: Hair Ornament

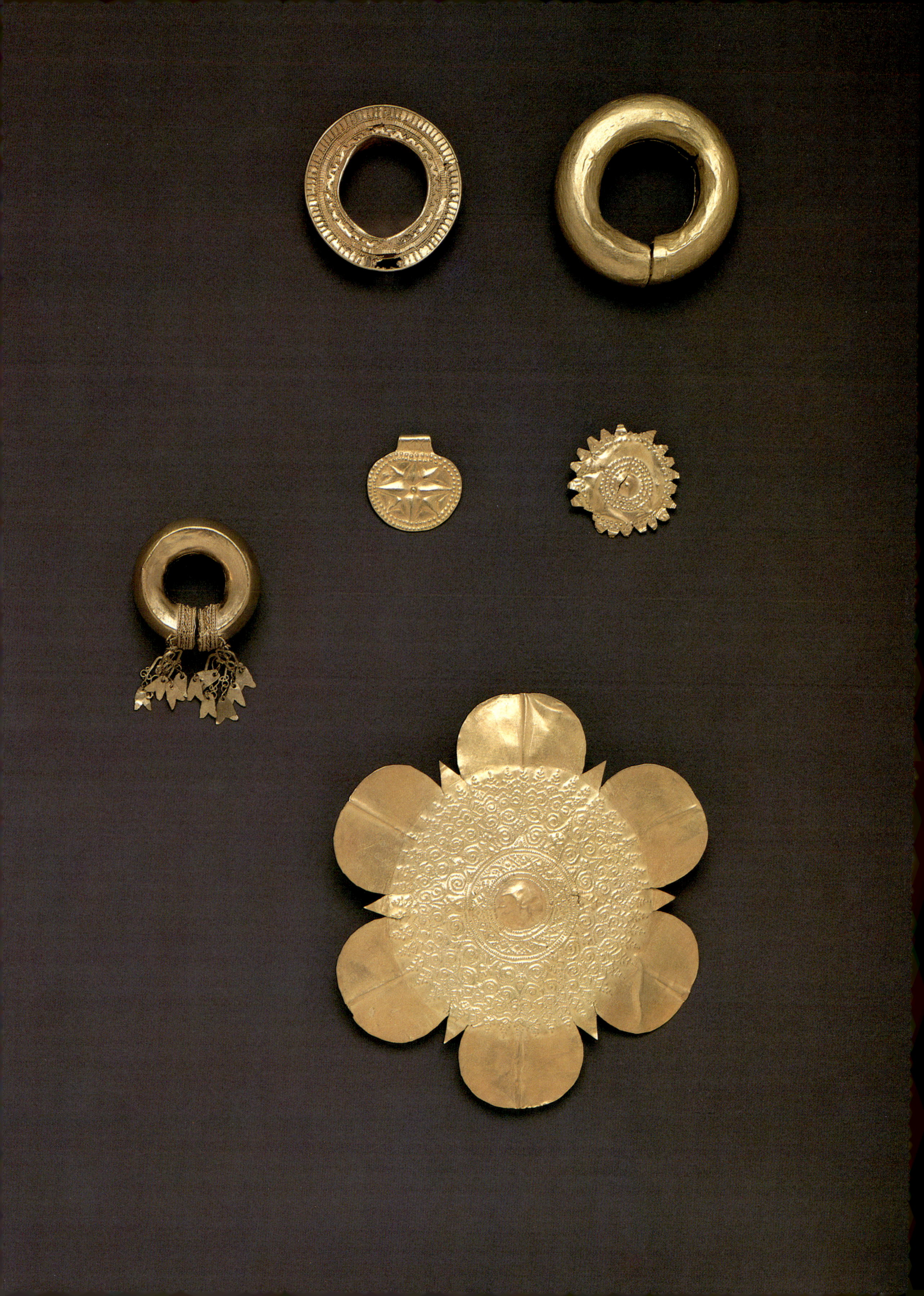

CHINA

QING DYNASTY COSTUME

The Manchu, a people of nomadic origin from the forests and plains of northern Asia, invaded China in 1644 and established the Qing Dynasty in Beijing, superseding the government of the Ming Chinese. The Manchu consolidated their rule in 1683 with the subjugation of the southern provinces and Formosa and remained in power until the inception of the Chinese Republic in 1912.

While the Manchu retained established bureaucratic institutions and preserved many Han (native) Chinese traditions, they also managed to maintain their own cultural identity and impose some of their customs on the Chinese. Among the most visible were the Manchu costume and hairstyle. Chinese men were required, partly as a symbol of submission, to wear their hair in a queue as did the Manchu, and ethnic Chinese in the service of the Qing government wore Manchu court attire.

The Manchu adapted Chinese symbolism to their own clothing styles which reflected nomadic origins in a northern climate. Robes, derived from animal skin prototypes, were close fitting and tightly belted. A curved flap over the chest fastened at the right with toggles and loops. (Vollmer, 1983:17) Men's robes were vented at the front and back for ease in mounting and sitting astride horses. Manchu women had traditionally walked alongside the horses in migrations, so their robes required side vents. Tapered sleeves with horseshoe-shaped cuffs, *madixiu (ma-ti hsiu)*, were designed to keep out the cold wind and cover the hands.

Qing Dynasty wardrobe was regulated by government edict as recorded in *The Illustrated Catalogue of Ritual Paraphernalia of the Qing Dynasty, Huangchao liqi tushi (Huang Ch'ao li-ch'i t'u-shih)*, 1759, during the celebrated reign of the Emperor Qianlong (Ch'ien-Lung), (1736-1796). All clothing was classified as official or non-official (or in some cases quasi-official), and within these categories were designations of dress as formal, semi-formal and informal.

Official formal court attire, worn by the emperor and upper echelon, was reserved for important ritual occasions such as the annual Sacrifices to Heaven and Earth. The ceremonial garment, called a *chaofu (ch'ao-fu)*, consists of hip-length coat worn with a lower body cover generally referred to as "paired aprons." For Manchu women, the *chaofu* became a single garment, resembling a robe, worn unbelted. At other official court functions the required attire, worn by men and women of all ranks, was the *qifu (ch'i-fu)* (lit. "festive," or "celebrated"), a full-length, semi-formal robe commonly called a "dragon robe" because of its principal design motif.

The dragon, bringer of rain, was a symbol of benevolence in China from ancient times. Early in the Qing Dynasty, when rules were rigidly enforced, the five-clawed *long (lung)* dragon, traditional Chinese symbol of imperial authority, was reserved for the robes of emperor, empress, consorts, heir apparent and those singled out for exceptional meritorious service to the government. In later years, especially the late 19th century, the five-clawed dragon might appear on robes worn by officials of almost any rank. However, an emperor's or empress' robe could be distinguished not by the five-clawed dragon alone, but by the yellow color and twelve embroidered symbols of imperial authority.

The *mang* dragon, a different species, was worn by members of the imperial nobility with the rank of third degree prince and below. Court officials, of Han Chinese as well as Manchu ethnicity, were also entitled to the four-clawed *mang* dragon. (Scott, 1958:16; Vollmer, 1986:22, based on Cammann, 1944:71-131)

The *qifu* is a terrestrial diagram. Diagonal bands form a wide lower border of water, topped with billowing waves, from which rises the earth mountain. Earth and a cloud-filled sky are inhabited by dragons, dominated by a large, curled, frontal dragon on the chest and center back. Birds, bats and other creatures frequently appear on the robes as well as Buddhist, Taoist and other auspicious symbols. The transition between the material world and the upper realm occurs symbolically at the neck opening of the garment, the "gateway to heaven." The head of the wearer represents the spiritual element. Only when the *qifu* was worn, therefore, did it symbolize the universe.

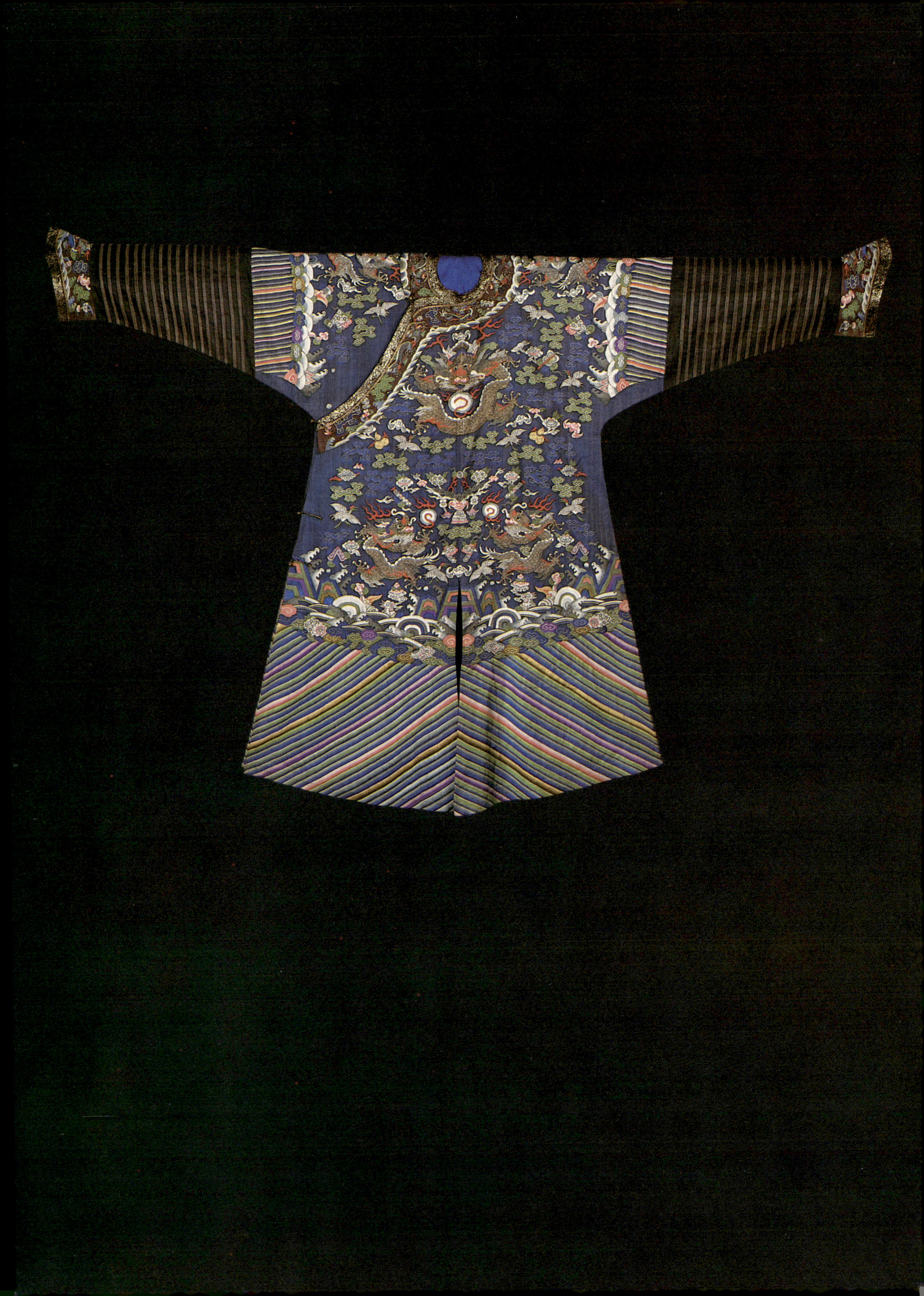

MAN'S SEMI-FORMAL
COURT ROBE, QIFU

1875-1911
Qing Dynasty
Manchu
Silk tapestry weave, kesi (k'o-ssu), gold wrapped thread, panjin (p'an-chin), gold braid, hand painted details
Center back 136.1 cm
Sleeve (width from sleeve tip to sleeve tip) 213.6 cm
A.80.6.2
Gift of Oma Umbel, 1980
Illustrated p. 90

Nine five-clawed dragons of gold wrapped thread (one is hidden underneath the front flap) are arranged on this blue silk *qifu*. The flaming pearl of knowledge, frequently associated with dragon imagery, is symbolic of the emperor's quest for wisdom and virtue.

Dragons and other design motifs are often couched in gold or silver thread. Couching, or anchoring thread to the ground fabric with an overcast stitch at intervals of about one-quarter inch, is the usual method of attaching metallic thread which tends to fray if it is stitched through. The metallic thread consists of a core, commonly of hemp, cotton or silk, which is wrapped in thin gold or silver leaf or, for economy, gold paper.

MAN'S SEMI-FORMAL
COURT ROBE, QIFU

1875-1900
Qing Dynasty
Manchu
Silk; gauze weave, *sha*; gold wrapped thread, *panjin*
Center back 141 cm
Sleeve 222 cm
A.1984.10.07
Gift of Oma Umbel, 1984

Silk gauze robes were officially designated for summer wear. The catalogue of ritual paraphernalia, *Huangchao liqi tushi*, of 1759 decreed that court robes, regardless of the wearer's rank, should be "quilted, lined, of gauze, or fur-trimmed, depending on the season." The actual date of change from one type of robe to another was determined each year by the Board of Rites. (Cammann, 1952:56)

This blue and gold gauze *qifu* is emblazoned with four-clawed dragons. Chung (1979:59) remarks on the skill of Chinese embroiderers who used a technique similar to modern petit-point for rendering designs on the very fine gauze mesh. The finished effect is much like embroidery on solid weave fabric. The edges of the dragons were usually couched with metallic wrapped thread.

MAN'S SEMI-FORMAL
COURT ROBE, QIFU

1875-1900
Qing Dynasty
Manchu
Silk; tapestry weave, *kesi*; gold wrapped thread, panjin
Center back 129.5 cm
Sleeve 203 cm
A.1982.08.03
Gift of Oma Umbel, 1982

Arranged among clouds, birds and five-clawed dragons on this purple *qifu* is the stylized character for *shou*, long life. This ubiquitous symbol is often depicted with another symbol associated with longevity, the bat. Together, they mean long life and happiness. The character *fu* (bat) is a homonym for *fu* meaning "happiness;" thus the bat is also an emblem of happiness and joy. (Williams, 1976:35)

MAN'S SEMI-FORMAL
COURT ROBE, *QIFU*
Qing Dynasty
China

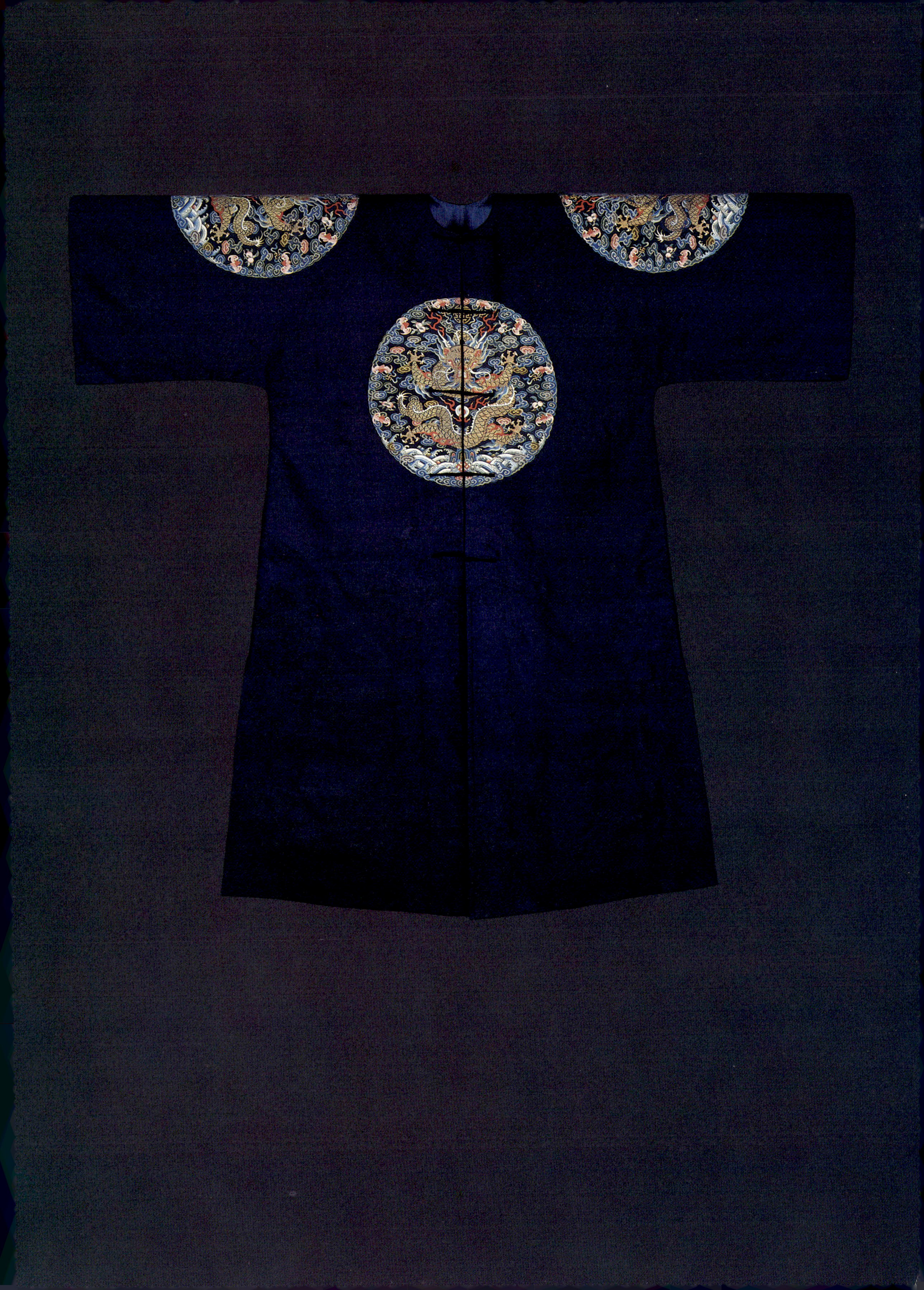

MAN'S SURCOAT,
PUFU (P'U-FU)

c. 1850
Qing Dynasty
Manchu
Silk; gold wrapped thread, *panjin*
Center Back 130.8 cm
Sleeve 138.4 cm
A.185.03.17
Gift of Mrs. Donald (Mary) Bartow, 1985
Illustrated p. 92

The *pufu (p'u-fu)* is a dark colored surcoat with wide sleeves worn over the *qifu* by all classes of court officials, including the emperor. The *long* dragon and other symbols of the imperial family were embroidered or woven in medallions (the circular form relating to the shape of heaven) on the *pufu*; the rank insignia of lesser nobility and court officials were depicted on separate "mandarin squares."

The *pufu* in this exhibition probably belonged to a person of very high rank, according to Mary Ellen Des Jarlais. Two of the twelve ancient symbols reserved for the emperor, empress and imperial family, the moon and the sun, appear on the right and left shoulder medallions. (The hare in the moon relates to an ancient Chinese myth. He stands under the sacred cassia tree grinding with mortar and pestle the elixir from which he will manufacture the pill of immortality. The three-legged bird, usually identified as a crow, lives in the sun. The number three is associated with the *yang*, or male principle, of which the sun is the essence.) Des Jarlais states that the very fine quality tapestry weave and gold wrapped thread found in this *pufu* further attest to probable imperial ownership.

According to the dress-code edicts of 1759, the *pufu* with rank insignia was part of the ensemble worn at annual annual sacrifices and other important occasions. The male costume consisted of the *qifu* with the wave and mountain border visible beneath the three-quarter length *pufu*, court beads, the court collar, *piling* (in the later years of the Qing Dynasty), knee-high black satin boots and a hat topped with a finial which indicated the rank of the wearer.

MANDARIN SQUARE,
PUZI (P'U-TZU)

c. 1875
Qing Dynasty
Manchu
Silk; gold wrapped thread, red coral, *shanhu*
Length 31 cm
Width 29 cm
A.1984.10.01a; 1984.10.01c
Gift of Oma Umbel, 1984

The Ming Dynasty custom of wearing badges to signify official rank was adopted by the Manchus. *Puzi*, "mandarin squares," were stitched to the back and front of the *pufu*. Emblems embroidered on the *puzi* were designated by law and corresponded with ancient Chinese tradition. The dragon (in a circular, not square, format) was worn by the Manchu nobility. Badges with different species of birds indicated the rank of civil officials, and animal badges were used for the military. The birds in the exhibited squares are most likely the silver pheasant, *baixian (pai-hsien)* and the lesser egret, *lusi (lu-ssu)*, symbols of fifth and sixth degree civil officials respectively.

MAN'S SURCOAT, *PUFU*
Qing Dynasty
China

COURT COLLAR, *PILING*
Qing Dynasty
China

COURT COLLAR, *PILING* (P'I LING)

1875-1911
Qing Dynasty
Manchu
Silk; satin, *duan (tuan)* and brocade weaves; gold wrapped thread, *panjin*
Center back 19 cm
Width 76 cm
62-8
Gift of Ada K. Erwin, 1972
Illustrated p. 94

The flaring, triangular-shaped court collar, *piling*, was worn by both men and Manchu women with the *chaofu* and sometimes on the surcoat, *pufu*.

The broad collar extended beyond the shoulders. The shape is most likely a vestige of the convertible collars on Manchu nomads' coats which were pulled up over the head and tied. (Vollmer, 1977:39)

Golden lotuses and cranes ornament this brocade court collar. The crane, a sign of longevity, good omen and happiness, is associated with the rank of first-degree court official.

HAT FINIAL

19th century
Qing Dynasty
Ivory; gilt metal
Height 5.2 cm
Depth 3 cm
Private collection

Qing Dynasty court costume was not complete without a hat on top of which was a knob or finial designating the rank of the wearer. At the apex of the hierarchy was the emperor, who wore a large pearl, and the nobility, down to the rank of fifth-degree, with ruby finials on their hats. Government officials of the first degree were entitled to coral knob, while ninth degree officials were identified by figured gilt ornaments attached to their hats. This hat finial is composed of a large ivory knob in a setting of fine filigree. Opaque white stones, such as the example in the exhibition, were designated for sixth degree government officials.

COURT BEADS, CHAOZHU (CH'AO-CHU)

Qing Dynasty, *Qianlong* period (1736-1796)
Bodhi seeds, amethyst, coral, aquamarine, yellow and pink tourmaline, jade, pearls, silk, metal filigree, kingfisher feathers
Length 74.3 cm
Private collection
Illustrated p. 96

Chaozhu were worn with court dress by nobles and higher officials, or by lesser officials for certain ceremonial occasions only. These court beads were status symbols but not actual indications of rank in the same manner as mandarin squares and hat finials. The choice of beads was left up to the individual except for the emperor, empress and dowager empress, who wore fresh water Manchurian pearls mandated by law for them alone.

The prototype of court beads is thought to be the rosaries used by Lama Buddhist monks of Tibet and Mongolia for counting repetitions of a prayer or mantra. (Cammann, 4:1979) In 1643, a year before the invasion of China, an envoy of the Dalai Lama presented the Manchu leader with a rosary.

The traditional rosary and the court beads which resemble them consist of 108 small counting beads, divided into four groups of twenty-seven by three large spacer beads called *fotou (fo-t'ou)*, or "Buddha heads." The ends of the cord then pass through a vase or pagoda-shaped bead from which extends a silken ribbon, a flat, rectangular stone, sometimes in a metal frame, *beiyun (pei-yun)* and several more inches of ribbon culminating in a drop pendant, *dazhui (ta-chui)*. This extension hangs down the wearer's back and acts as a counter-weight so the beads will be more evenly balanced between front and back and more comfortable to wear. Suspended from the back of the necklace are an additional three strands of ten beads each, *jinian (chi-nien)*, ending with a drop pendant.

BELT BUCKLE, DAIKOU (TAI-K'OU)

16th century
Ming Dynasty
White jade
Length 9.1 cm
Width 4.6 cm
Depth 1.3 cm
Private collection
Illustrated p. 99 top row, left

According to the *Shiji*, when King Wuling, who ruled the state of Zhou (Chou), 325-299 B.C., developed a mobile cavalry like that of his enemies to the north, he also adopted barbarian dress, including trousers and belt buckles. The latter soon became an important costume accessory with a number of uses according to type. In addition to functioning as buckles, some were used to fasten lapels of traditional Chinese robes, others to attach various objects to a belt.

This belt buckle consists of two interlocking pieces with loops to attach the belt. The white jade is incised with two horned dragons chasing the flaming pearl within a background of swirling clouds.

BELT BUCKLE, DAIKOU

16th century
Ming Dynasty
White jade with brown markings
Length 12.2 cm
Width 5.2 cm
Collection of Roger Lau
Illustrated p. 99 bottom row, right

The hook of this two-piece belt buckle is in the shape of a dragon's head. Two *chi (ch'ih)* dragons are carved in high relief open work on the front of the hook, and the reverse has two plain studs for attaching the ornament to the belt. Buckles of this type have been recovered from Yuan and Ming archaeological sites.

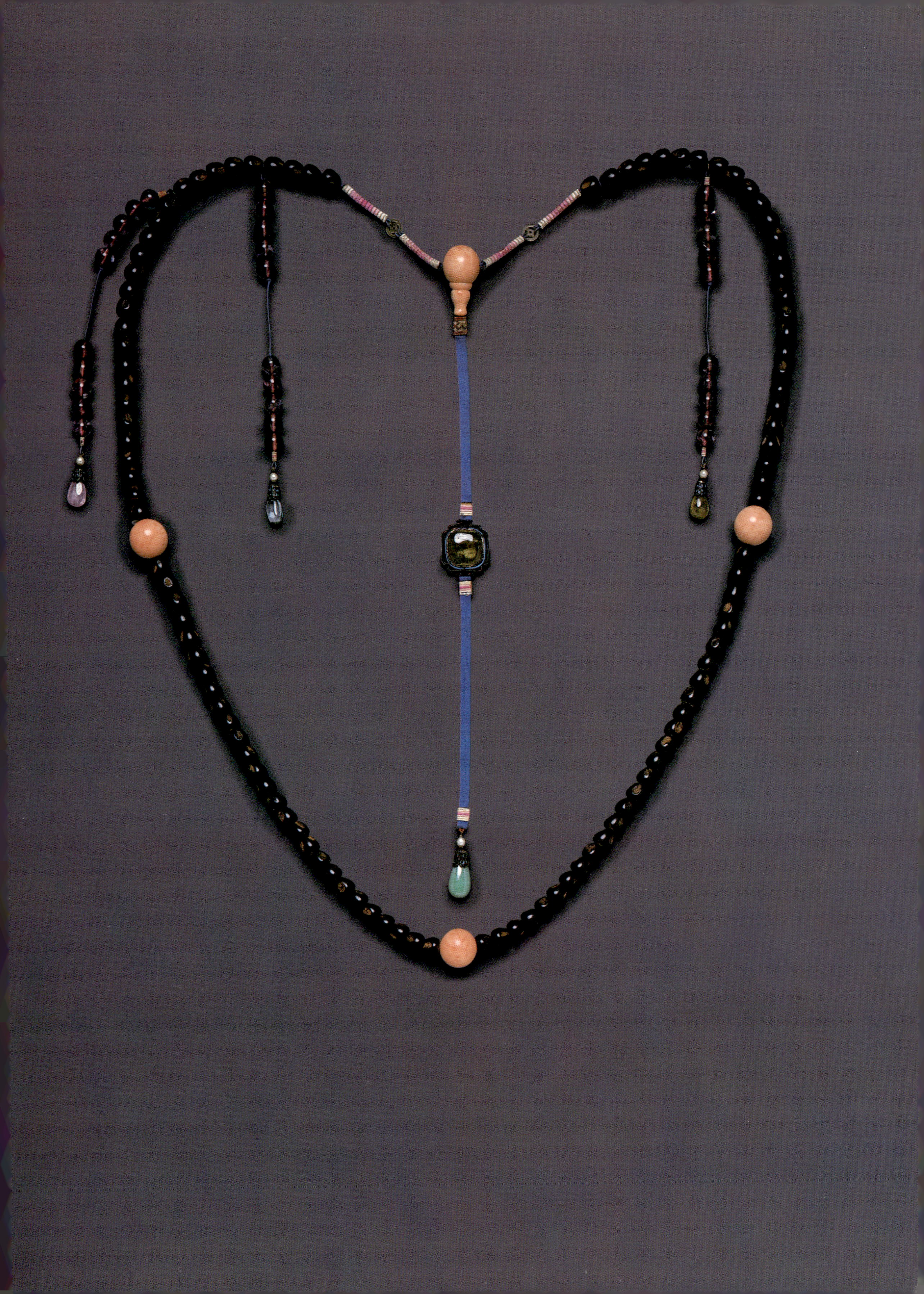

Belt Buckle, DAIKOU

17th-18th century
Ming or Qing Dynasty
Mutton fat jade
Length 4.9 cm
Width 9.1 cm
Collection of Virginia B. Randolph
Illustrated p. 99 second row, center

This undecorated oval shaped belt buckle is created in white jade called "mutton-fat," *yangzhiyu*, and reflects the Chinese appreciation of unadorned pebbles. According to *Ge Gu Yao Lun*, the treatise on the essential criteria of antiquities, the most valuable type of jade is mutton fat.

Belt Buckle, DAIKOU

15th century
Ming Dynasty (1368-1644)
Greenish-white jade
Length 7 cm
Width 5.8 cm
Collection of Virginia B. Randolph
Illustrated p. 99 second row, left

A lioness and her cub cavort among cloud-patterned open work on this jade belt buckle. The motif of lions playing became very popular during the Ming period and is often seen on blue and white porcelain and other decorative arts of that period. The reverse button and hook are carved in the shapes of a bat and sacred fungus, *lingzhi*.

Belt Plaque, DAISHI (TAI-SHIH)

16th century
Ming Dynasty
White jade
Length 14.2 cm
Width 5.5 cm
Depth .9 cm
Private collection
Illustrated p. 99 third row, right

Decorative plaques were often attached to belts. Made of precious materials, the plaques became symbols of status. In this belt plaque, a four-clawed, horned *mang* dragon, flanked by a bat and a skylark, is carved in high relief in a setting of peonies and clouds. According to Chen Boquan of the Jianqxi Provincial Museum, a full set of jade belt plaques of the Ming Period consists of nineteen pieces: two rectangular plaques similar to this example, seven square, four long and narrow, and six peach-shaped. The ground of this type of plaque is also carved in open-work. (Watt, 1980:198)

Belt Plaque, DAISHI

16th Century
Ming Dynasty
White jade
Width 2.5 cm
Height 2.8 cm
Private collection
Illustrated p. 102 second row, right

This rectangular belt plaque is carved in two layers of open work with a design of flowering prunus and a peony on a foliated ground, framed by a border of "pearls."

Belt Plaque, DAIBAN (TAI-PAN)

Early 19th Century
Qing Dynasty
White jade
Length 7.8 cm
Width 5.6 cm
Private collection
Illustrated p. 99 top row, right

Carved from a single piece of jade, this plaque was attached to a belt, and a pendant, pomander or purse was suspended from the movable hoop formed of double dragons. The upper section is incised with the sacred fungus of immortality, *lingzhi*.

Belt Hook, DAIGOU (TAI-KOU)

16th Century
Ming Dynasty
White jade
Length 9.4 cm
Width 1.8 cm
Collection of Roger Lau
Illustrated p. 99 second row, right

Hook-type belt buckles served to fasten the lapels of Chinese robes as well as belts at the waist.

Court beads, CHAOZHU
Qing Dynasty
China

BUTTON

Yuan Dynasty (1260-1368)
Greenish white jade
Diameter 7.7 cm
Collection of Virginia B. Randolph
Illustrated p. 102 top row, right

This large chrysanthemum button with a border of *rui* lappets, would probably have been used as a fastening for a man's robe. The reverse, carved in the form of overlapping petals, is similar to examples reportedly excavated from Yuan tombs. The chrysanthemum is the flower of mid-autumn and the symbol of joviality.

BUTTON OR BELT ORNAMENT

14th-15th century
Yuan or Ming Dynasty
Greenish-white jade
Length 9 cm
Width 5 cm
Collection of Virginia B. Randolph
Illustrated p. 102 third row, right

Two overlapping chrysanthemums are carved on both the front and reverse. Small holes for attaching the ornament to a garment or belt are integrated into the design in such a way as to be virtually invisible.

BUTTON

15th century
Ming Dynasty
White jade
Diameter 4.3 cm
Collection of Virginia B. Randolph
Illustrated p. 102 top row, left

This chrysanthemum button has a double row of delicate petals created in openwork carving. Small jade flowers ornamented women's robes but earlier, during the Tang Dynasty (618-906), they were worn in the hair.

BUTTON

14th-15th century
Yuan or Ming Dynasty
Mutton fat jade
Diameter 3.8 cm
Collection of Virginia B. Randolph
Illustrated p. 102 third row, left

Made for a woman's garment, this small button is in the form of a five petaled prunus, or plum, blossom. Five-petaled jade prunus flowers have been recovered from Yuan tombs.

CHINESE JADE ORNAMENTS
(Left to right)
Top row: Belt Buckle, *daikou*, 16th century; Belt Plaque, *daiban*, early 19th century
Second row: Belt Buckle, *daikou*, 15th century; Belt Buckle, *daikou*, 17th-18th century; Belt Hook, *daigou*, 16th century
Third row: Archer's Ring, *banzhi*, 17th-18th century; Belt Plaque, *daishi*, 16th century
Fourth row: Bead Pendant, 17th-18th century; Belt Buckle, *daikou*, 16th century

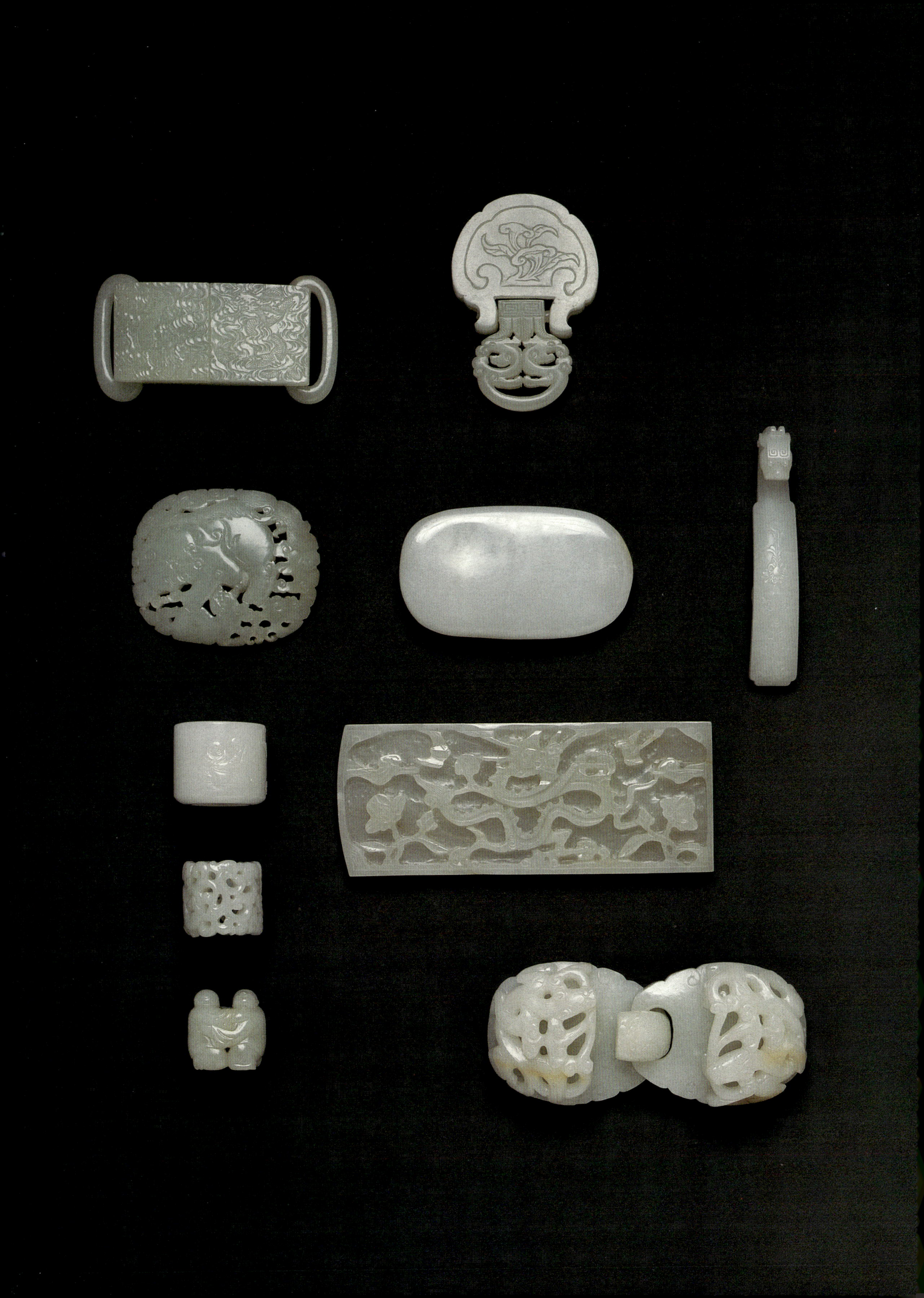

BUTTON

14th-15th Century
Yuan or Ming Dynasty
White jade
Depth 2.8 cm
Private collection
Illustrated p. 102 second row, left

This small button has five delicately carved concave petals.

HAIRPIN

15th century
Ming Dynasty
White jade
Length 9.2 cm
Width .8 cm
Collection of Virginia B. Randolph

Beautifully sculpted in the shape of a bow, this jade ornament is similar to the piece listed below. Hairpins such as these were placed in a woman's chignon. They were normally worn in pairs, one crossing the other, with the curved points downwards.

HAIRPIN

Ming Dynasty
White jade
Length 8.9 cm
Width 1.1 cm
Collection of Virginia B. Randolph

WOMAN'S BANGLE, ZHUO, (CHUO)

15th century, possibly earlier
Ming Dynasty
Greenish white jade
Length 7.4 cm
Width 6.8 cm
Collection of Virginia B. Randolph
Illustrated p. 102 bottom row, right

This simple but elegantly fashioned oval bangle conforms to the natural shape of the wrist and was comfortable to wear.

WOMAN'S BANGLE

Late 19th-early 20th century
Qing Dynasty
Amber; gilt metal
Diameter 7.8 cm
Collection of Virginia B. Randolph

The symbol for prosperity, *jixiang (chi-hsiang)*, is worked in repoussé gilt metal strips which ornament this bangle of rich, glowing amber.

BANGLE

19th Century
Qing Dynasty
Gilt silver; black coral
Diameter 7.0 cm
Width 0.9 cm
Collection of G. Pang

This bangle bracelet of black coral is decorated with the "three friends" motif: bamboo, peony and plum.

BRACELET

19th Century
Qing Dynasty
Gilt silver
Diameter 6.9 cm
Width 1.9 cm
Collection of G. Pang

Blossoming chrysanthemums on a stippled ground decorate this bangle. The terminals, which portray the accomplishments of a literary man, are carved in high relief surrounded by a key fret border that bears the shop mark Baocheng (Pao-ch'eng).

BANGLE

20th Century
Qing Dynasty
Reconstituted amber; brass
Depth 7.5 cm
Width 0.6 cm
Collection of Virginia B. Randolph

This bangle is decorated with the character for "good fortune" in a stylized seal script on a stippled ground.

BEAD PENDANT

17th-18th century
Late Ming or early Qing Dynasty
Greenish-white jade
Height 2.9 cm
Width 2.9 cm
Collection of Virginia B. Randolph
Illustrated p. 99 bottom row, left

Boys wrestling was a popular motif during the late Ming period. Linked arms of two little Chinese boys wrestling or playing form the opening of this bead which would have been strung on a silk cord. It was suspended from a girdle around the waist.

BEAD PENDANT

Yuan Dynasty
Black jade
Length 3.2 cm
Width 3.4 cm
Collection of Virginia B. Randolph

Shaped like the head of a mythological beast, probably associated with military prowess or having some protective connotation, this bead pendant would have been suspended by a cord from the girdle of a man's robe.

PLAQUE PENDANT

18th century
Qing Dynasty
Yellow Jade
Length 6.2 cm
Width 4.2 cm
Collection of Virginia B. Randolph

The *zhaijiepai (chai-chieh-p'ai)*, or abstinence plaque, was worn at the girdle to indicate that the wearer was fasting as part of a religious observance. Bordered by open "C" scrolls, one side has the word *zhaijie* ("abstinence"), the other the Manchu translation, *Bolgomi Targa*.

ARCHER'S RING, *BANZHI* (PAN-CHIH)

Kangxi period (1662-1723)
Qing Dynasty
Mutton fat jade
Height 2.9 cm
Diameter 3.4 cm
Collection of Virginia B. Randolph
Illustrated p. 99 third row, left

The thumb ring, or archer's ring, evolved from a leather band worn by archers in ancient times to aid in drawing the bow. It became an ornament made of precious material which is worn by a man on his right thumb.

Carved in relief on this archer's ring are two boys in a garden shaded by a banana tree, who seem to be peering into a large goldfish bowl. The motif of boys playing in a garden is commonly seen in late Ming period wood block prints and inspired jade carving of the early Qing period.

ARCHER'S RING, *BANZHI*

Early 18th century
Qing Dynasty
White jade
Height 2.6 cm
Diameter 2.9 cm
Collection of Virginia B. Randolph
Illustrated p. 99 Fourth row, left

An open work *chi (chih)* dragon and a *fenghuang* (phoenix) decorate this 18th century archer's ring.

HAIR PIN, *ZAN* (TSAN)

19th Century
Qing Dynasty
Gilt silver
Length 8.0 cm
Depth 4.0 cm
Collection of G. Pang

This hair pin consists of a stylized *shou* (good luck) medallion done in open-work.

HAIR PIN, *ERWAZAN* (EHR-WA-TSAN)

19th Century
Qing Dynasty
Silver
Length 21.4 cm
Width 2.3 cm
Collection of G. Pang

Stylized longevity designs and *rui* scepter motifs ornament this reticulated hair pin with ear pick.

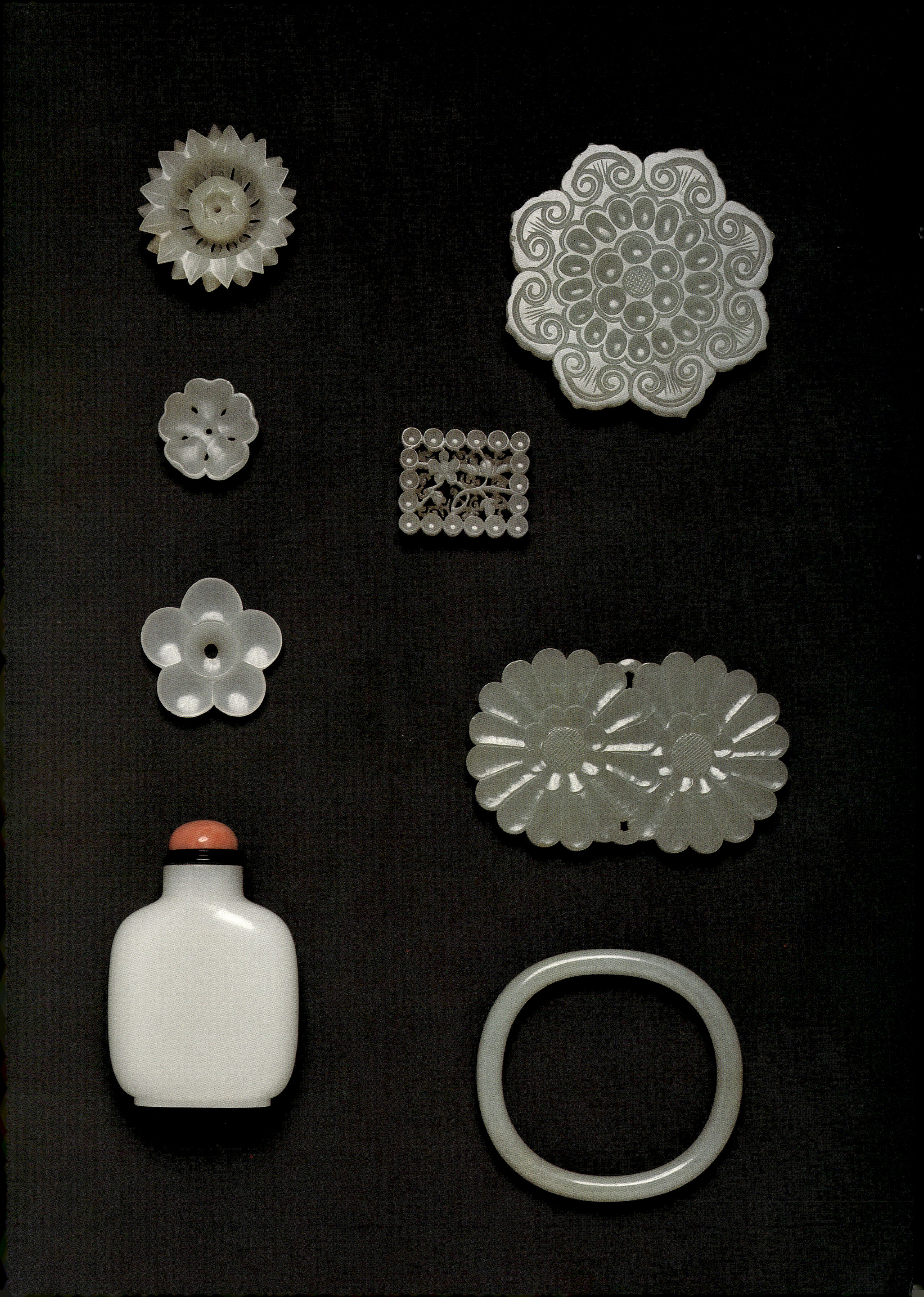

Hair pin, zan

19th Century
Qing Dynasty
White jade
Length 12.5 cm
Width 1.3 cm
Collection of G. Pang

This hair pin is simply carved with a bat and *shou* design, which are symbols of longevity.

Hair pin, zan

19th Century
Qing Dynasty
Gilt silver; enamel
Length 8.9 cm
Width 1.0 cm
Collection of G. Pang

This bow-shaped hair pin has a floral motif on a blue enamel ground.

Hair pin, zan

19th Century
Qing Dynasty
Gilt silver
Length 4.6 cm
Width 3.4 cm
Collection of G. Pang

This pin is done in open work with a repoussé butterfly on a floral ground.

Hair pin, chai (ch'ai)

19th Century
Qing Dynasty
Length 8.5 cm
Width 10.1 cm
Collection of G. Pang

Hair pins with two or more shafts are known as *chai*. This example consists of seven lotus pods, symbolic of purity and perfection.

Hair pin, zan

19th Century
Qing Dynasty
Silver, enamel
Length 11.8 cm
Width 2.5 cm
Collection of G. Pang

This pin has a butterfly in repoussé with a floral design on a blue enamel ground.

Hair pin, erwazan

19th Century
Qing Dynasty
Gilt silver; kingfisher feather
Length 16.7 cm
Width 2.0 cm
Collection of G. Pang

This hair pin, with an ear pick on the end, is decorated with stylized chrysanthemums in a flower pot made of inlaid kingfisher feathers or *cuidian* (*ts'ui-tien*).

Ornament of Kingfisher Feathers

1875-1900
Qing Dynasty
Kingfisher feathers, gilt brass
Length 5.4 cm
Width 2.7 cm
A.1984.10.03
Gift of Oma Umbel, 1984

Peacock feather holder, lingguan (ling-kuan)

19th Century
Qing Dynasty
Grayish-white jade with russet markings
Length 7.2 cm
Width 1.8 cm
Collection of G. Pang

The *lingguan*, made in a variety of materials, held a peacock feather, which was awarded to officials for meritorious service.

Chinese jade ornaments
(Left to right)
Top row: Button, 15th century; Button, 13th-14th century
Second row: Button, 14th-15th century; Belt Plaque, *daishi*, 16th century
Third row: Button, 14th-15th century; Button or Belt Ornament, 14th-15th century
Fourth row: Snuff Bottle, 18th century; Bangle, *zhuo*, 15th century

SNUFF BOTTLE, *BIYANHU (PI-YEN-HU)*

18th Century
Qing Dynasty
White jade; coral
Height 7.5 cm
Width 5.0 cm
Private collection
Illustrated p. 102 bottom row, left

Snuff bottles were carried in the voluminous sleeves of robes or in drawstring pouches suspended from the girdle. This bottle of a flattened, rectangular form is well-hollowed and has a coral stopper.

ROBE FOR TEMPLE IMAGE

c. 1900
Silk damask; ramie, gold wrapped thread, mirrors, brass
Center back 155 cm
Sleeve 294 cm
A.1984.06.01
Gift of the Department of Asian and Pacific Studies, University of Hawaii, 1984

Temple images were often draped in silk robes. The robe in this exhibition is believed to be the type which adorned the image of the God of War, Guandi (Kuan Ti), since the color ascribed to him was green. (Cammann, 1952:132) Guandi is the deified legendary military hero of the Han Dynasty, Guanyou (Kuan Yu), who received the title of God or Emperor posthumously in 1594. (Williams, 1976:211)

This image robe has several distinguishing characteristics as noted by Mary Ellen Des Jarlais: It is nearly twice as wide as it is long and is open from the hem to the sleeves on both sides for ease in placing it on the image. A small but very heavy piece of wood is attached to the underside of each side slit to add weight to the fabric and help keep the robe in place. On the lower part of the sleeve front is a another unusual feature—a wide section of fabric without embroidery. The omission of ornamentation suggests that this part of the robe would be obscured by the arm position of the image. Embroidery enhanced with gold wrapped thread was costly and was most likely eliminated for economic considerations. Blue satin insets, which increase the girth of the robe, cover the side openings. The robe is lined with coarse handwoven ramie in a coral color.

The imagery of this quasi-official robe is similar to the *qifu*. There are, however, eight dragon medallions instead of the usual nine. (On a court robe, *qifu*, the ninth dragon is located under the front flap and thus is not visible; in this robe it is simply omitted.) Four facing *mang* dragons are placed on the center front, center back, and shoulders. On the front and back of the robe, at knee height, are medallions with four walking dragons. Within the diagonal wave pattern on the hem, are auspicious symbols including musical jade stones and coins. In the central area, representing the earth, are curly-maned guardian lions frolicking with a beribboned sphere, symbol of the Buddhist wheel of law.

WOMAN'S FORMAL SURCOAT

1875-1900
Qing Dynasty
Manchu
Silk twill
Center back 143 cm
Sleeve 180 cm
A.1977.01.12
Gift of Adelaide Beste, 1977

Non-official costumes were worn at family celebrations and festive occasions other than court functions. Intended to be worn over a robe, this surcoat has wide sleeves, deep armholes and a center front opening. It is ornamented with floral roundels. Decoration arranged into circles is one of the five principal design layouts for robes. Circles, associated with the nobility, are an indication of formality. (Vollmer, 1983:60) The surcoat has a wave and mountain lower border and wave borders at the sleeves. It is embroidered with butterflies, peony and plum blossoms, auspicious symbols, objects associated with the Eight Taoist Immortals, and the sacred fungus, *lingzhi (ling-chih)*, from which is concocted the elixir of immortality.

WOMAN'S ROBE

Qing Dynasty
Manchu
Silk; satin weave
Center Back 122 cm
Sleeve 152 cm
A.1986.11.01
Gift of Herbert Y. C. Choy, 1986

An embroidered cloud collar, wide sleeve bands, and lower border enhance this dark blue robe with a floral medallion motif. The Chinese cloud collar, *yunjian (yun-chien)* dates to the Jin (Chin) Dynasty (1115-1234), and is based on the stylized cloud motif, an ancient symbol of heaven and long life. It is an irregular square with the four points, or lobes, arranged at the front, back and shoulders. Flowers in vases, and a variety of auspicious symbols are displayed on the sleeves. Sleeves and borders have tiny embroidered "pictures" of flowers, fruit, and human figures in landscape within irregular "frames" that remind one of looking through windows into a Chinese garden.

(Detail)
WOMAN'S FORMAL ROBE
Qing Dynasty
China

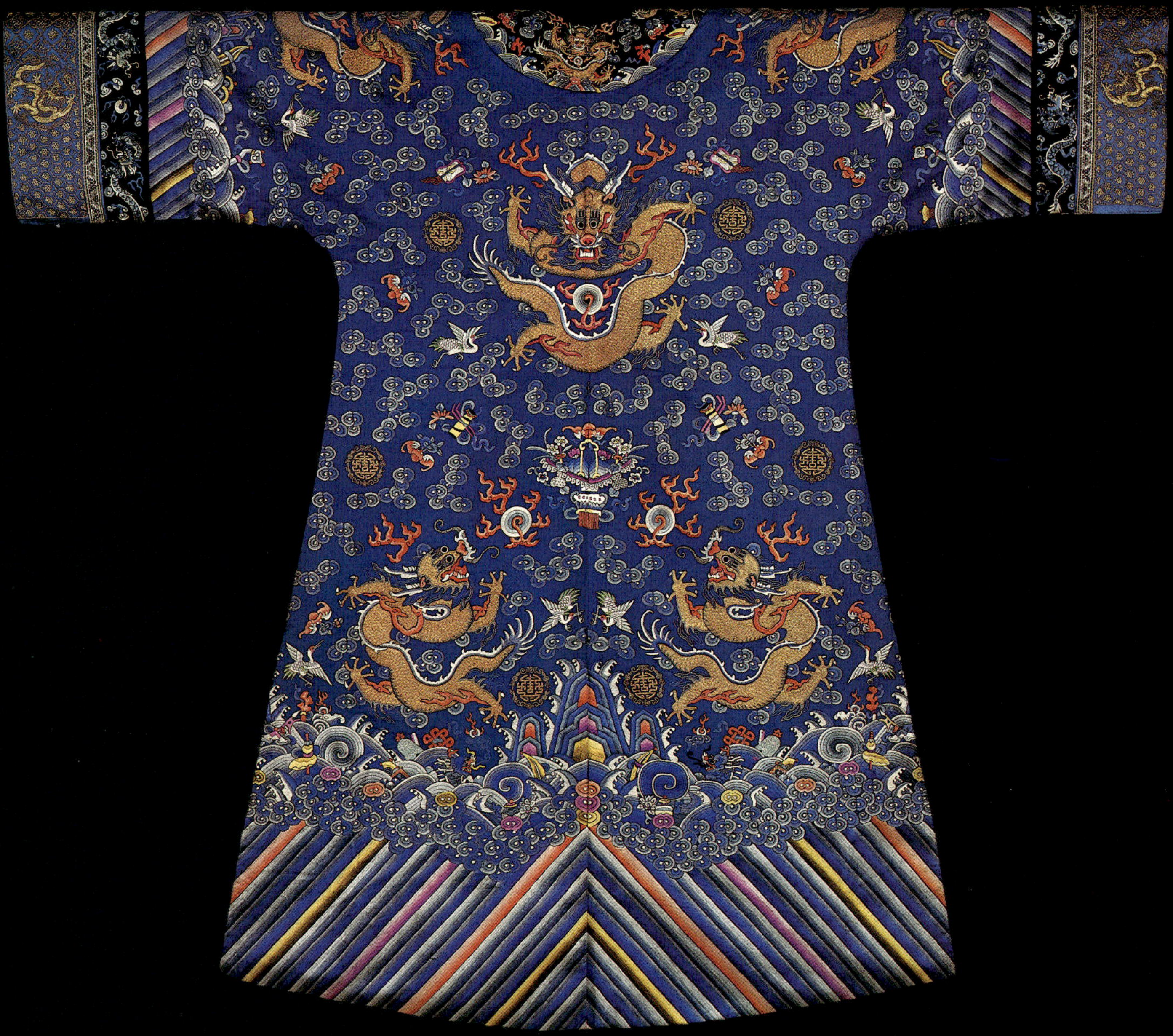

WOMAN'S SEMI-FORMAL ROBE

Late 18th-early 19th century
Qing Dynasty
Manchu
Silk twill
Center back 137.7 cm
Sleeve 200 cm
A.1982.12.01
Gift of Ellin Burkland Reynolds

Manchu women sometimes wore non-official robes with wide, Chinese-style sleeves. This wide-sleeved robe fastens on the right, in the Manchu tradition, with loops and gold buttons; the side seams are slit and bordered with appliquéd embroidered satin in blue and black. The robe extends to the floor, concealing the Manchu woman's unbound feet and platform shoes. The long sleeves are lined with white embroidered silk bands, probably intended to be turned back as cuffs. Silk floss embroidered flowers and butterflies are scattered across the robe. Red, the color of happiness, was worn for family celebrations and was favored for bridal costumes.

WOMAN'S FORMAL ROBE
Qing Dynasty
China

WOMAN'S FORMAL ROBE

1875-1900
Qing Dynasty
Han Chinese
Silk twill; gold and silver wrapped thread, ribbons
Center back 117 cm
Sleeve 138 cm
A.1985.06.01
Gift of Elizabeth Ho, 1985
Illustrated p. 105 (detail) and 106

Han Chinese men who were officials in the Qing government wore Manchu costume but their wives, who did not participate in court functions, were allowed to wear what they pleased. Most Chinese women wore the *paofu* (*p'ao-fu*), a voluminous robe in the traditional style, with a center front opening and wide sleeves. Because these garments were not governed by court edict, Han Chinese used symbolic ornamentation similar to that found on imperial "dragon robes" of both the Ming and Qing dynasties, conferring on the robes a quasi-official status. Worn for festive occasions, most quasi-official costumes were bridal robes. Others of this category are theatrical robes, liturgical robes, and large robes made to clothe temple images.

This quasi-official robe, ornamented with imperial symbolism and imagery, would be worn on formal occasions. Made of silk twill, the robe has a center front opening, and wide sleeve bands featuring gold embroidered dragons and phoenixes. In addition to the five-clawed dragons are embroidered auspicious signs associated with the Buddha: the umbrella, endless knot and canopy; and emblems of the Eight Taoist Immortals: the drum, gourd, stone chime and basket of flowers. Also represented are the *shou* symbol of longevity, the sacred fungus, *lingzhi*, and the phoenix, *fenghuang*.

WOMAN'S COAT

Late 19th-early 20th century
Qing Dynasty
Han Chinese
Silk damask, satin
Center back 94 cm
Sleeve 143 cm
A.1984.10.06
Gift of Oma Umbel, 1984

This non-official hip-length coat in floral patterned turquoise damask has a satin-edged, Manchu-style front overlap, with loops and gold buttons. The sleeves are bordered with purple satin embroidered with flowers, birds and bats in a predominantly aqua colored silk floss.

WOMAN'S COAT

c. 1900
Qing Dynasty
Han Chinese
Silk
Length 98.5 cm
Center back 150 cm
A.1986.11.01
Gift of Herbert Y.C. Choy, 1986

Satin stitch silk covers the entire surface of this aqua silk coat. The garment would have been worn with paired aprons.

BRIDE'S ENSEMBLE; COAT AND PAIRED APRONS

c. 1875
Qing Dynasty
Han Chinese
Silk satin; gold wrapped thread
15-12 a,b
Gift of Ada K. Erwin, 1972
Illustrated p. 109

COAT
Center back 109.8 cm
Sleeve 137.2 cm

PAIRED APRONS
Length 94.5 cm
Waist 88 cm

A bride was considered an "empress" on her wedding day, and quasi-official bridal attire often had imagery adapted from Manchu court costume, including the imperial dragon and the phoenix, *fenghuang*, associated with the empress. A mythical bird associated with the sun, the *fenghuang* presides over the heavens. Earthly appearances occur only in times of peace and prosperity. (Williams, 1976:325)

On the center front of this red silk satin coat is embroidered a *puzi* with a mandarin duck, emblem of a seventh-degree civil official. Wives of court officials were entitled to wear mandarin squares corresponding to the rank of their husbands.

The calf-length, Chinese-style coat has a center front opening and wide sleeves banded in white embroidered satin. The coat is patterned in a scattered scheme of flowers and birds; stylized waves and the earth mountain form the lower border. Paired aprons in red silk brocade, bordered in blue and accented with white, have straight end panels with couched gold wrapped thread *long* dragons and *fenghuang*.

The terms "paired aprons," *shuangqun*, and "skirt," *qun*, are both used (often interchangeably) to describe the lower body cover worn by Han Chinese women with their hip-length or calf-length coats. Paired aprons were also part of the Manchu man's formal court costume, *chaofu*. This garment consisted of two sections, each made up of a straight, vertical panel and pleats attached to a plain waistband. The paired aprons concealed trousers or leggings. The Han Chinese woman's version is of similar construction; the straight end panels are worn at front and back with gores or pleats at the sides. Embroidery and other ornamentation is found mostly on the lower half of the garment because the top portion would be covered by the jacket. Pants or leggings were worn underneath.

WOMAN'S PAIRED APRONS

Late 1800's
Qing Dynasty
Han Chinese
Silk brocade, satin; silk ribbons
Length 100.2 cm
Waist (adjustable) 68.8 cm - 80.2 cm
A.80.6.4
Gift of Oma Umbel, 1980

Some paired aprons have extremely fine side pleats and are defined by the term *yulin baizhequn*, literally "fish scale, one-hundred-pleat skirt." The embroidery on the pleated portion is arranged in such a manner that design motifs are intact with pleats either fanned out or closed.

Red silk brocade is contrasted, in these paired aprons, with narrow, pale green satin straight panels banded in white satin embroidered with scenic imagery. Reminiscent of a Chinese hanging scroll, the panels depict water, lotuses, a pavilion, pine tree and rock, and a pagoda.

WOMAN'S PAIRED APRONS

c. 1900
Qing Dynasty
Han Chinese
Silk brocade, satin; silk ribbons
Length 96.2 cm
Waist 109 cm
Ham.Lib.1
Hamilton Library Collection,
University of Hawaii

This *yulin baizhequn* is in rose-red with borders of black and aqua. The straight panels are appliqué and embroidered with a floral design.

WOMAN'S PAIRED APRONS

Late 19th - early 20th century
Qing Dynasty
Han Chinese
Silk damask, satin; gold wrapped thread, *panjin*
Length 102.8 cm
Waist (adjustable) 74 cm - 81 cm
A.80.6.5
Gift of Oma Umbel, 1980

Appliqué and reverse appliqué ornament these paired aprons with red damask end panels bordered in black satin and "one hundred pleats" in eight colors. Multi-colored embroidered designs feature peonies, lotuses and plum blossoms, the butterfly and the pomegranate.

BRIDE'S ENSEMBLE,
COAT AND PAIRED APRONS
Qing Dynasty
China

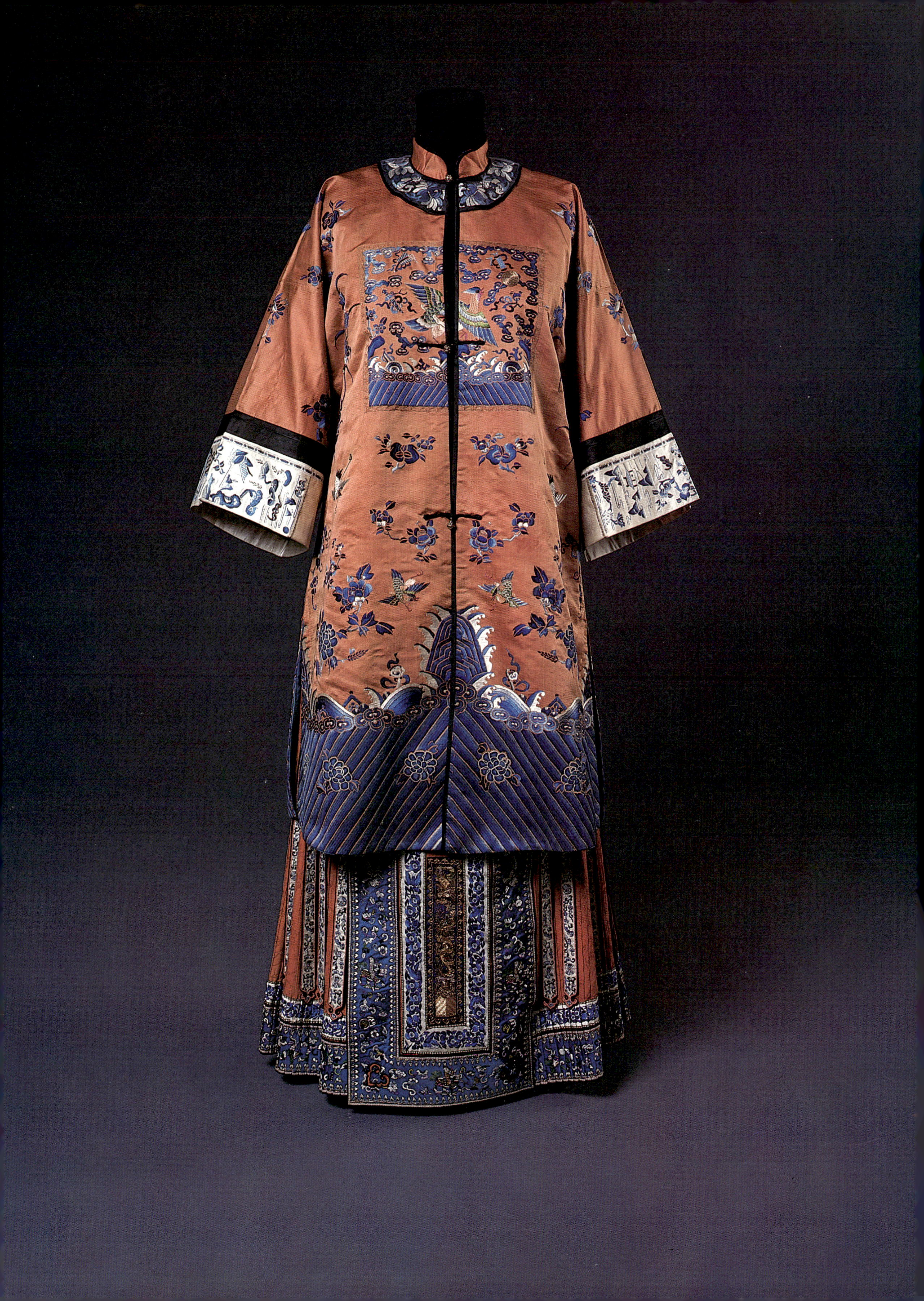

WOMAN'S PAIRED APRONS

c. 1900
Qing Dynasty
Han Chinese
Silk damask, satin; gold wrapped thread, *panjin*, silk ribbons, sequins
Length 102.9 cm
Waist 118.5 cm
A.1983.06.01
Gift of Paula S. Waterman, 1983

Butterflies and flowers, including peonies, the flowers of spring, are embroidered on pink silk damask in paired aprons with twelve gores on each side bound in blue.

PERFUMER, *XIANGHEBAO* (HSIANG-HO-PAO)

c. 1900
Qing Dynasty
Silk satin; gold and silver wrapped thread
Height 7.2 cm
Width 7 cm
A.1980.06.09
Gift of Oma Umbel, 1980

Perfume, medicine bottles, amulets, precious gems, signature seals and other small possessions were carried in small, decorative drawstring bags which came in a variety of shapes and styles appropriate to their purpose. Ornamented with intricate embroidery, semi-precious stones, silk ribbon and tassels, these bags were special gifts given by family members on important occasions.

This heart-shaped, black silk satin pouch has a couched gold and silver bat (?) and four yellow silk tassels. It probably held fragrant herbs and resins.

PEFRUMER

19th century
Qing Dynasty
Silk; petit point, *nasha*, glass
Length 11.7 cm
Width 10.2 cm
Private collection

This exquisite pomander was worn suspended from a ceremonial or court belt; the silk ribbons would probably have been attached to a belt clasp, often of gold ornamented with precious stones. It is made of petit-point, *nasha*, over gauze and decorated with stylized *shou*, longevity characters, among a ground of floral patterns, clouds and waves. The pink glass beads imitate tourmaline. Yellow cords were generally reserved for members of the imperial family.

WOMAN'S SHOE

1850-1900
Qing Dynasty
Silk; cotton
Length 13.3 cm
Width 4.8 cm
64-3
Departmental purchase, 1965

Tiny feet, shod in delicate satin shoes known as "lily slippers," were fashionable among the Han Chinese. A little girl's foot was tightly bandaged from early childhood. The toes were bent under the foot and bound, ultimately resulting in a deformity. The bindings were never completely removed during a woman's entire lifetime.

A contemporary Western view of the effect of bound feet on Chinese women comes from a 1855 edition of *Godey's Lady Book:* "...Of course, such a distorted foot makes the gait of a Chinese lady very awkward. She sways her arms to and fro as if walking on her heels, and is greatly aided by the shoulder of an attendant or an umbrella, carried as a walking stick. But these Chinese ladies do very little walking. It is supposed by some that the practice of compressing the feet was originally imposed by the men to keep the women at home..." (*Arts of Asia*, Sept/Oct, 1979:143)

Among the numerous theories on the Han Chinese custom of binding women's feet is, in fact, that it originated as a tribal practice intended to keep women close to home and in relative seclusion. A popular legend has it that women bound their feet to emulate the favorite concubine of an Emperor (or, variously, a prince). Her very small feet apparently "aroused his erotic desire." (Scott, 1958:28-29; Chambers (ed.) 1981:62) It was not until the onset of the Chinese Republic in 1912 that the practice was finally abolished.

BABY BOY'S TIGER HATS
Qing Dynasty
China

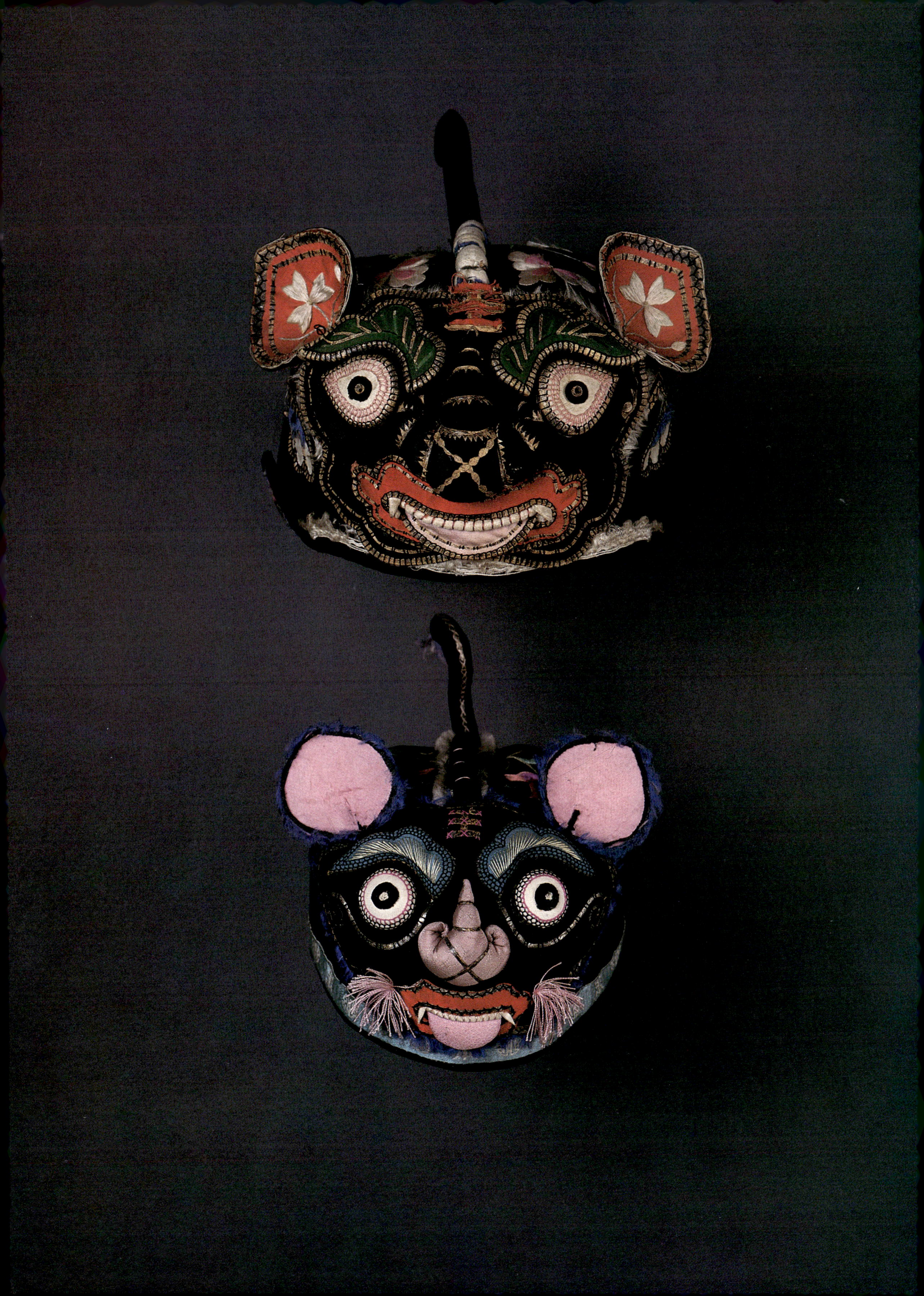

Woman's Shoe

Probably 1850-1900
Qing Dynasty
Silk
Length 7.6 cm
Width 3 cm
64-2
Gift of Mary Bartow, 1965

The ideal length of these little shoes is said to have been about seven and a half centimeters (three inches). The woman who wore this rose and green embroidered slipper had the most desirable foot size.

Woman's Shoes

Silk
Length 10.1 cm
Width 3.7 cm
A.80.6.7 a,b
Gift of Oma Umbel, 1980

The top portion of these tiny handmade shoes has a floral design embroidered on brown satin, and a white inset in front, bordered in blue. Lily slippers were not practical for wear outside the house; the soles of these shoes are lavender and purple silk.

Woman's Shoe

Early 20th century
Black leather
Length 15.3 cm
Width 5 cm
64-1
Gift of Leanne Luke, 1963

This shoe is one of a pair worn by a Chinese woman who unbound her feet after emigrating to Hawaii. This may account for the shoe's relatively large size.

Baby Boy's Tiger Hat

1850-1875
Qing Dynasty
Han Chinese
Silk; gilt paper, silk ribbon
Height 6.2 cm
Circumference 41.5 cm
A.1987.02.02
Departmental purchase, 1987
Illustrated p. 111 bottom

Baby Boy's Tiger Hat

1850-1875
Qing Dynasty
Han Chinese
Silk; gilt paper, silk ribbon
Height (back including mask flap) 14.5 cm
Height (front) 9.5 cm
Circumference 54.5 cm
A.1987.02.03
Departmental purchase, 1987
Illustrated p. 111 top

It was customary for Chinese baby boys to be presented with a hat (usually by their maternal grandmothers) which would be worn on special occasions such as birthdays or the Lunar New Year Festival until the child was about the age of five. The caps come in a variety of shapes but were known generally in most regions as "tiger hats," because many have tiger ears sewn on top and some, such as these from the exhibition, have tigers' faces.

Tseng Yuho Ecke (1977:36) makes an analogy between the design of some of these little silk hats and the prototype bronze tiger helmets worn by Shang Dynasty royal guards in the 12th century B.C. Both have the same protective connotation. In China, the tiger, whose forehead is emblazoned with a mark resembling the Chinese character for "king," is known as the king of beasts rather than the lion. While the tiger is sometimes related to the forces of darkness, it can also be persuaded to use its power to control and destroy evil spirits, and frighten away demons. The tiger is a favorite motif of Chinese folk art and frequently appears on children's clothing, including hats and shoes.

The base of these whimsical hats tiger hats is black silk satin embroidered with flowers and other motifs. Both hats have tails. One, with ear and neck flaps, is a type known as *fengmao*, "wind hat." The hat without such protectors is called *liangmao*, or "cool hat." (Stevens, *Arts of Asia*, January-February, 1982:92)

HAT ORNAMENTS

19th-early 20th Century
Qing Dynasty
Silver, copper, Gilt silver
Height 3.6 to 8.3 cm
Private collection

Charms made of repoussé silver or copper or, sometimes, gilt or gold, were often sewn to the front band above the eyes of tiger hats and wind hats. Larger amulets were worn with dangling bells and charms sewn onto the center of the back of the hats. The charms represent stellar deities and various immortals.

Most common was Shouxing, the God of Longevity, who is easily recognized by his tall, domed, bald head, a beard, and the peach and staff he carries. He is accompanied by a deer. The Eight Immortals are identified by the objects they carry: Li Tieguai has a gourd and crutch; Zhong Lichuan, a fan; Lan Caihe, a flower basket; He Xianggu, her lotus flower; Zhang Guolao a drum; Han Xiangzi, a flute; Lu Dongbin, a sword and fly whisk; and Cao Guojiu, his scholar-official hat and a pair of castanets. Other deities depicted include Fu Hu Lohan riding his tiger; Mi Le Fo, the jolly Buddha of the future recognized by his fat, bare stomach; Laozi riding his water buffalo; and Hehe Erxian, the Twins of Harmony.

(Detail)

BED COVER
Qing Dynasty
China

CHILD'S NECKLACE

19th Century
Qing Dynasty
Silver
Length 63.5 cm
Private collection

Children wore pendants around their necks in the form of the traditional Chinese lock, symbolically signifying that the child would remain *"locked"* to life. This lock pendant features Wen Shu, who is worshiped in China as the God of Wisdom, riding a unicorn. The reverse has the saying, *fushou kangning,* in seal script, wishing wealth, longevity and good health.

BABY BOY'S BIB, *DOUDU (TOU-TU)*

Early 20th century
Silk brocade; ink
Length 39.5 cm
Width 36.2 cm
Private collection

The bib is inscribed with names of Buddhist and Taoist deities. Amulets and prayers could be placed in the bib through the slit pocket located at the upper right.

BED COVER

c. 1900
Qing Dynasty
Silk satin weave
Length 286.7 cm
Width 262.9 cm
A.1984.01.01
Gift of Paula S. Waterman, 1984
Illustrated p. 113 (detail) and 115

Birds, flowers, insects and butterflies in multi-colored silk embroidery are scattered over this white silk bed cover. Also represented are Taoist and Buddhist symbols and the Eight Ordinary (secular) Things: the pearl, a wish-granting jewel; a coin for wealth; a open lozenge, symbol of victory; a pair of books, a painting and musical stone, the accomplishments of the scholar; rhinoceros horns and artemisia leaf, symbols of health and good omen. (Chung, 1979:167) The bed cover is fringed in silk and has two large tassels at the lower corners.

BED COVER
Qing Dynasty
China

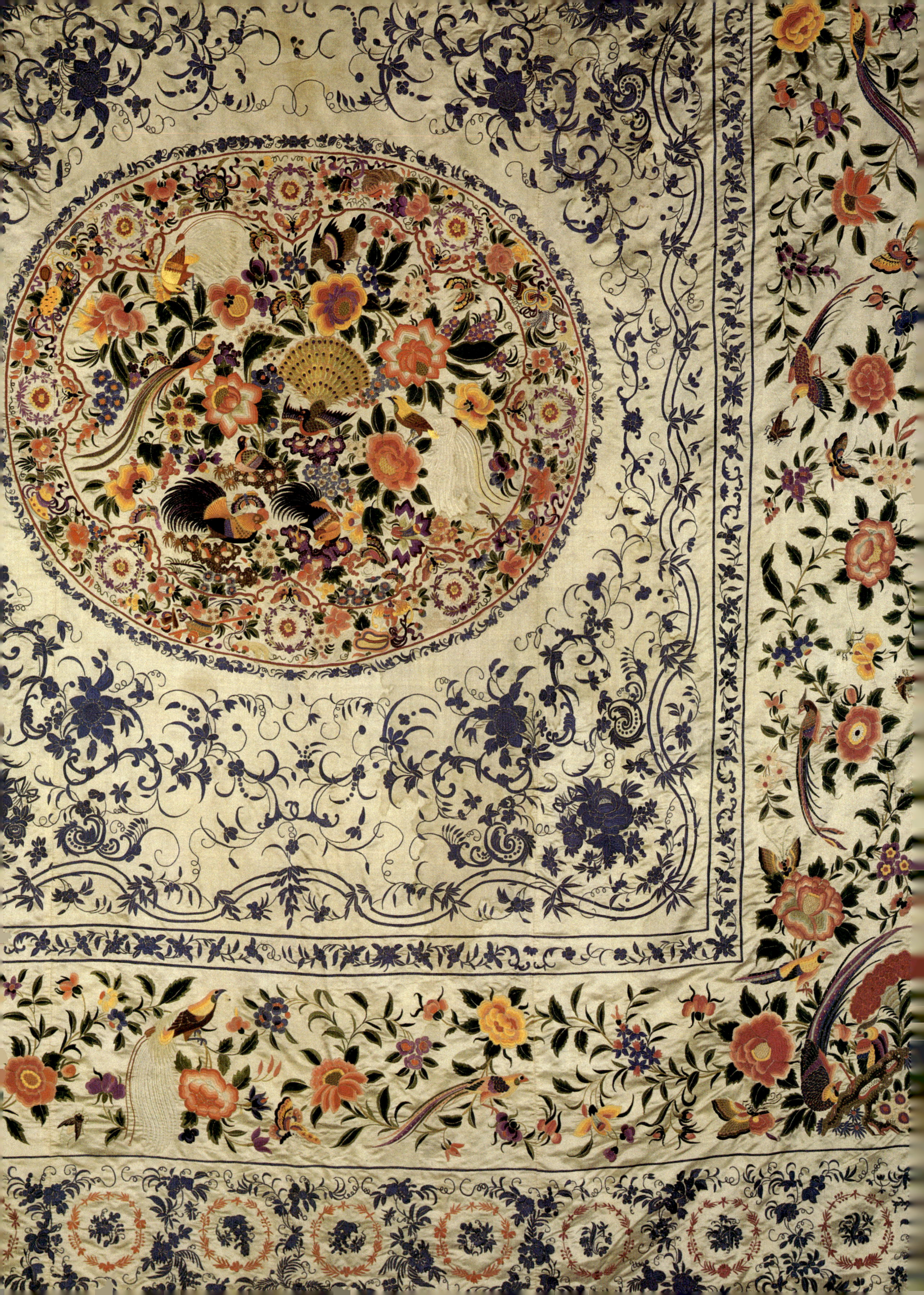

KOREA

TRADITIONAL KOREAN CLOTHING, HAMBOK

Ancient Korean clothing is believed to be influenced by nomadic Manchuria. In the first millennium, B.C., immigrants from Manchuria and southern Siberia settled in the Korean peninsula and elements of their clothing styles were integrated with that of the local inhabitants. The Koguryo Kingdom (37 B.C.-668 A.D.) established its territory in the area of present day southern Manchuria and northern Korea, and their clothing continued to reflect the influence of Manchurian tribes. A record of ancient Korean dress has been documented on the wall paintings of the Muyongchong tomb, or "dancers' tomb," in modern Jian Prefecture, dated to about 500-650 A.D.

On these tomb murals, some of which illustrate costumes from the first century A.D. (Kim, 1979:234), it is known that ancient peoples' clothing included baggy pants tied at the ankles, loosely fitted, tunic-style robes which tie over the left breast, and sleeves trimmed with wide bands extending past the hands. Heavily pleated, wide skirts trailed on the ground; ankle-length robes were belted at the waist.

In the Old Silla Kingdom, notably during the reign of Queen Jindok (647-653), fabric types and colors were mandated as a means of separating the nobility from commoners. Royalty and other members of the court wore cotton, hemp and silk, inspired in part by the importation of Tang Dynasty Chinese textiles. Commoners were limited to cotton and hemp. Men wore thick, woven hemp clothing with a black hemp hood and robe-like upper body covers. Skirts of white or natural colored hemp were worn by women. Noblewomen decorated their hair with jewels but female commoners twisted their unadorned hair into plaits.

The costumes of the 13th century Koryo Dynasty, characterized by Mongolian cultural influence, had the most impact on present day traditional Korean clothing. For example, the word *chogori* (or *jogori*), which refers generally to the male or female upper body cover, is taken directly from the Mongolian language. (Kim, 1970:235)

Royal intermarriages between Koreans and the Mongolian rulers of China affected Korean costume during the middle of the Koryo period. The change was initiated when a princess from the court of Kublai Khan became the consort of King Chongyol of the Koryo Dynasty. Mongolian influences, with some alteration, were retained through the late Yi Dynasty (1392-1910) and remain in the traditional Korean costume of today. Women's *chogori* are raised high above the waist and bound tightly about the chest with a long ribbon instead of a belt, and sleeves are shaped with a definite curve. The jacket has a narrow, V-shaped collar band. The skirt, or *chima*, shortened to ankle length, is gathered to a bosom-band snugly fastened under the arms, usually with three widths of fabric. Under the *chima*, women wear voluminous pants, *paji*, and a petticoat, *sokchima*.

Men's traditional dress generally consists of baggy pants, *baji*, which have cuffs and are tied at the ankles with fabric strips, *tae nim*. The jacket-like shirt with loosely fitted sleeves, called *chogori*, is double-breasted, and longer and fuller than the woman's *chogori*. (Both men and women fasten *chogori* and similar garments from left to right.) Over this is worn a sleeveless vest, *chokki* (or *jokki*), and a jacket, *magoja*, or a top coat, *torumagi*.

The manner of ornamentation distinguished men's shoes from women's. According to historical records, leather shoes were worn during, and perhaps before, the Three Kingdoms period (57 B.C.-668 A.D.). Traditional shoes of leather are now rare; they are generally made of rubber. Everyday footwear, however, usually consists of white socks and black slippers.

MAN'S ENSEMBLE

Seoul
Departmental purchase, 1963
Illustrated p. 121

SHIRT, CHOGORI
Silk; bleached muslin
Center back 61 cm
Sleeve 156 cm
15-5

SLEEVELESS VEST, CHOKKI
Silk; satin brocade
Center back 60.3 cm
Shoulder width 33.4 cm
15-6

JACKET, MAGOJA
Silk; satin brocade
Center back 62.2 cm
Sleeve 160.8 cm
15-7

PANTS, BAJI
Silk; bleached muslin
Length 138.5 cm
Waist 107 cm
15-4

The stylized character for "longevity," is woven into the aqua silk satin brocade of a full-sleeved, dropped shoulder jacket, *magoja*. The *magoja* is worn with a matching, fitted vest, *chokki*, over an off-white long-sleeved shirt, *chogori*. The shirt is tied at the right with a half bow, the ends of which hang below the jacket. The wide waist of the gray silk trousers, *baji*, is folded over at center front and bound with a belt of light gray silk. The full-cut *baji* taper to a snug fit at the ankles and are tied with ankle ties, *tae nim*, of the same aqua brocade used for the vest and jacket.

MAN'S SHOES, KOMUSIN

1963
Rubber
Length 26 cm
Width 8.5 cm
64-9 a,b
Departmental purchase, 1974

Komusin (or *gomushin*) are often worn by both men and women with present day traditional clothing. The off-white rubber shoes with turned up toes are intended as a substitute for a type of white leather, flat-heeled shoe, worn in the Yi Dynasty, which had sharply raised toes and were fashioned with narrow pieces of leather that left the top of the foot partially uncovered. Left and right shoes were an identical shape. Leather shoes were worn by officials and aristocrats, but country folk and commoners wore footwear made of straw. (Kim, 1970:239)

MAN'S HAT, KAT;
INNER CAP, KUMTOO

1960
Bamboo and horsehair
Height 12.5 cm
Diameter (brim) 32.5 cm
Height (inner hat) 5 cm
Diameter 13 cm
62-2
Departmental purchase, 1973
Illustrated p. 121

Structured of split bamboo and black horsehair, these brimmed hats have a semi-transparent, net-like quality. The wider brimmed of the two hats has a petal motif woven into the top. Horsehair hats are secured under the chin with black silk ties, which are sometimes ornamented with dangling amber beads. Each hat has a brimless inner hat which is constructed of similar materials. In order to accommodate a man's hair, which was fashioned into a topknot, the front section of the inner hat is higher than the back. The inner hat alone was suitable for indoor wear. The hats were stored in lacquered papier-maché hatboxes, sometimes constructed with the addition of horsehair.

Traditionally, long-bearded aristocrats, *yangban*, scholars of Confucian classics, had the honor of wearing these brimmed hats. The width of the brim was an indication of status; the wider the brim the higher the status of the wearer. Hat brims could extend to eighty centimeters. Because these extremely wide-brimmed hats distanced one man from another, intimate personal conversation was not always expedient. (Kim, 1970:238; Moes, 1983:plates 95-97)

MAN'S HAT, KAT;
INNER CAP, KUMTOO

1960
Bamboo and horsehair
Height 13 cm
Diameter (brim) 51 cm
Height (inner cap) 5 cm
Diameter 20 cm
62-1
Gift of Halla Huhm

Man's Robe

1964
Silk, gauze weave
Center back 129 cm
Sleeve 158 cm
15-15
Departmental purchase, 1974

This garment is the traditional bridegroom's robe. The intense magenta lining is visible under the bright blue gauze fabric which is woven with a variety of large floral designs. The wide and flowing sleeves comprise almost two-thirds the length of the robe itself. Interesting highlights are the small ties at the underarm points of the sleeves, one knotted button below the white collar, a large bow arranged at the right of the front panel and the embroidered mandarin square, *hyungbae,* at the front and back of the robe. The front square depicts a simple, yet colorful landscape and two cranes with long, interlocking beaks; they fly amidst stylized mountains, trees and clouds.

During the Yi Dynasty, these squares indicated the rank of a court official, a Chinese tradition adopted by the Koreans. A pair of cranes signifies a civil official of the first to third degree. A single crane identifies a junior official of fourth to ninth rank. Military officials had tigers embroidered on their chest insignia; a pair of tigers symbolizes senior ranking and lesser military official had a single tiger. (Moes, 1983:97 and Suk, 1984:180) A belt wrapped over the squares, baggy trousers, black boots and the double-winged hat, *samo,* are worn by the traditionally costumed bridegroom with this robe.

Man's Undergarment Vest

Split bamboo
Center back 54 cm
Shoulder width 36 cm
30-4
Gift of Barbara B. Smith, 1961

Circular designs of finely split bamboo are arranged in an all over pattern on this vest. This type of vest, worn in summer, was constructed for the purpose of separating outer garments from the perspiring body. A collar of woven split bamboo extending above the nape of the neck insulates the neck as well. Similarly, split bamboo wristlets prevented layered garments from sticking to the arms. (Hoefer, 1981:332) Bamboo undergarments, some constructed from bamboo tubes, were also known in China and served the same purpose. (Ecke, 1977:14)

Little Boy's Ensemble

Silk
Gift of Halla Huhm, 1961
15-1 a-e
Illustrated p. 121

PANTS, *BAJI*
Length 64 cm
Waist 72 cm

SHIRT, *CHOGORI*
Center back 34.7 cm
Sleeve 74 cm

VEST, *CHOKKI*
Center back 33.4 cm
Shoulder width 24.4 cm

SURCOAT, *JUN BOK*
Center back 44 cm
Sleeve 25 cm

HOOD, *BOKGON*
Length 58 cm

Boys' costumes consist of the traditional, full, gathered pants and shirt with loose, flowing sleeves worn by adult males. The pants in the exhibition are light aqua tissue silk with a woven brocade pattern and are bound about the ankles with pink ties. The shirt, in matching silk, is trimmed with a white collar band that fastens at the right with a bow. The sleeveless purple silk vest is block printed with gold flake characters expressing the joy of parenting a boy child.

Over the vest is worn a calf-length, sleeveless, purple tissue silk surcoat, *jun bok,* decorated with gold flake block printed characters and floral designs. It is fashioned with slits at the sides for ease of movement. According to Mary Ellen Des Jarlais, the surcoat is styled in the same manner as a garment worn as a component of a military uniform. Now, however, it is worn as part of the traditional costume for celebrations, including birthdays. Completing the costume is a pointed black hood, *bokgon,* with a capelet extending just below the shoulders. It fastens with ties at the neck and is decorated with gold flake rectangular motifs, characters, and seven-petaled flowers.

WOMAN'S JACKET, CHOGORI, AND SKIRT, CHIMA

Ramie; silk
Center back 37.6 cm
Sleeve 144 cm
Length (skirt) 135 cm
15-16
Departmental purchase, 1963
Illustrated p. 121

For centuries royalty and commoners alike used bleached ramie, *moshi,* and natural, straw-colored hemp for everyday clothes and for mourning clothes. This white *chogori* fastens with a frog and loop with a pendant of silver silk cords and tassel.

WOMAN'S JACKET, CHOGORI AND SKIRT, CHIMA

Probably hemp, *sambae*
Center back 34.6 cm
Sleeve 132.6 cm
Length (skirt) 113.3 cm
15-19 a,b
Gift of Halla Huhm, 1968

This unadorned *chogori* and *chima* displays a natural richness in its golden, straw-like fabric which appears to be *sambae*, a coarse, hemp fiber used to tailor everyday clothing. It is a cool and comfortable fabric desirable for wear in the hot and humid summer. (Hoefer, 1981:332) It has been lined with a net-like fabric. The neck is trimmed with a narrow white band. Typical of everyday *chogori* is the simple frog and fabric loop closure at upper right rather than the half-loop bow used to fasten the multi-colored *chogori*.

WOMAN'S JACKET, CHOGORI, AND SKIRT, CHIMA

Silk, gauze weave
Center back 32 cm
Sleeve 144.8 cm
Length (skirt) 119.9 cm
15-11 a,b
Departmental purchase, 1964

The bright yellow *chogori* of this traditional woman's costume is strikingly contrasted by deep purple trim and ribbons and a purple *chima*, or skirt. Woven into the silk gauze fabric is a pattern of large floral motifs. Gold medallions with the character for "double happiness" are stamped around the neckline and applied in elaborate fashion on the gussets.

WOMAN'S JACKET, CHOGORI, AND SKIRT, CHIMA

Silk, satin brocade
Center back 37.4 cm
Sleeve 137 cm
Length (skirt) 117.9 cm
1977.04.18 a,b
Gift of Lola Stone, 1977

A red satin brocade skirt with a colorful pattern of floral designs is combined with a yellow *chogori*. The slightly curved, multi-colored sleeves, stenciled characters for "longevity," and colorful quilted squares on the front of the bodice exemplify the combination of diverse color elements, decoration and structural techniques often found on traditional Korean clothing.

This *chogori* and *chima* has the celebrated Korean feature of striped sleeves (*saech-dong sam-hwae jang chogori*). The striking use of color is not arbitrary but an intentional expressive element characteristic of Korean clothing and Korean folk art in general. Children and women entertainers, *kisang,* wear bright colors, and, appropriately, mature women often wear pastels. White or natural hemp is suitable for everyday clothing and also for the lengthy, three year period of mourning.

One function of color is to represent the five directions or points: black for north; red, south; white, west; blue, east; and yellow for the central point. Craftsmen are not reticent in arranging color, as demonstrated in the striped sleeves of the woman's robe, *wansam* (15-10), and little girl's *chogori* (15-2) in the exhibition. These multi-colored striped sleeves are a Korean innovation.

To coordinate complementary colors, such as violet and lemon yellow, used in the *chogori* and *chima,* 15-11, above, meets an aesthetic objective. Contrasting strong, acrid colors achieves a kind of emphatic harmony. Admiration for directness, and a lack of subtlety which marks some Korean art as distinctly separate from that of China and Japan, is evident in the selection and arrangement of colors in traditional clothing.

TRADITIONAL CLOTHING, HAMBOK
Korea

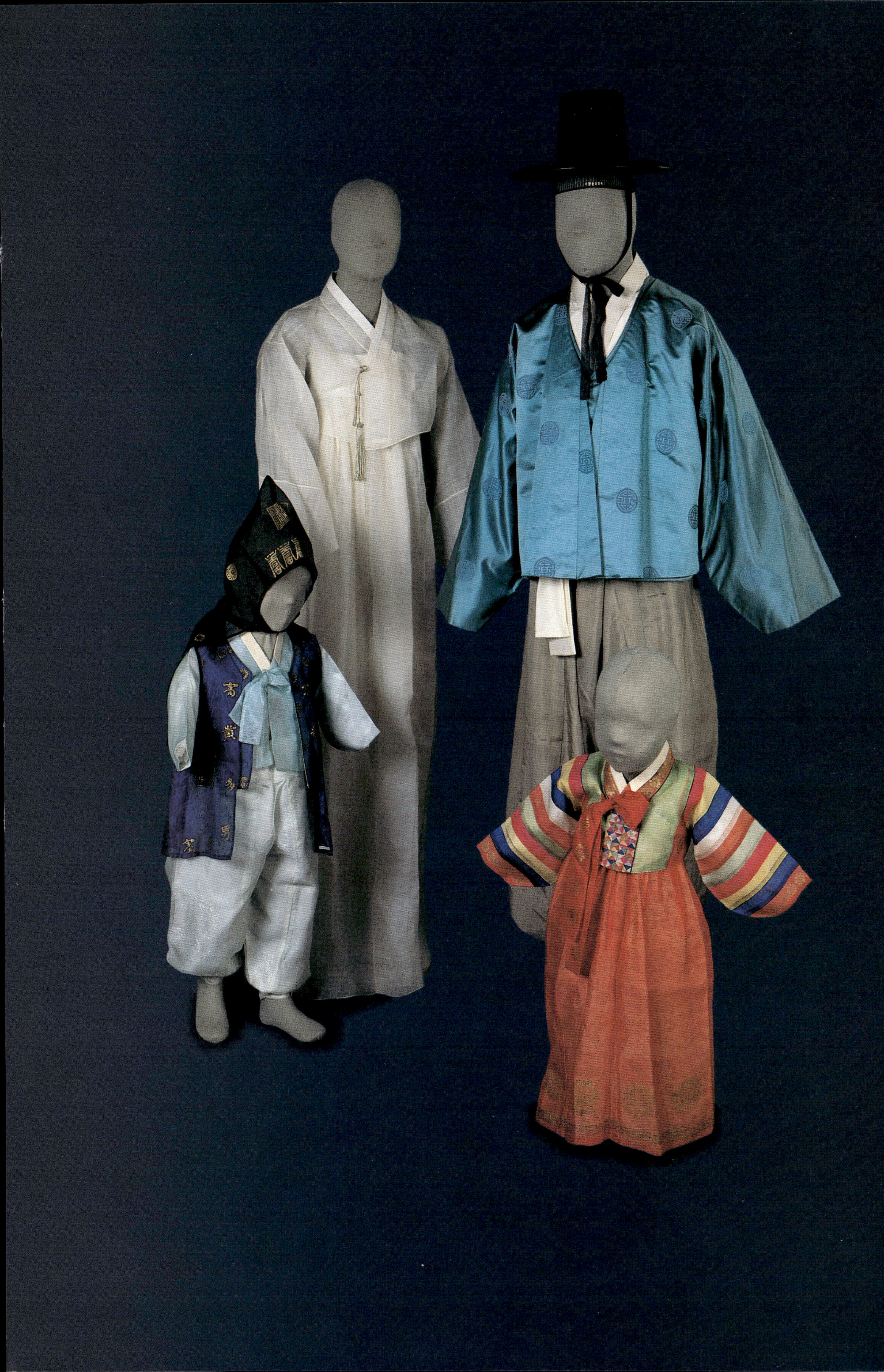

LITTLE GIRL'S JACKET, CHOGORI, AND SKIRT, CHIMA

1980
Seoul
Tissue silk
Center back 26.5 cm
Sleeve 75 cm
Length (skirt)
A.1988.32.01 a,b
Gift of Mary Ellen Des Jarlais, 1988
Illustrated p. 121

Curved, multi-colored sleeves and colorful, geometric patchwork on the front of the *chogori* are interesting features on this traditional festive costume for a little girl. Gold, block printed, stylized floral motifs decorate the bodice just below the neck band, on the lower edge of the sleeves and on the skirt, *chima*, which also has a cloud/thunder pattern along the hem. The bow of red tissue silk has gold floral motifs and the characters for "family" and "prosperity." The sheer *sokchima*, or underskirt, is allowed to show at the center back opening of the skirt.

LITTLE GIRL'S VEST, CHOKKI

Silk, satin weave; rabbit fur
Center back 27 cm
Shoulder 15 cm
15-18
Departmental purchase, 1963

White rabbit fur lines and trims this winter vest of red brocade with floral and geometric embroidery.

CHILD'S SOCKS

Cotton
Length 14 cm
64-2 c,d
Gift of Halla Huhm, 1961

A simple but brightly colored floral scheme is embroidered on these white quilted child's socks. The toe of each is accented with a magenta tassel.

GIRL'S SHOES

Leather; silk satin brocade
Length 18 cm
64-3 a,b
Departmental purchase, early 1960s

This type of shoe is known as "phoenix-eyed" due to a green triangle flanked by two narrow pieces of blue appliquéd on the turned-up toes. (Suk, 1984:188) Other girls' shoes have detailed floral designs or are simple brocaded satin with a contrasting patch of color at the toe.

BOY'S SHOES

Leather; silk, satin brocade
Length 19 cm
64-2 a,b
Gift of Halla Huhm, 1961

Boys' shoes have bold, stylized geometric patterns which are repeated at toe and heel. A design of turquoise brocade is applied over orange silk ground. Unlike the girl's shoes, these have rounded toes. In both instances there is no distinction between right and left shoes.

WOMAN'S ROBE, WANSAM

Silk, gauze weave; gold stenciling
Center back 96 cm
Sleeve 186 cm
15-10
Departmental purchase, 1964

During the reign of Queen Jan Duk (647-654) the Korean emissary to China, Kim Chun Chu, returned to Korea with gifts of costumes and textiles of the Tang Dynasty (618-906), noted for high-fashion extravagance. These costumes inspired the development of the early *wansam*, precursor of the traditional Korean bridal robe, *hwal-ot*. In the Unified Silla Dynasty (668-918), an imperial decree allowed commoners the privilege of modeling their wedding clothes after the court *wansam*. Royalty, however, had sole authority to embroider imperial designs and add luxurious materials such as gold leaf and precious stones. The traditional *wansam* continues to be based on the 13th century Korean design with only slight changes. Women wear this type of robe over a *chogori* and *chima* for festive celebrations such as birthday banquets. *Wansam* are also worn as part of the bride's ceremonial costume.

The red and green silk gauze *wansam* in the exhibition has basic ornamentation indicating it is not an imperial robe. (Chung, 1979:83-85; Suk, 1984:84-87; 187) It is embellished with gold stencil designs of stylized flowers and the character for "blessing." The ornamentation of the garment should be appreciated in its entirety, including the decorated underarm sections of the sleeves, which are displayed when the wearer opens her arms. The sleeves flare into wide, sweeping curves ending in large cuffs.

CROWN, CHOCTURI

Black satin; beads, imitation pearls
Height 8 cm
Diameter 12 cm and 11 cm
62-4
Departmental purchase, 1983

Women wore this type of black satin crown during part of the wedding ceremony. The *chocturi* in the exhibition is enhanced with a finial of colored beads projecting from the center of the soft, cushion-like crown. Except for a few beads, the sides of the crown are left unadorned to emphasize the texture of the shiny black satin. Historically, this type of crown may be traced to Tang Dynasty Chinese influence. (Chung, 1979:84)

FLOWER CROWN, HUA GUAN

Glass and plastic
Crown 10 cm
Diameter 11 cm
62-5
Departmental purchase, 1984

Women wear this dainty crown-like ornament high on the head. The glittering decorations, strung on springy, flexible extensions, give the impression of flowers dancing in space. Royalty used a colorful array of precious metals and stones to comprise the flower crown. Gold and silver embroidery or stamped gold designs, pins with jade pieces attached, and other jewels ornamented these crowns. In a part of the traditional Korean wedding ceremony, a bride, wearing this crown, formally bows to her husband. (Chung, 1979:86)

HAIRPIN, PINYO

19th century
Gilded brass, coral
Length 37 cm
60-4
Gift of Barbara B. Smith

The dragon on this hairpin has a tall, flat horn and a beard under his chin comprised of thin wires wound into coils; there is a red, wing-like projection at either side. The dragon's body is incised with undulating lines and scales. These two-dimensional design elements combine well with the modeled quality of the head. The dragon has caught a coral ball, which it holds in its mouth. The animated expression, especially in the wide, peering eye, gives emphasis to the theme: the dragon chasing the flaming pearl of wisdom and immortality.

In present day traditional Korean hairdressing a hairpin is a practical tool inserted to hold a woman's chignon in place at the nape of the neck, a hairstyle said to have developed as a result of an early Yi dynasty king's dislike for the disorderly piling of hair on the top of heads. "King Hyonjong issued an instruction that wives of officials below the senior third rank must wear a chignon with a hairpin when in full dress. Furthermore, the hairpin, or bar, was to be simple and not made of gold, silver or precious stones in an attempt to discourage the excessive hair decorations prevalent at the time. From that time married women wore their hair in a chignon coiled at the nape of the neck." (Huh, 1987:21)

However, by the later half of the Yi dynasty, twenty different kinds of hairpins are known to have developed. Women considered hairpins as well as other accessories important decorative additions to demonstrate individuality because little variation was allowed in the standard *chogori* and *chima*, and chignon hairstyle. Hairpins worn by court women were often made with precious materials such as jade, gold or silver, and decorated with cloisonné. Commoners usually had hairpins made of undecorated brass. (Huh, 1987:21)

PENDANT

Seoul
Kingfisher feathers; silk embroidery
Length 27 cm
Width 6 cm
60-1
Departmental purchase, 1963

This pendant is comprised of two five-strand sections of cylindrical beads made of kingfisher feathers attached to colorful pieces of lightly quilted silk. These are embroidered with the character for "double happiness," the peach, for fertility and long life, the peony, for summer and wealth, and other flowers. The brilliant, aqua blue feathers compliment the predominant soft orange of the embroidered hanging pieces. Silk tassels probably hung from the embroidered work, adding another colorful element to this pendant. Delicate, ornamental knotting of silk threads would have linked these tassels to the pendant. (Huh, 1987:20)

This type of decorative accessory could be pinned to either a knot or one-loop bow at the top right of the *chogori*, the traditional upper body garment. It is also known to have been attached at the waist. The embroidered pieces, kingfisher beads and tassels were strung independently allowing the pendant to gently ripple and flow with the movement of the wearer. Colorful hanging pendants have been said to enliven the invariably traditional *chogori* and *chima*.

The length of the tassels defined social status. Young women and girls attached short tassels whereas women of the upper echelon could wear pendants with medium length tassels. (Huh, 1987:21) These kinds of dress ornaments were to be worn on significant occasions and bestowed appropriately as wedding and ceremonial gifts. Other pendants could function as cases for acupuncture, sewing needles, small knives, incense and medicine. The family's eldest daughter received a pendant as an heirloom. (Huh, 1987:20; d'Argence, 1979:152)

Woman's Bag

Seoul
Ramie; metallic gold threads, cording
Height 19 cm
Width 20.5 cm
72-1
Departmental purchase, 1963

Woman's Bag

Silk, satin weave; metallic gold threads, cording
Height 19 cm
Width 19 cm
72-4
Gift of Barbara B. Smith

A stylized "longevity" character flanked by characters meaning "double happiness" adorn this red silk satin bag. "Double happiness" is also the main motif embroidered on the white ramie bag. On the bottom of both bags is a border featuring a variation of the cloud/thunder pattern, adapted from ancient Chinese bronzes. The pouch bags are closed by a drawstring at the top, which creates folds. Nine folds indicate the bag belongs to someone of court status. Commoners' bags would have only three folds.

A woman's traditional garment has no pockets. She can fasten a bag by its drawstring to the tie of her bodice or within her skirts, which are layered over billowing pants. The celebrated genre painting, "Collecting Alms on the Road," one of five album leaves on silk by Sin Yun-bok (b. 1758), illustrates a woman taking out a donation from her purse to give to a beggar. (d'Argence, 1979:plate 28) Red was the color most used to indicate that a bag functioned as a purse, *chumoni*. However, bags had numerous functions and could contain other items: a spoon, chopsticks, fan, medicine, incense, as well as soybeans which were an expression of happiness. A few of the motifs commonly embroidered on decorated bags include peonies, chrysanthemums, plum blossoms, and Chinese characters for longevity and good fortune. (Huh, 1987:54-57)

Fan

Oiled paper, bamboo, wood
Length 34.5 cm
Width 25 cm
68-1
Gift of Halla Huhm, 1981

Decorated, rounded fans made of oiled paper on a structure of bamboo ribs which radiate from a wooden handle are noted for durability as well as aesthetic quality. The interlocking forms combined in a circle is the *taegu* (Chinese *yinyang*) motif expressing the Taoist perspective of duality of negative and positive principalities. Folk artists put the *taegu* on many objects for daily use, such as fans.

Fan

Oiled paper, bamboo, wood
Length 33.5 cm
Width 25 cm
68-2
Gift of Halla Huhm

Encircled in the middle of this fan is the character for "double happiness." It is surrounded by sections of bold, complementary colors, dark green against vermillion, which divide the fan diagonally. In this fan, as well as the example above, stylized floral designs ornament the area above the black wooden handle.

Headrest

Seoul
Bamboo; silk
Length 20 cm
Width 12 cm
Depth 10 cm
80-1
Departmental purchase, 1963

Bamboo and straw headrests were comfortable for the summer season. Long strips of natural bamboo are bent to fashion the end pieces of this headrest, which are trimmed in black and red silk with embroidered floral designs.

Headrest

Seoul
Woven straw; silk, brocade weave
Length 21 cm
Width 14.5 cm
Depth 10 cm
80-2
Departmental purchase, 1963

As in the bamboo headrest above, the craftsperson has combined natural materials with simple floral and leaf embroidered designs on brocade. This headrest is made of straw matting that has been woven in horizontal rows.

Japan

Kimono

The kimono is the traditional garment of Japan. Worn by both men and women, the kimono is a long, full robe without buttons or ties, that has wide, long sleeves. It is made from a variety of fabrics including silk, linen, and cotton. For adults the kimono is a standard shape and size, and is secured with a long sash called obi. With this versatile feature almost any figure can be accommodated, as the excess length of the kimono is adjusted by tucking it under the obi. Kimono (singular and plural in Japanese) for children have small tucks sewn at the shoulders and waist which are removed as the child grows. For cleaning, a kimono must be taken apart, washed, and then resewn.

A kimono is classified according to the type of occasion for which it is worn. Kimono for formal wear may be made of fine silk or brocade created with various techniques including resist-dyeing, tie-dyeing, appliqué, and embroidery with silk, gold, or silver threads. For daily wear in the home the kimono may be made of cotton, wool, or lesser quality silk. While the type of kimono must be appropriate for the occasion, there are other considerations in selecting a kimono. For example, the color and patterning of the fabric must be appropriate for the time of year. Since the changing seasons are very important in Japanese culture, certain colors and motifs traditionally associated with a particular season are requisite. The season may also dictate the type of lining, or wadding for warmth.

The modern kimono has its roots in the Kamakura Period (1185-1392) when the warriors, or samurai class, rose to power. Worn beneath multiple layers of flowing robes, the undergarment of the nobility of the elegant and refined Heian Period (794-1185) became an outer garment for both men and women of the samurai class. Shunning the opulence and extravagance of their Heian predecessors as a sign of weakness, the samurai class opted for a garment that reflected a lifestyle of simplicity and frugality. This preference for austerity continued throughout the Muromachi Period (1336-1568). As samurai and *daimyo* (landowners) became more affluent and attained positions of power and authority during the Momoyama Period (1568-1603), they could afford elaborate kimono which served as means of displaying their wealth.

Colorful, lavish kimono with bold designs worn by popular *kabuki* actors, entertainers, and famous courtesans influenced kimono fashion during the Edo Period (1603-1868). By the middle of the Edo Period, the obi began to gain prominence as a decorative element of the kimono. Until then, the obi was simply a narrow cord that kept the kimono in place and attracted little attention. Interest was vitalized with the ornamental potential of the new, wide obi and different ways of tying the bow.

Influence from the West during the Meiji Period (1868-1912) made many people eager to adopt Western dress, although the kimono was often worn. Kimono designers incorporated Western-inspired ideas into their creations.

For the first twenty years following World War II, there was little interest in wearing the kimono. Today, there are a few Japanese who prefer the kimono for everyday attire. While most wear Western clothing, many are beginning to rediscover and appreciate the significance of Japan's national costume.

WOMAN'S KIMONO, KOSODE

1825-1850
Yokohama
Silk, gold wrapped threads
Center back 153 cm
Sleeve 128.0 cm
A.1981.02.01
Gift of Dr. and Mrs. W. Glenn Marders, 1981
Illustrated p. 127

Fashioned of royal blue silk satin couched in gold, this kimono with short sleeves, *kosode,* is reputedly associated with an important historical event: the second expedition to Japan of Commodore Matthew Perry of the United States Navy in 1854 which resulted in a treaty that opened Japanese ports to American trade. During negotiations there was an exchange of gifts. Presented to Perry and members of his landing party were rice, lacquer ware, ceramics and silks. This satin-weave, wadded kimono is said to have been a gift to one of Perry's men.

The kimono was donated to the Asian Costume Collection by Dr. and Mrs. W. Glenn Marders. According to notes on file in the Department of Human Resources, the Marders received the robe from a friend who is a descendant of one of Perry's crew. This kimono is said to have been handed down to family members.

The featured design, *shochikubai,* a combination of plum, pine, and bamboo is commonly known as *saikan no san'yu,* "the three friends of the cold season." Done in couched, gold-wrapped threads, they are ancient emblems of longevity, integrity, and fidelity. These three trees were used as examples in Confucian classics of the virtues a man should pursue as he faces the afflictions of life. The plum, the only blossom to brave the cold of February, symbolizes courage. Bending but not breaking, the bamboo is noted for its durability and resilience. Long life is associated with the evergreen pine.

YOUNG WOMAN'S SUMMER KIMONO, FURISODE

1935
Silk
Center back 156 cm
Sleeve 128 cm
Sleeve length (vertical length from shoulder) 76 cm
15-38
Departmental purchase, 1977

A kimono such as the one in the exhibit may be worn at home as well as for visiting friends. Unlined and made of light weight fabric, it was probably worn during summer. Kimono with long, swinging sleeves are called *furisode. Furisode* are worn by unmarried women and girls; it is said that the beautiful, fluttering sleeves can attract a husband. Married women wear the *kosode,* the small-sleeved kimono.

This *furisode* is an example of *kasuri,* a tie-dye technique that originated in India. (This process is generally known to Westerners by the Malay-Indonesian term *ikat.*) The pattern is designed and the threads dyed before the fabric is woven. Stripes, checks, and other geometric shapes are the basic patterns for *kasuri.* The process also permits the weaving of bold and creative designs such as concentric circles.

WOMAN'S KIMONO, KOSODE
1825-1850
Japan

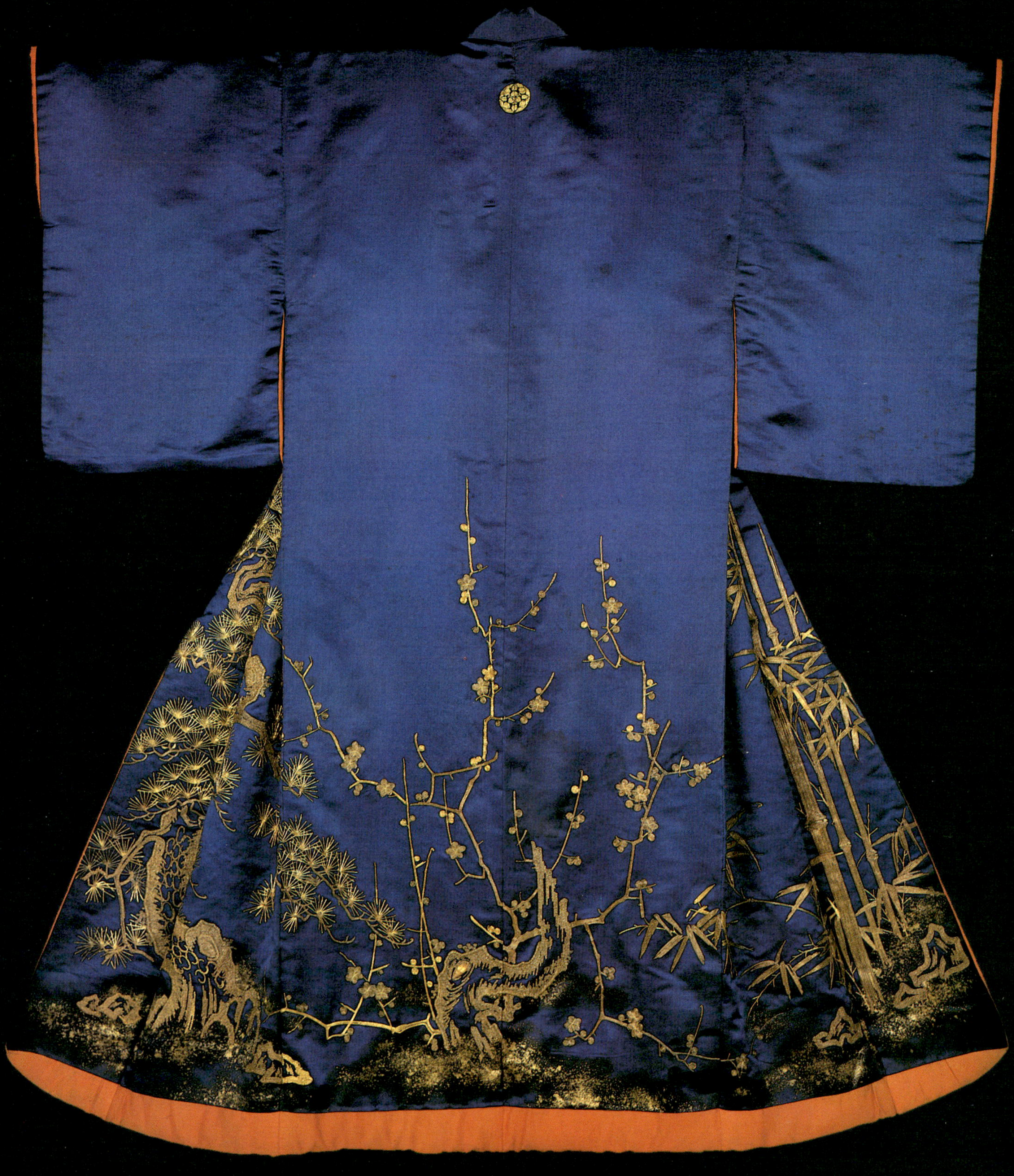

Woman's Kimono, Kosode

1935
Japan
Silk
Center back 156.5 cm
Sleeve 132 cm; sleeve length 57 cm
15-37
Departmental purchase, 1977

The delicate geometric pattern of this kimono was created by the stencil process called *katazome*. Stencils were also used for the leaf design on the front panels. According to Des Jarlais, this *kosode* is appropriate for a middle-aged, married woman.

Man's or Woman's Kimono, Yukata

1960s
Japan
Cotton
Center back 154 cm
Sleeve 126 cm
15-9
Gift of Barbara B. Smith 1969

Made of thin bleached cotton, the *yukata* was traditionally worn by both men and women after a hot bath. It is now worn during the summer months, especially at festivals and celebrations.

Patterns on the *yukata* are often done in *komon*, or small stencil. This indigo and white *yukata* creates an impression of coolness and informality. The sense of coolness is emphasized with a bold pattern of waves.

Woman's Kimono for Visiting, Homongi

1930s-1940s
Silk; gold wrapped threads
Center back 168 cm
Sleeve 124 cm; Sleeve length 56 cm
15-3
Departmental purchase, 1964

When a woman is visiting, the *homongi*, a formal kimono, is the proper attire. An unmarried woman will wear *homongi* with *furisode*, swinging sleeves. The small sleeves, or *kosode*, on the *homongi* in the exhibition indicate that it would be worn by a married woman.

Homongi are usually lined with a fabric that is different from the kimono itself. This example is lined with red silk in the sleeves, and a section each of white and beige silk in the center. The pattern of the fabric is often designed to incorporate the seam lines. Bamboo leaves and diagonal bands of bamboo stems flow smoothly over the seam in this kimono.

The design of the bamboo and deer spot pattern was developed by the use of three techniques; tie-dyeing, weaving, and embroidery. The tie-dye method used to create the deer spot pattern, *kanoko*, is called *shibori*. Here, the pattern was achieved by tightly tying small sections of fabric before it was dyed. Other parts of the pattern were woven into the fabric with gold threads. Couched, gold-wrapped thread embroidered in various areas accent the pattern.

Bride's Kimono, Furisode

Early 1960s
Japan
Silk crepe
Center back 183 cm
Sleeve 130 cm; sleeve length 107 cm
15-21
Departmental purchase

This silk *furisode* features a pattern of wisteria, flowers, and leaves on a black background. Embroidery in silver and gold-wrapped threads accents some of the motifs. There are three *mon*, or family crests, in a paulownia design, stenciled on each shoulder and the center back of the kimono.

According to Department of Human Resources records, this kimono was worn by a bride in the early 1960s. Des Jarlais suggests that the kimono may have been worn during autumn because the colors of orange and rust are appropriate for that season. She also states that the fabric is *yuzen*, a dyed silk that was first produced in Kyoto and could be afforded only by the wealthy.

Yuzen is made using a rice paste resist process. Rice paste, placed in a paper cone fitted with a brass tip, is squeezed onto the silk fabric. The areas covered with the paste remain unaffected by the dye.

BRIDE'S KIMONO, FURISODE

1970
Silk, gold foil
Center back 174 cm
Sleeve 131 cm; Sleeve Length 104.5 cm
1979.04.02
Departmental purchase, 1979

Because of the weight of the fabric, the maple leaf and chrysanthemum motifs, and the orange, rust, and yellow colors, this bride's kimono from a 1970s wedding was, according to Des Jarlais, probably worn in the fall.

Several different techniques were used to produce the designs on this kimono. The maple leaves and clouds were woven into the fabric. Broad, horizontal bands in purple were created by the tie-dye process. Within the purple bands, patterns were produced with stencil, gold foil, tie-dye, and rice paste resist. These bold bands may have been influenced by Noh costumes, which were often made with bands of different fabrics sewn together.

The multiple tiny circles, called *kanoko*, or deer-spots, were created with the tie-dye method, *shibori*. The flowers and *seigahana*, or stylized wave patterns, were made using stencils and gold foil. The stencil was placed on the fabric and a paste was applied through the stencil. Then gold foil was pressed over the paste. The use of the rice paste resist process, *yuzen*, and handpainting of the flowers and leaves was also noted by Des Jarlais.

STENCILS, KATA

Early 1960s
Paper
48 cm x 31 cm
A.1988.12.04,.07
Departmental purchase, 1988

These paper stencils, *kata*, are used in the Japanese method of resist-dyeing known as *katazome*. In this process, a sticky paste made of steamed rice flour and rice bran is forced through the *kata* and on to the fabric. The stencil is removed and the paste is permitted to dry. Then a sizing liquid made from soybeans is applied to the fabric. After this dries, dye is brushed over the fabric. Washing the fabric removes the paste and exposes the areas that resisted or were protected from the dye.

Kata are made from stencil paper, *katagami*, which consists of two to four layers of Japanese handmade paper that are laminated and treated with persimmon juice. The *katagami* are dried in the sun and then cured in sawdust smoke. This treatment strengthens and waterproofs the paper which allows it to be used many times. The patterns are cut by skilled craftsmen using special tools.

There are four traditional methods for cutting stencils: *Kiribori* is the method used for designs made completely of small dots cut with an awl; *tsukibori*, in which the cutter turns the knife away from him and moves it with upward and downward strokes, is used for floral and arabesque designs; *dogubori* uses tools with various shaped ends to punch out the pattern, and *hikibori* is the method used for designs of fine stripes in which the cutter pulls the knife toward himself. *Kiribori* and *tsukibori* are used to create the patterns in the stencils displayed in the exhibition.

Small patterns, known as *komon* and medium-sized patterns, called *chugata* were popular. Dyed indigo blue, the patterned fabrics were often used to make *yukata* and bedding covers.

WOMAN'S FORMAL ENSEMBLE

1970s
Honshu
A1979-01.01a,b
Gift of Shizu Naganuma, 1979

KIMONO, *UCHIKAKE*
Silk; synthetic yarns
Center back 191 cm
Sleeve 132 cm; sleeve length 104 cm

UNDER-KIMONO
Silk
Center back 180 cm
Sleeve 134 cm; sleeve length 108 cm

Made of wadded silk, the *uchikake* is a full-length outer robe with long flowing sleeves and padded hem. It was worn only by women of the nobility or warrior class for ceremonial occasions until the Edo Period (1615-1868). Since that time, other classes wear the *uchikake*.

This *uchikake* was reportedly worn for a wedding ceremony held in Honolulu during the 1970s. Instead of the more common wedding kimono motifs of cranes or bamboo, it is patterned with silver embroidered peacocks. The bright pink fabric of the kimono worn underneath is woven in the geometric *saya* pattern. It features designs of fans, maple leaves, and flowers.

BRIDE'S OVER-KIMONO, *UCHIKAKE*

Silk, metallic thread
Center back 163 cm
Sleeve 131 cm; sleeve length 103 cm
A.1985.11.01
Departmental purchase, 1985

Clouds and cranes are embroidered in dyed and metallic-wrapped threads on this silk *uchikake*.

WOMAN'S UNDER-KIMONO, *NAGAJUBAN*

1960s
Japan
Silk crepe
Center back 138 cm
Sleeve 129; sleeve length 43.5 cm
30-1
Departmental purchase

Worn over a cotton undershirt and half-slip, the *nagajuban* is a full-length under-kimono. It may be lined or unlined depending on the season. The texture, color, and pattern of the *nagajuban* must be coordinated with the kimono, although white and cream are the preferred colors for formal occasions. This pattern features irises, fans, stylized water, and deer spots, or *kanoko*. These *kanoko* were probably stenciled.

BRIDE'S ACCESSORIES

The following four accessories were used by a Japanese bride. The wedding ceremony was held during the 1960s.

WEDDING FAN

1960s
Paper, wood
Length (closed) 20 cm
Width 31 cm
68-1
Departmental purchase

FAN WITH FAN CASE

1960s
Silk brocade, bamboo, paper
Length 22.5 cm
Length (cord and tassel) 76 cm
72-3
Departmental purchase

PURSE, HAKOSEKO

1960s
Silk; metallic thread, silver, mirror
Length 12.5 cm
Width 8.5 cm
72-4
Departmental purchase, 1967

When wearing a kimono, a woman may carry a small kimono purse or ornamental wallet called *hakoseko*. It is tucked into the kimono at the chest. Made of woven silk or velvet, the *hakoseko* often contains vanity items such as a small mirror, some tissue and hairpins. Included is a small bag which, according to Des Jarlais, was used as a perfume container.

OBI TIE, *OBI-JIME*

1960s
Silk;, metallic thread
Length 145 cm
Diameter 1.5 cm
66-13
Departmental purchase, 1967

The *obi-jime* is a braided or sewn cord which is used to support and secure the obi. It is passed through the tied obi and then looped into a knot in the front. A clasp of precious metal and semiprecious stones, called *obi-dome*, may be fastened at the knot.

Specially prepared yarns may be braided in various ways to produce a round, flat, or square cord. Silk, satin, or brocade is used for the sewn *obi-jime*. For a ceremonial kimono, the preferred *obi-jime* is sewn of gold brocade.

COSMETIC BRUSH

1950s
Wood; lacquer, gold, natural bristle, silk
Height (including knot) 5 cm
Diameter 4.4 cm
74-1
Gift of Mary Bartow

A pale complexion was and is considered a sign of beauty for Japanese women. According to records of the Department of Human Resources, this type of brush was used to apply *oshiroi*, a white facial powder.

MAN'S PANTS, *HAKAMA*

Early 20th century
Silk
Length 98 cm
15-25
Departmental purchase

Formal attire for men consists of *hakama*, kimono, and *haori*. Worn over the kimono, the *hakama* is a sort of loose trouser, or divided skirt that is fastened with two pairs of long bands. To complete the ensemble, the *haori* is worn over the kimono and *hakama*.

Hakama are usually made of stiff, high quality silk, or occasionally, thick cotton. They may be lined, but are never wadded. Somber colors such as black, brown, and grey are proper choices for this garment. Combinations of these colors in thin, vertical stripes are also appropriate.

After the kimono is donned and secured with the obi, the front section of the *hakama* is tied with bands at the back of the waist. A small tab at the *koshi-ita*, the trapezoid-shaped piece stiffened with paper or cardboard at the back waist, is tucked into the obi to hold the *hakama* in place. The bands from the back are brought to the front and tied, and then folded into the shape of a cross.

Obi

The obi is a long narrow strip of fabric which is used to secure the kimono. It is made of a variety of textiles that include woven patterns, dyed patterns, and patterns accented with techniques such as gold foil and embroidery. Obi are categorized by the placement or arrangement of the pattern; some have patterning over the entire area, some have patterning only on specific areas, and others have no patterning. Like the kimono, the obi is classified on the basis of the occasion at which it will be worn. Men have only two types of obi, the *kaku*, or stiff obi, and the *heko*, or soft obi, while women have many more choices.

Before the Edo period (1603-1868), the obi was a thin, blindstitched cord that basically served the functional purpose of securing the kimono. The use of the obi as a decorative part of the kimono began during the early Edo period. The obi was tied at the side, the back, or the front depending on the wearers' preference. By the middle of the Edo period the obi had become wider and was tied in the front. Later, the style changed and a woman's marital status could be distinguished by the obi; married women tied the obi in the front and unmarried women in the back.

There are hundreds of ways to tie the obi, and some of the styles can be traced to innovative Kabuki actors. The *tateya*, the standing arrow, and the *chidori*, the plump sparrow, are bows which the people copied from actors that are still worn today.

Obi (Fragment)

c. 1950
Kyoto
Silk, metallic gold wrapped yarns
Warp 32.5 cm.
Weft 25.0 cm.
40.4
Departmental purchase

The maple leaf design, done in a tapestry weave, suggests that this obi was worn during autumn.

Woman's Obi

c. 1895-1917
Silk
Length 376 cm
Width 30.5 cm
66-31 B--75-49
Gift of Mrs. Adelaide Beste, 1975

A plaid pattern is featured on one side of this obi and, on the other, a design of leaves on blue-grey damask. According to Des Jarlais this is an appropriate obi for a middle-aged woman.

Woman's Pre-Tied Obi

1936
Silk
Length 342 cm
Width 76 cm
Width (bow) 31 cm
66-7
Gift of Mrs. Howard R. Starke

This partially patterned obi developed at the end of the Taisho period (1912-1926) and is called Nagoya obi after the city of its origin. The unpatterned section is covered after the wrapping and tying of the obi is completed. Depending on the type of fabric and the design, this obi is can be worn for many occasions. For the most formal occasions, however, obi such as *maru obi*, made of silk brocade, are more appropriate.

Man's Obi, *Heko Obi*

1960s
Silk crepe
Length 317.5 cm
Width 53.3 cm
66-30
Gift of Mary Bartow

While women have a wide choice of obi styles, there are only two for men: the stiff obi, *kaku obi*, for formal occasions and the soft obi, *heko obi*, for informal wear. The *heko obi* is a more recent development and can be worn with the *yukata*. This obi is made of soft white silk crepe treated with the *shibori* tie-dye technique which is achieved by folding, stitching, or binding the fabric before it is dyed.

Farm Woman's Jacket and Pants

Early 1960s
Tokyo
Cotton
15-13, 14
Departmental purchase

Jacket
Center back 68 cm
Sleeve 125 cm

Pants
Length 97.5 cm
Waist 80 cm

This type of outfit is worn by farm women, according to Des Jarlais. Consisting of a jacket or blouse and a pair of pants, it is made of cotton that has been dyed and woven in the *kasuri* technique.

Man's Coat, *Kuro Montsuki Haori*

Pre-1940s
Silk
Center back 109.5 cm
Sleeve 134 cm
15-16
Gift of Mrs. Howard R. Starke, 1965

A light-weight coat, the *haori* is worn by men and women. Its origins may be found in the *dochu-gi,* a cape used for traveling. *Haori* is a form of the word haoru, which means "to put on." Unlike the kimono, which is double-breasted, the *haori* is open in front and loosely fastened with cords.

For men, the *haori* is an essential part of ceremonial dress. *Haori* did not become fashionable for women until the Edo Period (1615-1868). Women did not wear the *haori* as part of ceremonial attire, but as a garment to protect their kimono. Upon arrival at their destination, it was usually removed.

Depending on the purpose, *haori* are made in different lengths and colors. Short length *haori* are worn at home, medium for ordinary or daily wear, and long for dressy occasions. *Haori* of black and various colors are used for formal and semi-formal wear.

This *haori* is an example of the *kuro montsuki haori*. Made of black silk, this type of *haori* has *mon*, family crests at the shoulders, and is worn for school ceremonies and for mourning. The color of the cords indicate the occasion, such as white for school events and black for mourning. For these events, it is not necessary to remove the *haori* while indoors. Lining the upper back of this *haori* is a depiction of Mount Fuji on gold-colored silk.

Little Girl's Winter Kimono with Vest

Early 1960s
Tokyo
Rayon crepe
Center back (kimono) 76 cm
Sleeve 70.5 cm
Center back (vest) 49.5 cm
15-10
Departmental purchase, 1963

Red and orange are popular colors for little girls' kimono. The fabric is often patterned with symbols of the season or of good luck. One of the many flowers featured in this kimono is the plum blossom, a symbol of winter. The cloud pattern is also included in the design. The kimono and vest are wadded for warmth.

Little Boy's Vest

1960s Japan Silk
Center back 41 cm
Shoulder 19.5 cm
15-33 Departmental purchase

The crane, fan, ingot, and Buddhist wheel are some of the auspicious symbols printed on the fabric of this little boy's vest. Small tucks at the shoulders can be removed to accomodate the child's growth.

Footwear

Tabi, geta, and *zori* are the types of footwear that are worn with the Japanese kimono. Generally made of white cotton or silk, *tabi* are split-toed socks that fit the foot snugly. Hooks secure the *tabi* at the ankle. Indoors, *tabi* are worn without other footwear. Outdoors, tabi are worn with *zori.*

Geta are raised, wooden sandals with straps that are worn with *yukata* and informal kimono. The kinds of wood used for *geta* include *kiri,* the light-weight paulownia wood, cedar, cypress, chestnut and oak. The wood may be painted, lacquered, or naturally finished. Geta straps are often made of leather or velveteen.

Flat-soled sandals, *zori,* are worn outdoors with formal and ceremonial kimono. *Zori* are made of fabric, leather, vinyl, or plant fibers. For ceremonial kimono, the *zori* are made of brocade with a heel-height of four to five centimeters. For formal kimono, the heel-heights were lower. Proper etiquette requires that the color of the *zori* match the base color of the kimono, or harmonize with the colors of the obi and *obi-age,* the cloth-covered bow pad.

Sandals, *Geta*

c. 1960s
Wood, velvet
Height 3 cm
Length 23.2 cm
Width 7.8 cm
Loaned by Sharon Tasaka

Child's Sandals, *Geta*

Early 1960s
Kyoto
Wood, lacquer, velvet
Height 2.5 cm
Length 14 cm
64-4
Departmental purchase

Child's Sandals, *Pokkuri*

Early 1960s
Kyoto
Wood, lacquer, straw, velvet, brocade, metal
Height 6.5 cm
Length 17 cm
64-3
Departmental purchase, 1963

Pokkuri, worn by geisha and small girls, are a variation of *koma geta,* a type of *geta* made with a solid wooden form which is lacquered and covered with fine rush or straw matting. These *pokkuri* have been hollowed on the inside to reduce the weight. The crane and pine pattern symbolize good luck and long life.

CHILD'S SNOW BOOTS, WARA GUTSU

Early 1960s
Tohoku, northern Hokkaido
Straw, cotton
Height 9 cm
Length 16 cm
64-6
Departmental purchase, 1963

BOOTS, JIKATABI

1960s
Tokyo
Rubber, cotton
Length 23 cm
Height 13 cm
64-2
Departmental purchase, 1963

Jikatabi are made of heavy drill cotton and thick cleated rubber soles. They are worn by farmers and fishermen. This pair is machine made. Like common *tabi*, metal hooks, located at the ankle placket, secure the *jikatabi*.

SANDALS, WARAJI

Early 1960s
Straw
Length 27 cm
64-5
Departmental purchase

Waraji, flat, plaited sandals made of coarse rice straw, are worn during dry weather. For a proper fit, the sandals are woven slightly shorter than the length of the wearer's feet and are secured by cords made of fine twisted straw that pass between the toes and around the ankles.

RAIN SANDALS, AMAGETA

1963
Tokyo
Wood; leather, artificial fur, lacquer, cotton, brass, plated metal
Length 22 cm
Width 11 cm
Height 15.5 cm
64-1
Departmental purchase, 1963

Amageta, sandals worn for rainy weather, are distinguished by high wooden cleats and protective covers for the toes, *tsuma-gake*. The extra height of the *amageta* allows the wearer to walk through puddles. The covers, constructed of lacquered cotton fabric and artificial fur, keep the toes warm and dry.

The fashionable *geta* with extremely high cleats worn by geisha, women trained in entertainment and the arts, are called *takegeta*.

BANNER, NOBORI

Cotton
Length 614.5 cm
Width 71.9 cm
A.1986.16.11
Gift of Mrs. George Ariyoshi, 1986

Tall, striking banners, called *nobori*, are made in the *tsutsugaki* technique. This is a resist process that is similar to that of *yuzen*: thick rice paste squeezed through a cone-shaped tube onto cotton or hemp fabric to create a pattern. The fabric is dried in the sun, and then painted with a soybean liquid that allows the dye to bond with the fabric. Bright colors are produced by pigments, which may be applied to the open areas of fabric. The fabric is dipped in dye and dried. This step can be repeated several times depending on the desired depth of color. After soaking in hot water to soften the rice paste, the fabric is placed in a river and scraped to remove paste. It is again soaked in hot water, stretched, and finally dried. The entire process may take twenty days to complete.

Nobori were frequently used for ceremonial purposes. Banners were marked with large family crests, *mon*, and served as identification for different warrior clans. The practice of displaying *nobori* on Boy's Day, (the fifth day of the fifth lunar month) may have also developed about the same time. The birth of a baby boy would often be announced by hoisting a banner fifteen or more feet into the air above the house. During the Edo period the samurai used *nobori* as a heraldic device.

The Peach Boy, Momotaro, a character from Japanese children's stories, is the subject of this *nobori*. When Momotaro went to battle on Devil's Island, he carried a *nobori*. The character on the flag he holds read "Japan number one." A *mon* consisting of a large circle surrounded by eight small circles, is visible above the mountain.

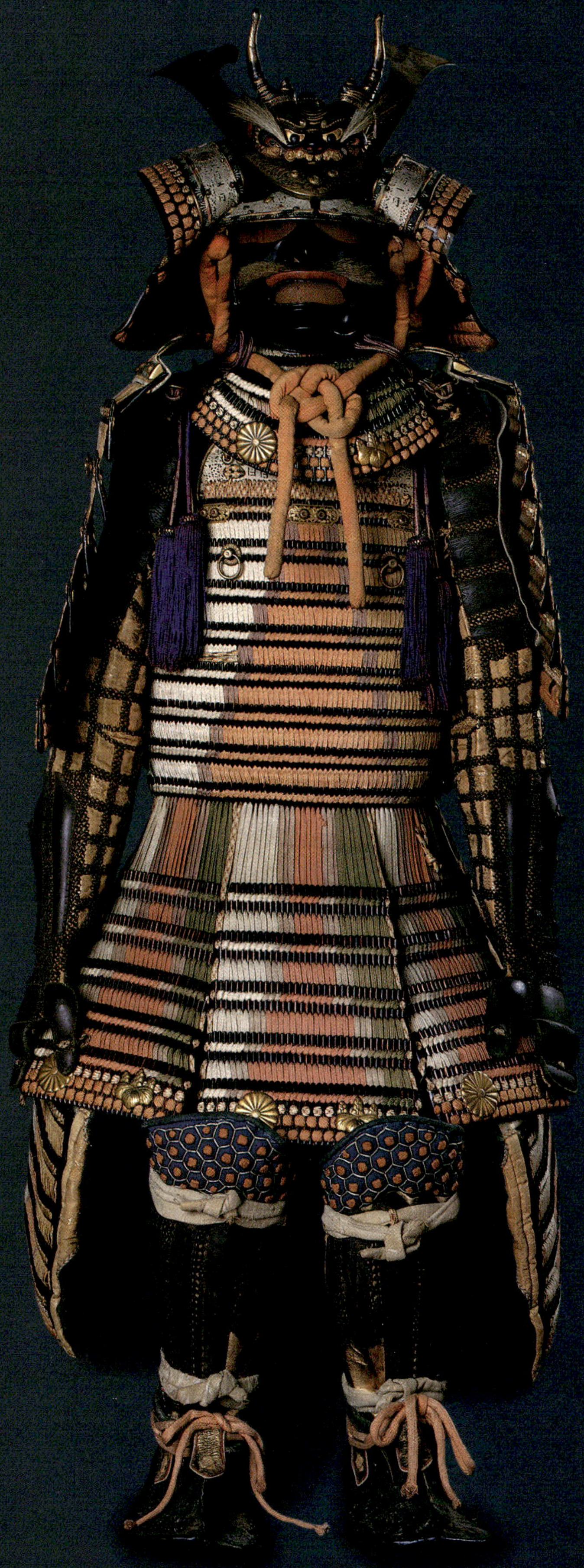

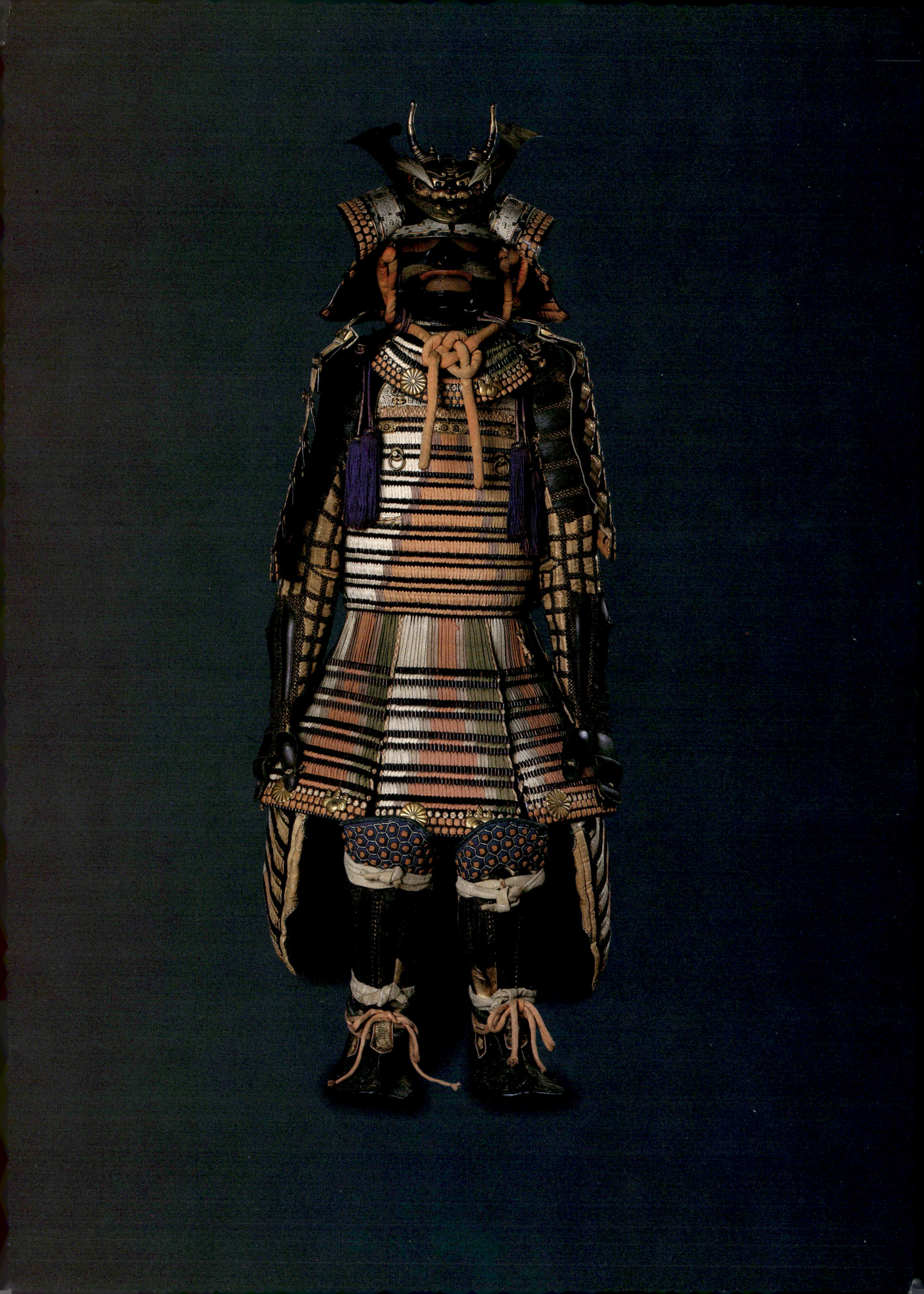

JAPANESE ARMOR

Japanese lamellar armor displays skillful craftsmanship in ironworking, lacquering, braiding, weaving and leatherworking to produce complex protective garments that are strikingly dramatic and beautiful. Body armor consisting of rows of rectangular plates of iron or hide laced together and protected with coats of lacquer can be traced back to early Persian examples that influenced much of the armor of Central Asia, China, Korea, and Japan. In Japan lamellar armor can be found as early as the Tomb period (AD 250-552). Through the centuries, many variations in armor developed in response to new methods and requirements of warfare. During the peaceful Tokugawa period (1615-1868), widespread interest in ancient armor led to the revival of older styles alongside modern versions attesting to the Japanese appreciation of the aesthetic as well as the functional aspects of armor.

The suit of armor in the exhibition resembles the *domaru*, or "wraparound" cuirass style. The *domaru* is characterized by a one-piece construction which wraps entirely around the body and ties at the right side with closely spaced lacing. The skirt is divided into tassets, *kusazuri*, usually seven, to facilitate movement. Although the wraparound style of armor can be seen in paintings of the twelfth century, it became particularly popular and widespread in the thirteenth through fifteenth centuries and, like the tenth-century "great armor," *oyori*, from which it evolved, continued to be made in the Tokugawa period.

Tosei gusoku, or modern equipment, developed in the second half of the sixteenth century. This armor is characterized by a close fit achieved through the use of hinges which bind two of five plates of armor together. Modern armor, like the *domaru* style, uses multiple tassets, but the cuirass is treated in a variety of ways. It can resemble the *domaru* armor when it employs closely spaced lacing, as in the example displayed here. Widely spaced lacing, however, is more common. Laced lamellar plates are sometimes replaced with solid sheets of iron in a style influenced by European armor of solid plate from the sixteenth century. These variations reflect both an attempt to simplify and lighten the armor while, particularly in the armor of the eighteenth and nineteenth centuries, emphasizing elaborate surface decoration.

In addition to the cuirass, high ranking soldiers were further protected by shoulder guards, *sode*, of lamellar construction, armored and chain mail sleeves, *kote*, shin guards, *koshiate*, and an armored skirt that protected the thighs, *haidate*.

Headgear included a half-face mask with a throat guard, but the most distinctive feature was the helmet, *kabuto*, with its pair of decorative horns, *kuwagata*, center ornament, *tatemono*, and rows of iron plates that hung from the back rim to protect the neck, forming turned back flaps at the sides of the face. Originally made of overlapping plates of lacquered iron held together by scores of rivets, the helmet was fashioned in various shapes, often imitating plant and animal forms. Even the simplest shapes, however, could have fanciful central ornaments and elaborate horns. The helmets impart a sense of individuality to the suits of armor and came to be appreciated as unique works of art.

LAMELLAR ARMOR
IN *NIMAIDO GOSOKU*
STYLE
Ca. 18th century
Japan

SUIT OF ARMOR, *NIMAIDO GOSOKU* STYLE

Ca. 18th century
Metal, lacquer, leather, silk
Loaned by the Center for Japanese Studies,
University of Hawaii. Donated in Memory of George Fujii.
Illustrated p. 136

CUIRASS
Length 58.8 cm (length of tasset 23.3 cm)
Width (chest) 25.7 cm

SHOULDER PROTECTORS
Length 44.3 cm
Width 38.5-39 cm

ARMORED SLEEVES
Length 71 cm

SHINGUARDS
Length 32.5 cm

ARMORED SKIRT
Length 60.5 cm.

HELMET
Height 35.5 cm
Depth 40.1 cm

SHOES
Length 28 cm

The hinged two-piece cuirass on this armor has lacquered metal plates on the upper portion and lacquered leather plates in the seven tassets. Closely laced with multi-colored silken cord in the *omodaka* pattern, it is further adorned with stenciled leather along the chest and arm bands, on the armored skirt and at the brim and turned back flaps of the helmet. The stenciled pattern incorporates the phrase *shohei rokunen, rokugatsu, ichinichi* which means the first day of the sixth month in the year 1351. This kind of leather was first presented to the court in that year and its makers continued to incorporate that auspicious date into the leather pattern in later centuries.

At the lower band of the tassets, the shoulder guards, throat guard and helmet are the crests of the imperial family, a sixteen-petaled chrysanthemum, and a paulownia crest that was used by several high-ranking families including the Toyotomi, Ashikaga and others.

The essentially ceremonial purpose of this suit of armor is revealed in details such as the gilding of the under surface of the cuirass, the decorative lacing patterns, and gilt bronze rivets and other metallic ornaments. The careful attention to detail can be noted also in the use of a brocade lining with the same patterns (paulownia and chrysanthemum) as used for the crests, the embossed wood grain pattern on the plates of iron and the complicated chain mail and floral bosses in the armoured sleeves.

The lacquered iron helmet with thirty-two flanges and brass horns has a central ornament of lacquered wood in the form of a demon head. This helmet also retains elements of an older tradition in the small hole in the crown which originally allowed the topknot of the warrior to protrude but which, in the 18th century, had no practical purpose. The name Yorimichi is inscribed in lacquer on the underside of the brim. Yorimichi, who worked in the second half of the sixteenth century, was one of the most famous members of the Myochin school of armorers and is credited with a set of armor very much like the one exhibited. However, this set of armor appears to be a revival intended for ceremonial purposes, an eighteenth century imitation that pays homage to Yormichi and the sixteenth century traditions.

HELMET

18th century
Iron, lacquer, wood
Height 26.2 cm
Depth 39.5 cm
Dragon ornament length 33.5 cm; height 15 cm
Loaned by the Center for Japanese Studies, University of Hawaii. Donated in memory of George Fujii.
Illustrated p. 139

This lacquered iron helmet is made up of fifty-eight narrow plates and is crowned by an open hole surmounted by concentric circles of floral designs. The multi-flanged helmet that omitted visible rivets was first made in the late sixteenth century. The brim and turned-back flaps are covered with a layer of leather stenciled with floral and butterfly designs. The Tokugawa crest executed in silver further adorns the flaps. Careful braiding and the decorative rivets all contribute a sense of splendor but the most remarkable element is a carved wood, gold and red lacquered dragon with glass eyes which appears between the brass horns.

The dragon was a popular choice for the central ornament. Minamoto Yoritomo, warrior-ruler of Japan in late twelfth century, wore such a helmet and later leaders continued the practice. Produced in the Tokugawa period, this elegant helmet reflects the beautiful craftsmanship so common in the apparel and accouterments of the warrior.

HELMET
Tokugawa Period (1615-1868)
Japan

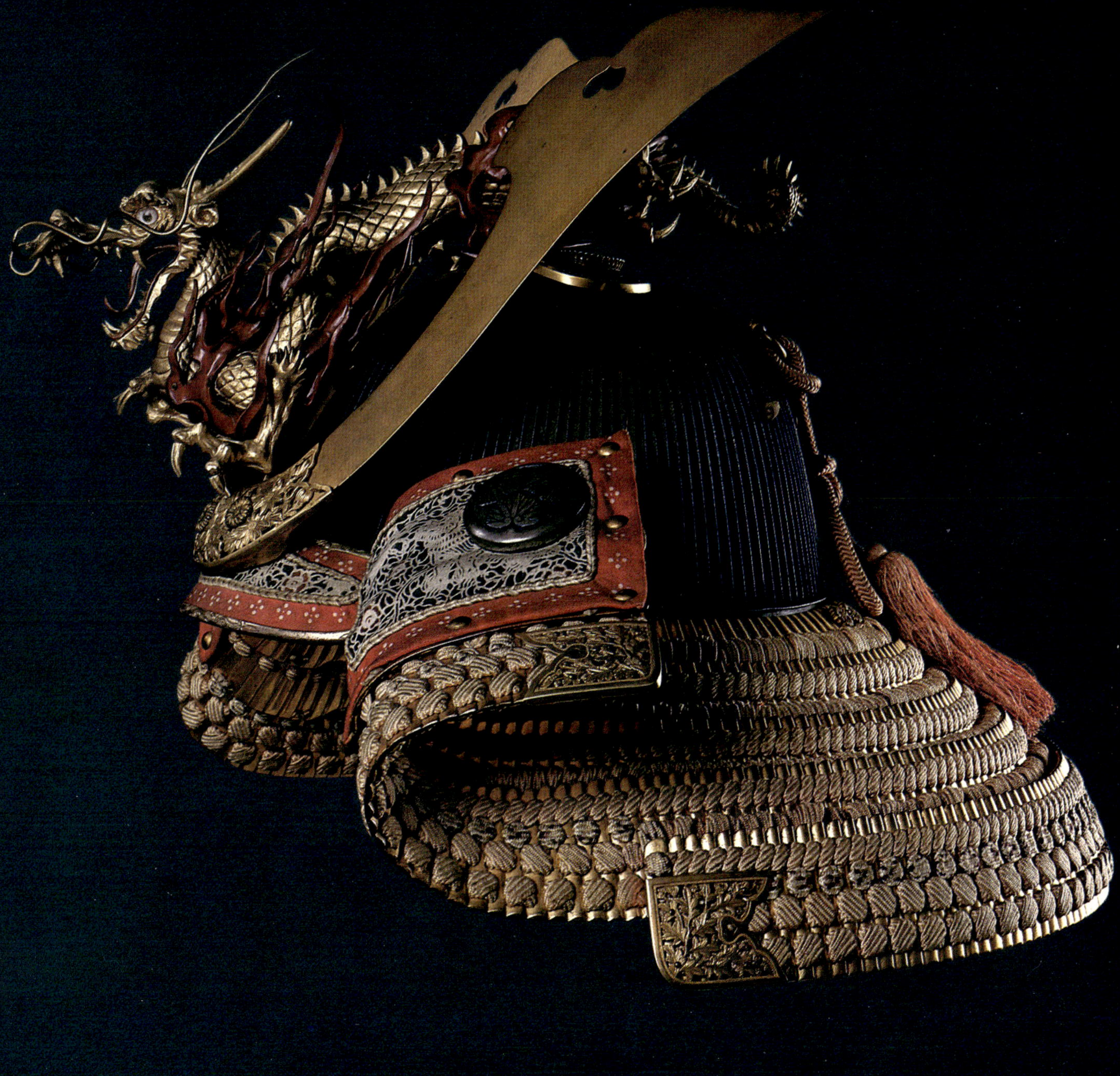

Okinawa

Dancer's Ensemble

Late 1940s
Loaned by Yoshino Majikina Nakasone

KIMONO, *TAIGATA*
Silk
Center back 155 cm
Sleeve 140 cm
Sleeve extension 75 cm

UNDER JACKET, *DOJIN*
Silk
Center back 83 cm
Sleeve 130 cm

PLEATED SKIRT, *KAKAN*
Polyester
Length 91 cm
Waist 128 cm

SASH, *MURUSAKI*
Cotton
Length 221 cm
Width 42.7 cm

SASH, *MURUSAKI*
Cotton
Length 257 cm
Width 37 cm

Costumes for Okinawan classical dance originated three hundred years ago and have not changed in style or color. Worn by women of high status, these costumes are made of silk and consist of a long-sleeved kimono *taigata*, worn over a short kimono-style jacket, *dojin*, and a white pleated wrap-skirt. The *taigata* is tied under the bust with a sash, and a head sash is worn under a large, red hat shaped like lotus petals, *hanagasa*.

Taigata are intended to be seen from a distance, and are brightly colored with bold patterning. This *taigata* is in yellow, a favorite color, lined with red silk. The traditional *taigata* design of flowers and birds is hand painted.

Dancer's Hat, *Hanagasa*

Cotton; gold paper, wire
Height 24.3 cm
Circumference 135 cm
A.1987.10.01
Gift of Ken and Diane Chung
Illustrated p. 141

Woman's Kimono

1960s
Cotton
Center back 144.5 cm
Sleeve 125 cm
15-2
Gift of Amy Shimabukuro, 1970

Curtain, *Noren*

1960s
Ramie
Length 39 cm
Width 87 cm
80-8
Departmental purchase, 1963

Noren are decorative paneled curtains which are hung in interior doorways. This *e-kasuri* (pictorial), *noren* of indigo blue ramie, has a design of bold checks and swimming ducks.

Curtain, *Noren*

Silk
Length 38.5 cm
Width 102 cm
Fringe 7.5 cm
80-2
Gift of Barbara B. Smith

This *noren*, with a double-knotted fringe, is of very sheer, natural colored silk.

Curtain, *Noren*

Banana fiber
Length 40 cm
Width 94 cm
80-3
Gift of Barbara B. Smith, 1961

Plantain or banana fiber is used for this three-paneled *noren* in a natural color with a geometric design in indigo and brown.

Dancer's Hat, *Hanagasa*
Okinawa

BIBLIOGRAPHY

Achjadi, Judi
1976 *Indonesian Women's Costumes*, Penerit Djambatan, Jakarta, Indonesia

Adams, Marie Jeanne
1969 *System and Meaning in East Sumba Textile Design*, Cultural Report Series, no. 16, Yale University, New Haven, Connecticut

Afghanistan
1988 *Encyclopedia Americana*, vol. 1:242-255, Grolier, Inc., Danbury, Connecticut

d'Argence, Rene-Yvon Lefebvre (ed.)
1979 *5,000 Years of Korean Art*, Asian Art Museum of San Francisco, San Francisco

Arney, Sarah
1987 *Malaysian Batik: Creating New Traditions*, The Malaysian Handicraft Development Corporation, Kuala Lumpur, Malaysia

Biswas, A.
1985 *Indian Costumes*, Publications Division Ministry of Information and Broadcasting, Government of India, New Delhi

Brandon, Reiko Mochinaga
1986 *Country Textiles of Japan, The Art of Tsutsugaki*, Honolulu Academy of Arts, Honolulu

Buhler, Alfred, and Urs Ramsayer and Nicole Ramsayer-Gygi
1975 *Patola und geringsing*, Museum fur Valdskunde, Basel

Cammann, Schuyler
1952 *China's Dragon Robes*, The Ronald Press Company, New York

Casal, Father Gabriel, and Regalado Trota Jose, Jr., Eric S. Casino, George R. Ellis, Wilhelm G. Solheim II
1981 *The People and Art of the Philippines*, Regents of the University of California, Los Angeles

Chandra, Moti
1973 *Costumes Textiles Cosmetics and Coiffure in Ancient and Medieval India*, Oriental Publishers on behalf of The Indian Archaeological Society, Pataudi House, Delhi

Ch'oe, Sun-u
Korean National Committee for UNESCO (ed.)
1983 *Traditional Korean Painting*, Si-sa-yong-o-sa Publishers, Inc., Seoul

Chung, Young Yang
1979 *The Art of Oriental Embroidery*, Charles Scribner and Sons, Inc., New York

Cruz, Eric V.
1982 *The Terno: Its Development and Identity as the Filipino Women's National Costume*, The U.P. College of Home Economics, Dilman, Quezon City, Philippines

Dar, S.N.
1969 *Costumes of India and Pakistan: A Historical and Cultural Study*, D.B. Taraporevala Sons and Co., Private Ltd., Bombay, India

Djebar, Assia
1961 *Women of Islam*, Andre Deutsch Limited, London

Dongerkery, Kamala S.
195_ *The Indian Sari*, The All India Handicrafts Board, Ministry of Commerce and Industry, Government of India, New Delhi

Ecke, Tseng Yuho
1977 *Chinese Folk Art II*, University of Hawaii Press, Honolulu

Elliot, Inger McCabe
1984 *Batik, Fabled Cloth of Java*, Clarkson N. Potter, Inc., New York

Elson, Vickie C.
1979 *Dowries from Kutch: A Women's Folk Art Tradition in India*, Regents of the University of California, Los Angeles

Emery, Irene
1980 *The Primary Structure of Fabrics*, The Textile Museum, Washington, D.C.

Fabri, Charles
1977 *Indian Dress: A Brief History*, Sangam Books, New Delhi

Fairservis, Walter A. Jr.
1971 *Costumes of the East*, The Chatham Press, Inc., Riverside, Connecticut

Femenias, Blenda and Cynthia Cort
1984 *Two Faces of South Asian Art: Textiles and Paintings*, Elvehjem Museum of Art, University of Wisconsin, Madison

A Festival of Fibers: Masterworks of Textile Art from the Collection of the Honolulu Academy of Arts
1977 Honolulu Academy of Arts, Honolulu

"The Filipino Gentleman's Guide To Dressing"
1978 *Archipelago* A 52, vol. 5 (May):39-41, Manila

Flynn, Dorris
1971 *Costumes of India*, Oxford and IBH Publishing Company, Calcutta

Forman, Bedrich
1978 "Javanese Batik: The Magic of Tradition and Individual Talent", *Orientations* 9, no. 5 (May):47-55, Pacific Magazines, Ltd., Hong Kong

Fraser, Sylvia
1976 "Indonesian Batik", *Arts of Asia* 6, no.5 (September-October):42-45, Arts of Asia Publications, Kowloon, Hong Kong

Fraser-Lu, Sylvia
1988 *Handwoven Textiles of South-East Asia*, Oxford University Press, Oxford, Singapore, New York

Hacker, Katherine F.
1982 "Bandha Textiles: India's Ikat and Plangi Expression", *Arts of Asia* 12, no. 4 (July, August):63-71, Arts of Asia Publications Ltd., Kowloon, Hong Kong

Haddon, Alfred C. and Laura E. Start
1982 *Iban or Sea Dayak Fabrics and Their Patterns*, Ruth Bean Publishers, Carlton and Bedford, Great Britain

Harrold, Robert
1978 *Folk Costumes of the World*, Blandford Press, Dorset, Great Britain

Hartman, Roland
1980 "Kingfisher Feather Jewelry", *Arts of Asia* 10, no. 3 (May-June):75-81, Arts of Asia Publications, Kowloon, Hong Kong

Hoefer, Hans Johannes
1981 *Korea*, APA Productions, Hong Kong

Huh, Dong-hwa
1987 *Crafts of the Inner Court: The Artistry of Korean Women*, The Museum of Korean Embroidery, Seoul

Imperial Robes and Textiles of the Chinese Court
1943 The Minneapolis Institute of Arts, Minneapolis

Ito, Motoko, and Aiko Inoue
1979 *Kimono*, Hoikusha Publishing Co., Ltd., Osaka, Japan

Kahlenberg, Mary Hunt
1977 *Textile Traditions of Indonesia*, Los Angeles County Museum of Art, Los Angles

Kartiwa, Suwati
1986 *Songket-Weaving in Indonesia*, Penerbit Djambatan, Indonesia

Koop, Albert James
1920 *Guide to The Japanese Textiles, Part II — Costume*, Victoria and Albert Museum, South Kensington, London

Kim, Jok-Dae (ed.)
1970 *Korea: Its People and Culture*, Hakwon-sa Ltd., Seoul

Kim, Won-Yong
1979 *The Arts of Korea: Painting*, Dong Hwa Publishing Co., Seoul

Langewis, Laurens, and Frits A. Wagner
1964 *Decorative Art in Indonesian Textiles*, Uitgeverij C.P.J. Van Der Peet, Amsterdam

Larsen, Jack Lenor, with Alfred Buhler, Bronwen and Garrett Solyom
1976 *The Dyer's Art*, Van Nostrand Reinhold Company, New York

Lee, Sherman E.
1982 *A History of Far Eastern Art*, Harry N. Abrams, Inc., New York

Link, Howard
1975 "Kimono", *Orientations* 6, no. 4 (April):29-38, Pacific Magazines, Ltd., Hong Kong

Levy, Howard S.
1966 *Chinese Footbinding*, Walton Rawls, New York

Lewis, Paul and Elaine
1984 *Peoples of the Golden Triangle*, Thames and Hudson, London

Lin, Lee Chor
1987 *Ancestral Ships: Fabric Impressions of Old Lampung Culture*, National Museum Singapore, Singapore

Mailey, Jean
1978 *Embroidery of Imperial China*, China House Gallery/China Institute in America, New York

Mailey, Jean
1980 *The Manchu Dragon: Costumes of the Ch'ing Dynasty*, The Metropolitan Museum of Art, New York

Makhlouf, Carla
1979 *Changing Veils*, University of Texas Press, Austin, Texas

McCune, Evelyn
1962 *The Arts of Korea: An Illustrated History*, Charles E. Tuttle Co., Rutland, Vermont

Mc Reynolds, Pat Justiniani
1982 "Sacred Cloth of Plant and Palm", *Arts of Asia* 12, no. 4 (July, August):94-100, Arts of Asia Publications Ltd., Kowloon, Hong Kong

Medley, Margaret
1964 *A Handbook of Chinese Art*, Harper and Row, New York

Medley, Margaret
1982 *The "Illustrated Regulations for Ceremonial Paraphernalia of the Ch'ing Dynasty"*, Han Shang Tang, Pesces Press, London

Mehta, Tustam
1970 *Masterpieces of Indian Textiles*, D.B. Taraporenela Sons, Bombay

Ministry of Foreign Affairs, Republic of Korea
1956 *Korean Arts, Vol.I: Painting and Sculpture*, Seoul

Minnich, Helen Benton with Shojiro Nomura
1963 *Japanese Costume and the Makers of Its Elegant Tradition*, Charles E. Tuttle Co., Tokyo, Japan; Rutland, Vermont

Moes, Robert
1983 *Auspicious Spirits. Korean Folk Paintings and Related Objects*, International Exhibitions Foundation, Washington, D.C.

Mookerjee, Agit (ed.)
n.d. *Designs in Indian Textiles*, Institute of Art in Industry, Calcutta

Nakano, Eisha with Barbara B. Stephan
1982 *Japanese Stencil Dyeing, Paste-Resist Techniques*, John Weatherhill, Inc., New York and Tokyo

Newman, Alex R. and Egerton Ryerson
1964 *Japanese Art, A Collector's Guide*, A.S. Barnes and Co., South Brunswick, New York

Newman, Cathy
1988 "Kyongju, Where Korea Began," *National Geographic* 174, no. 2 (August): 259-268, National Geographic Society, Washington, D.C.

Nguyen-Ngac and Nguyen-Van-Luan
197__ *Un Siecle D'Histoire de la Robe Des Vietnamiennes*, Direction des Affaires Culturelles, Saigon

Noma, Seiroku
Translated by Armins Nikoviskis
1974 *Japanese Costume and Textile Arts*, The Heibonsha Survey of Japanese Art, vol. 16, Heibonsha Co. and Weatherhill Inc., Tokyo and New York

Nordquist, Barbara K., and E. Jean Mettam and Kathy Jansen
1986 *Traditional Folk Textiles and Dress*, Kendall/Hunt Publishing Company, Dubuque, Iowa

Peebles, Merrily
1981 *Court and Village: India's Textile Traditions*, Santa Barbara Museum of Art, Santa Barbara, California

The Peoples and Cultures of Cambodia, Laos and Vietnam
1981 Center for Applied Linguistics, Washington, D.C.

Priest, Alan
1935 *Japanese Costume, An Exhibition of Noh Robes and Buddhist Vestments*, The Metropolitan Museum of Art, New York

Ramseyer, Urs
1977 *The Art and Culture of Bali*, Oxford University Press, Oxford

Reischauer, Edwin O. and John Fairbank
1960 *East Asia, the Great Tradition*, vol. 1, Houghton Mifflin, Inc., Boston

Rites of Passage: Textiles of the Indonesian Archipelago from the Collection of Mary Hunt Kahlenberg
1980 Mingei International Museum of World Folk Art, La Jolla, California

Sadikin, Ali
1974 *Batik*, The Municipal Committee of PATA 74, Indonesia

Sahay, Sachidanand
1975 *Indian Costume, Coiffure and Ornament*, Munshiram Manoharlal Publishers Pvt. Ltd., New Delhi

Samut phap ying Thai
1965 Phranakhon: Rongphim Samnak Thammiap Nayok Ratthamontri, Thailand

Scott, A.C.
1958 *Chinese Costume in Transition*, Donald Moore, Singapore

Secret Splendors of the Chinese Court
1981 Denver Art Museum, Denver

Sichel, Marion
1987 *Japan*, BT Batsford Limited, London

Sim, Katharine
1963 *Costumes of Malaya*, Donald Moore for Eastern Universities Press Ltd., Singapore

Solyom, Bronwen and Garrett
1984 *Fabric Traditions of Indonesia*, Museum of Art, Washington State University, Washington State University Press, Pullman, Washington

Steinberg, J. David
1957 *Cambodia: Its people, its society, its culture*, Human Relations Area Files, Inc., New Haven, Connecticut

Suk, Joo-sun
1984 *Clothes of the Joson Dynasty*, Folk Art Reasearch Collection Series III, The Suk Joo-sun Memorial Museum of Korean Folk Arts, Dankook University, Korea

"The Terno: Regal Philippine Dress"
1974 *Archipelago* A 7, vol. 1 (July):38-41, Manila

"The Textile Industry in Cambodia"
Kambuja, 1st Year, no. 7 (October 15, 1965):47, Phnom Penh, Cambodia

Turnbull, Krista Jensen
1982 "Recollections: Elizabeth Bailey Willis and Her Collections", *Arts of Asia* 12, no. 4 (July, August):106-119, Arts of Asia Publishing, Kowloon, Hong Kong

Treasures of Indian Textiles
Calico Museum, Ahmedabad
1982 Humanities Press, Atlantic Highlands, New Jersey

Van Dijk, Toos, and Nico de Jonge
1980 *Ship Cloths of the Lampung South Sumatra*, Galerie Mabuhay, Amsterdam, Netherlands

Vollmer, John E.
1977 *In The Presence Of The Dragon Throne*, The Royal Ontario Museum, Toronto, Canada

Vollmer, John E.
1981 *Five Colours of the Universe*, The Edmonton Art Gallery, Edmonton, Alberta, Canada

Warming, Wanda and Michael Gaworski
1981 *The World of Indonesian Textiles*, Kodansha International Ltd., Tokyo

Wastraprema, Himpunan
1976 *Kain Adat Traditional Textiles*, Djambatan, Jakarta

Watt, James C.Y.
1980 *Chinese Jades from Ming to Ch'ing*, Asia Society, New York

Wikan, Unni
1982 *Behind the Veil in Arabia*, Johns Hopkins University Press, Baltimore, Maryland

Wilcox, R. Turner
1965 *Folk and Festival Costume of the World*, Charles Scribner's Sons, New York

Williams, C.A.S.
1976 *Outlines of Chinese Symbolism and Art Motives*, Dover Publications, Inc., New York

The World and Its Peoples: Southeast Asia I
1969 Greystone Press, New York

Yacopino, Feliccia
1977 *Threadlines Pakistan*, The Ministry of Industries, Government of Pakistan, Pakistan

Yamanaka, Norio
1982 *The Book of Kimono*, Kodansha International Ltd., Tokyo

Yang, Seung Mok
1963 *Social Customs in Korea*, The University Club, Seoul

Thomas Tsuhako
Catalogue Design

Nathan J.D. Chung,
Nate's Photography
(cover), P. 16, 19, 44-45,
69, 94, 105, 106, 113,
115, 127
Man To Wan
P. 12, 21, 26, 29, 32,
35, 36, 48, 51, 53, 56,
60, 63, 64-65, 67,
72-73, 76, 80, 87, 90,
92, 96, 99, 102, 109,
111, 121, 136, 139, 141
Catalogue Photography

Jeanne Wiig
Catalogue Editor

Carol Langer
Catalogue Proofreader

Studio Graphics
Typesetter

General Printing Corporation
Printer

Quality Graphics
Color Separations

The University of Hawaii Art Gallery
Department of Art
Honolulu, Hawaii 96822
USA